Improve and Modify Golf/Jetta

Mks I & II - including GTi

Lindsay Porter and Dave Pollard

Foulis

Haynes

A FOULIS Motoring Book

First published 1988

© Porter Publishing & Haynes Publishing Group 1988

Published by:
Haynes Publishing Group,
   Sparkford, Nr Yeovil,
   Somerset BA22 7JJ, England

Haynes Publications Inc.,
   861 Lawrence Drive,
   Newbury Park,
   California 91320 USA

Produced by:
Porter Publishing,
The Storehouse, Little Hereford Street,
Bromyard, Herefordshire HR7 4DE, England

British Library Cataloguing in Publication Data
Porter, Lindsay, 1949-
Improve & Modify: Jetta, Golf & Golf GTi.
1. Cars, Maintenance & repair - Amateur's manuals
I. Title   II. Pollard, Dave
6.29.28 '722
ISBN 0-85429-669-7

Library of Congress Catalog Card No: 88-80841
ISBN 0 85429 748 0 (Softback)

Editor: Lindsay Porter

Design, typesetting and artwork:
   Typestyle, Sea King Road, Lynx Trading Estate, Yeovil,
   Somerset BA20 2NZ, England

Printed in England by: J. H. Haynes & Co. Ltd.,

Contents

Contents

Acknowledgements

Thanks go to John Humphries for spending endless hours fitting various bits and pieces for photographing and to his wife Carole for supplying her daughters Laura and Lucy for the child seat section.

J. Giles & Son of Northampton provided invaluable advice and assistance with regard to the photography and equipment used during the preparation of this book.

Volkswagen UK, from their Milton Keynes HQ, provided masses of help, not just by providing equipment for inclusion, but also by providing skilled technicians and workshop time in order to show how various tasks should be handled.

Burt and his crew at Continental Coachworks of Northampton were particularly helpful and took great pains to make sure that nothing was missed during the 'Fitting a body kit' section.

Working with Brian Ricketts and his right-hand men Ross and Mark, was a pleasure, not least because of his total knowledge of his subject. What Brian doesn't know about tuning a GTi isn't worth knowing.

Roy Craggs is (or was!) a personal friend who made several 200 mile round trips in his Mk I 1500 Golf so that urgent photo sessions could be completed.

At Turbo Technics, Eddie Kimble was most co-operative in providing a Golf Turbocharger in kit form, along with all the necessary technical descriptions. In addition, it was most interesting to be in at the start of their 16-valve project.

DAVE POLLARD,
Buckinghamshire

Introduction

This is a book for Golf and Jetta owners who want to add some of their own individuality to what is already an outstanding car in its own right. Many of the sections in this book are about how to carry out your own mods on a DIY basis, while others set out to show what is available and what the specialists can do to your car for you; the choice is yours.

Naturally enough, owners are drawn to their Golfs and Jettas because of their cars' build quality and their sheer dependability, but the cars are also renowned for their sportiness and verve on the road, even the 1300cc models being capable of quite a respectable turn of speed and having cornering ability and handling that make them a pleasure to drive. And when you get up to the level of a GTi, the levels of performance are a revelation to those not used to scorching acceleration and pin-point precision steering. Yet, at the same time, Golf and Jetta GTis have an ease of use and comfort that would put many an everyday 'shopping' car to shame.

In spite of all that, no-one would claim that Golfs and Jettas, in the form in which they leave the factory, could ever be unique. It's up to the individual owner to stamp his or her own hallmark onto the car in one of the many hundreds of ways suggested by this book. Volkswagen themselves are more than pleased to help the owner do so in a responsible manner, which is why they have given their invaluable assistance and advice in many parts of this book.

The range of improvements and modifications that you can make to your Golf and Jetta is vast. Among the simplest are styling stripes for the bodywork, mats for the interior and performance-boosting exhaust pipe swaps for the engine. For more serious modifications, you can buy body styling kits from your Volkswagen dealer (or have them fitted there), Recaro seats from the same source, or go to Turbo Technics and give your Golf incredible acceleration - at a price. All of these modifications, and more, are included in this book. We have not pretended that everything shown here can be DIY fitted; indeed, we recommend that some of it should not be for reasons of safety or specialist skills required.

Improvements and modifications to Golfs and Jettas cover a huge field and we hope we have done it justice. We certainly could not have done so without the close assistance of all the specialists and suppliers shown in this book. In every case, we selected the specialist company which we believe has the most to offer the Golf and Jetta owner in their particular field; that's why you'll recognise some of the biggest 'names' in the business in this book, alongside some less well-known names who deserve to be better known. We hope and believe that the combination of top specialists, experienced motoring writing and enthusiastic Golf ownership has brought you a book that you, as a Golf or Jetta owner, will want to turn to again and again.

Introduction

The modifications and improvements shown in this book cover a very wide spectrum, from the smallest item such as wheel nut covers right through to full-blown bodywork, engine and suspension modifications.

▲
I.1
Acknowledging their owners' interest in those Golfs that are that little bit different, Volkswagen celebrated the ten millionth Golf with a 'special equipment' package in 1988. Special features included new alloy sports wheels, half-darkened rear light clusters and three new metallic paint colours.

I.2 ▶
Changes to suspension and tyres can make some of the most exciting Golf improvements. Here, the outstanding P600 tyres are put on test at Pirelli's Vizzola test track, near Milan.

◀ **I.3**
Apart from its Pirelli 'P' wheels, this Golf GTi would look like any other on the road. The Turbo Technics turbocharger beneath the bonnet would make it perform like **no** other however!

◀ I.4
Another approach to engine tuning is taken by BR Motorsport, whose much admired engine work is featured in many of the pages in this book.

I.5 ▶
Excellent though Volkswagen's anti-rust treatment is, there's no reason why older Golfs shouldn't benefit like this one, from the application of preservation fluid such as the Corroless sytem shown here.

◀ I.6
Branyl styling stripes give instant styling appeal.

Pride of Golf or Jetta ownership can be reflected in a number of ways: Improvements can cover performance or appearance aspects of the cars, but it can also include modifications that will have a bearing on longevity or practicality, such as the addition of a delay windscreen wiper control or a Volkswagen-approved storage box.

A far more expensive but, in all honesty, a more exciting package, because every Golf or Jetta will be unique, is the Designer Paint approach offered by Glasurit and Autotech ...

I.7
▼

◀ I.8
Very few of the improvements and modifications shown here apply only to the Golf; most of them apply equally to the Jetta and many are shown being fitted to that model.

Chapter One
Improving the appearance

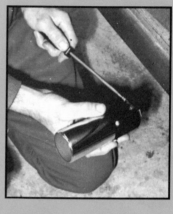

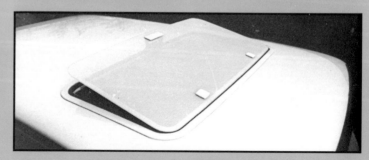

Fitting a grille panel with lamps

◄ IA1.1
Remove the VW roundel from the original grille. It is held by three simple lugs, which can be eased gently out with a screwdriver. Place the roundel on one side for use with the new grille.

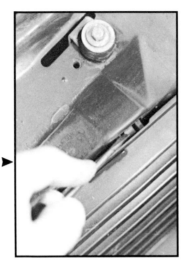

IA1.2 ►
The grille is held by six plastic spring clips. Again, use a screwdriver inserted as shown to apply the required pressure, whilst pulling the grille forward. There are four clips along the top edge.

Fitting a replacement grille panel with driving lamps is one way of making a standard Golf look like a GTi. All Mk II GTis have a twin lamp system and many of the Mk Is as well. The grille we fitted here is a well-made Hella item which took little time to fit. Like the new driving lamps, the existing headlamps were also Hella. As always when dealing with car electrical systems we disconnected the earth lead from the battery before starting work. Once the lamps have been fitted and connected, it is very important that they should be correctly set, so as not to blind oncoming traffic.

▲
IA1.3
There is also a clip in each end of the grille at the corner of the wing. These are removed in the same manner. With all the clips released, the whole grille will simply lift forward and off. The headlamps stay in position.

▲
IA1.4
The body colour trim strip must be taken from the old grille. This is held by a series of clips as before. Once removed, this is transferred to the Hella grille by repeating the removal process.

IA1.5 ►
Fit the new Hella grille, making sure that the wiring for the driving lamps is not trapped in any way. As can be seen, there is a short wire complete with connectors already fitted.

Fitting a grille panel with lamps

The grille cannot be fitted to cars with air conditioning and on 'GTi' or 'GTD' models, it is necessary to cut a hole in the cardboard panel to accommodate the driving lamps.

◄ IA1.6
Unlike the original grille, the new one has only four spring clips. Two of the top fasteners are replaced by self-tapping screws. These feed into plastic inserts supplied which themselves fit directly into the original spring clip holes.

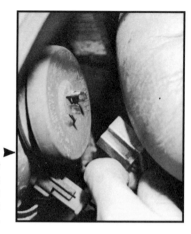

IA1.7 ►
The wiring is extremely simple. The headlamp connectors should be disconnected by pulling them straight off.

IA1.8 ►
The Hella wiring loom supplied is then inserted between the headlamp connector and the new driving lamp. A matter of a few minutes completes both sides. The wiring connects the new lights directly into the existing circuitry and means that it is fused via the fusebox. The new lights come on when main beam is selected.

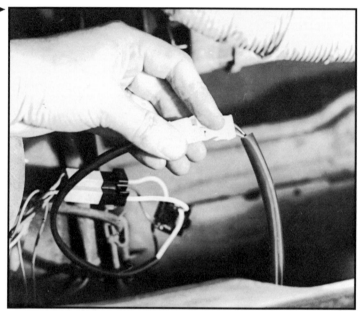

IA1.9
With the VW roundel replaced the finished result is most pleasing, immediately giving the car an 'upmarket' look. Similarly, night time vision is considerably improved by using four, rather than two, lamps.

▼

Fitting wheel arch extensions

IA2.1 ▶
The existing plastic trim around the front of the rear wheel arch is removed. This is held by plastic lugs which fit into plastic inserts in the bodywork. It can be pulled out by hand, although a screwdriver placed under one edge may be necessary to start with. Care must be taken here not to damage the paintwork. Though not obvious, there is a lug on the underside of the car.

Another way to achieve the 'GTi' look is to fit wheel arch extensions. We fitted original equipment items as supplied by Volkswagen UK Ltd. The whole kit consists of the four arches, two self-adhesive sill strips and twenty black-headed rivets. The arches are handed and moulded to fit the bodywork exactly. The rivet holes are pre-punched in the bodywork and need only cleaning out to remove any build up of road dirt and/or wax.

◀ **IA2.2**
The sill strip must be applied first as the new wheel arch mouldings will overlap it at either end. The strip is flexible, tough black plastic which sticks onto the sill of the car. The sill was prepared by thoroughly cleaning with spirit wipe. The peel-off backing is in three sections. Peel off the top section and position carefully.
With just this section removed, the strip is offered up along the sill, taking care to get it exactly level. As can be seen, the top edge aligns inside the car. Two pairs of hands are very useful to ensure that the strip is level all the way along.

▲
IA2.4
After cleaning any dirt out of the rivet holes, you are ready for your second pair of hands to hold the arch exactly in place whilst you insert the first rivet in the hole at the top of the arch. This effectively holds the arch in position and makes fitting the other four rivets much easier. Repeat this for the other three arches and the job is complete. To see the finished result, take a look at Section IA7.

IA2.3 ▶
Smooth it down like wallpaper, ensuring there are no bubbles or creases, and that it is straight. Having stuck down the strip with just one section, the second section can be peeled off and the operation repeated. This is much easier, although care must still be taken to make sure that it is flat. The same applies with the third section removed.

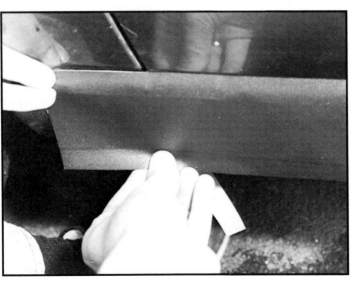

Fitting wheel trims

Fitting a set of wheel trims is an inexpensive method of getting the 'alloy wheel' look. They will also cover up rusty old wheels that really need a respray! Volkswagen UK Ltd can provide several different styles, three of which we show here. All are claimed to be aerodynamically effective. Trims are only available for 13 inch wheels.

◄ IA3.1
The three styles of trim alongside the standard wheel. The two on the left are Volkswagen products and the third a Votex item. The latter has a central Wolfsburg crest.

IA3.2 ►
The Volkswagen trims are supplied with five fixing lugs per wheel. These are fitted at any one of three different heights which allow the trims to be fitted to any 13 inch wheel in the VW range.

◄ IA3.3
A rear view of a VW trim with the five lugs fitted.

IA3.4 ►
The Votex trim comes in one depth and has six very strong, sharp metal retaining grips. Having had to remove one, we would be very surprised to hear of trims working their way off whilst driving!

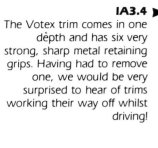

Great care should be taken when fitting wheel trims. Make sure that they are securely fastened on; an errant trim flying off the car at speed could be highly dangerous, especially since the clips are extremely sharp and could easily inflict a nasty cut.

◄ **IA3.5**
Both Volkswagen trims have extra wide openings to permit access to the tyre valve. The Votex does not, however, and therefore a valve extension is supplied.

IA3.6
The 1.3 Golf CL complete with double headlamp grille, wheel arch extensions and now, wheel trims. Already looking much more distinctive.
▼

Fitting a front spoiler with lamps

Some non VW-approved spoilers may cut off the flow of air to the front brakes, causing them to overheat and malfunction. Those, such as Hella, designed for use in the German market will be 'TUV approved' which means that they make the car inherently more efficient with no detrimental effects - as well as looking prettier! Fitting a spoiler should not only make the car look better but also improve the aerodynamics and hold the front of the car down at high speeds. The Hella spoiler that we fitted had the added advantage of having their DE series foglamps built in.

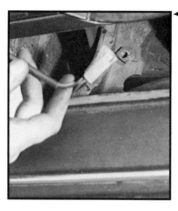

◄ IA4.1
Remove the bumper which is held by two bolts, accessible from under the car. The indicator wires must be disconnected as shown.

IA4.2 ►
Next remove the plastic trim from under the bumper. This is held by plastic lugs which are released by slight pressure with a screwdriver.

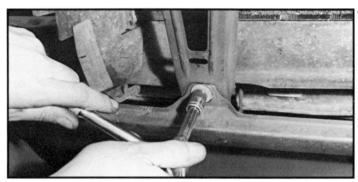

◄ IA4.3
The scuttle is held by three self-tapping screws and the spoiler is attached to the scuttle. Shown here is the centre mounting, just in front of the radiator. However, the assembly cannot be taken off until the self-tapping screws which fasten to the wings at each end of the spoiler have been removed.

IA4.4 ►
Your pride and joy should now be reduced to this. Although it looks fairly drastic, there are no load bearing items removed. Note how it is not necessary to separate the spoiler from the scuttle.

◄ IA4.5
The spoiler is designed to bolt onto the underside of the bumper. The hole positions are marked but not drilled through. We used a pilot drill first for greater accuracy. Note that the lights are ready wired complete with connectors.

IA4.6 ▶
With the spoiler held in place via the two bolts which pass through the number plate indent, we then used a right angled scriber to mark the hole positions through onto the bumper. With the spoiler removed again, the holes were drilled as marked.

The light from the Hella DE lamps is not produced by the usual means of using a parabolic reflector and lens, but by means of a special lens - like that in a slide projector - which produces a wide, even beam.

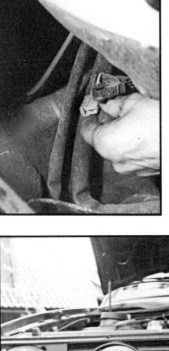

◀ **IA4.7**
The wiring was just a matter of connecting in the loom supplied. Volkswagen thoughtfully supplied not only a two position foglamp switch, as standard on the car, but also most of the wiring to fit front fog lamps. (A standard toggle switch is provided by Hella for cars not already wired this way.) We patched into it at the left-hand rear of the bulkhead as shown. In practice, neither the standard rear or the newly fitted front foglamps will function unless the parking lights are illuminated. With the parking lights on, the first switch position brings on the front foglamps and the second brings on the rear lamp also.

IA4.8
It was a simple matter to bolt the bumper and spoiler together and slide the whole assembly back into position, the design of the spoiler allowing it to curve around the wheel arch. As we had just fitted wheel arch extensions (see Chapter 1, section 2), we had two extra jobs to do. First, drill out the front lower rivet on the wheelarch, to allow a self-tapping screw to be fitted which holds both the arch and the spoiler. Second, as the extension sat proud of the bodywork, we had to 'doctor' the spoiler slightly with a craft knife to make a flush fit.
▼

Fitting rear screen transfers

The makers claim that these transfers act as a theft deterrent because the car is instantly recognisable as it is being driven away from the scene of the crime. Food for thought! No-one need be in any doubt as to the make of your car with one of these fitted! Although no mention is made of it in the instructions, we thought it wise not to put the transfer over the heated rear window.

IA5.1 ▶
It is essential that the glass area be clean and free of stickers. We used a spirit wipe and a razor scraper to attain this. The transfers come on a protective paper backing which is peeled off and the transfer stuck onto the glass. Some care must be taken to ensure that the logo is central and level.

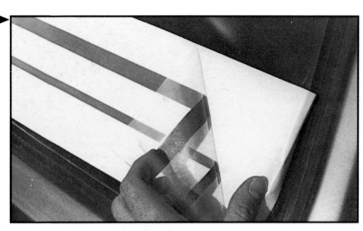

◀ **IA5.2**
Once in position the red logo and stripes can be pressed firmly into place ensuring that there are no air bubbles or creases. When this has been done, a craft knife can be used to remove the excess from each end.

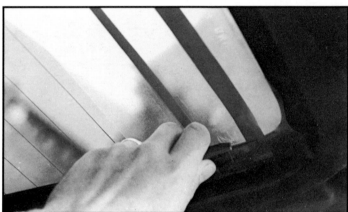

IA5.3 ▶
The clear plastic backing should be pulled back slowly. If the previous instructions have been followed the logo and stripes will be left perfectly positioned.

◀ **IA5.4**
We chose 'Golf' as the logo for this car. Mitchell Marketing can also supply 'VW' and 'GTi' logos in the same style. If none of these are to your liking, you can specify your own logo, up to twelve characters.

Fitting headlamp transfers

◀ IA6.1
'Protectaline' transfers consist of a series of lines, in this case red ones, on a clear plastic adhesive backing. It is important that the lines be exactly horizontal. Place the sheet gently on the centre of the lamp for positioning.

These headlamp transfers, known as 'Protectalines', are also designed to give a distinctive look to your car. Also, should a headlamp get broken they will help to prevent glass from dropping out so you can keep the car on the road until a replacement light unit is fitted.

IA6.2 ▶
When this has been done, the sheet can be cut roughly to shape and then pressed firmly in place pressing outwards from the centre. There should be no bubbles or creases. Then the excess can be cut away with a sharp knife. Unlike the 'backflash' transfers fitted earlier, the clear backing sheet remains in place. We found that there was enough to do both of the headlamps and the driving lamps in the Hella grille.

Sum of The Parts ...

IA7.1 ▶
The front end has a totally new look and there is no excuse for not being able to see in the dark or on foggy days. Though physically small, the lamps in the Hella spoiler throw out an incredible beam of light.

The modifications detailed in the first part of this book were all carried out on one car, a rather ordinary Mk II, 1300 model. We were interested to see what could be done to enliven its appearance and the pictures here show the results.

◀ IA7.2
All the items were an excellent fit and the benefit is obvious. None of the modifications look like tagged-on afterthoughts. The wheel trims have the dual effect of looking good and covering up slightly rusty wheels.

Designer paint

Design your own colour styles

Mr Stan Constable works as a 'Designer Paint' consultant to several leading car manufacturers and to Glasurit paint. He visited the Volkswagen-approved bodyshop, Autotech of Belbroughton where he went through the design process with the proprietor, Graeme Barson. Graeme and partner Chris Reynolds began their working lives in motor car design studios, so were no strangers to this process!

The next six pages describe just one of an infinite number of individual paint designs which could be applied to your Golf or Jetta, making it not just different but absolutely unique. This high-class service is offered by Autotech of Belbroughton in conjunction with designer, Mr Stan Constable. This section also shows how a more straightforward colour-coding operation is carried out.

◄ DPW1
The first stage is to discuss with the customer his or her basic requirements.

DPW2 ►
Stan Constable produces, on Autotech's behalf, a number of designer paint options, incorporating a selection from the vast range of Glasurit Paint options available.

DPW3 ►
Stan Constable's finished 'rendering' looked most impressive. Compare it with Autotech's interpretation on page 23, making due allowance for the fact that the project car is a four-door whereas this one is a two-door Golf.

◄ DPW4
Once in the workshop, front and rear bumpers were removed from the Autotech project car along with the radiator grille.

DPW5 ►
Autotech's Jason removes the stuck-on side mouldings after heating them with a hot air blower to soften the adhesive. He later removed the styling stripe in the same way.

x

◄ DPW6
Jason uses a spoon-shaped trim remover to lever off the rear wheel arch trims. He levers against a plastic filler spatula to avoid damaging paintwork.

The Glasurit 2-pack paint shown being used in this section gives the finest Volkswagen-approved paint finish available. However, it is potentially toxic and must never be used by the DIY enthusiast but only by fully-trained professionals.

DPW7 ►
This gives an idea of the huge amount of plastic finish bodywork that has to be removed for this project or for conventional colour-coding work.

◄ DPW8
After conscientiously rubbing down every square inch with Glasurit Pre-Paint Treatment, components were hung up in a spray booth that was beginning to take on the appearance of part of the Tate Gallery!

DPW10
Without a coat of clear plastic primer, ordinary paint would simply peel off the plastic surfaces in no time at all.

DPW9
Painter Steve Molineux mixes the Glasurit Plastic Primer with the activator required.

Design your own colour styles

There's far more to colour-coding - which means painting all of the cars 'black work', usually to the same colour as the rest of the car - than meets the eye. There is a great number of small components to remove while their preparation and painting can take many hours of work.

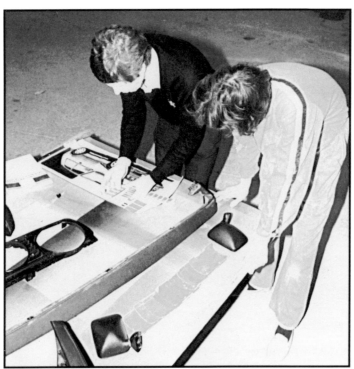

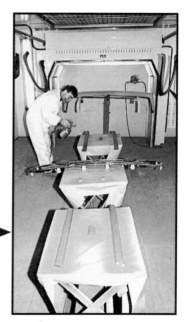

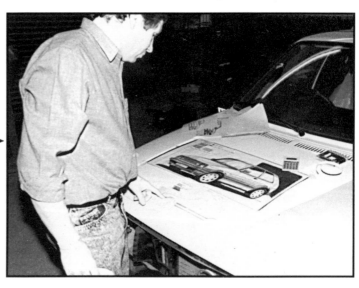

◀ **DPW11**
Stan Constable came up with a colour scheme which involved three different shades of red being used. Graeme goes through the Glasurit colour 'chips' to match up the Glasurit paint required with the shade selected by Stan.

◀ **DPW12**
Straightaway, Steve Molineux mixes the paint, activator and thinners, using the standard measuring stick method to ensure that the proportions are correct.

DPW13 ▶
With the plastic primer dried off, it is back into Autotech's immaculate spray booth to put on two coats of colour as specified by Stan Constable.

DPW14 ▶
Stan Constable's 'rendering' - his finished full-view drawing of how his design will appear - is taped to the bonnet of the Golf to assist Graeme in carrying out the next stage of the work, masking the car ready for the styling stripes to be sprayed on.

DPW15 ▶
Masking up, which involved interpreting Stan Constable's design, was a major operation. Upper and lower styling stripes had to be painted in different shades of course.

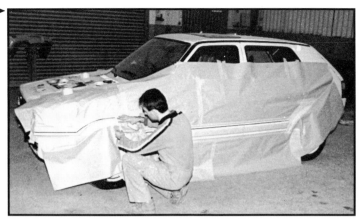

◀ **DPW16**
After masking them both up, the lower styling stripe was itself masked off leaving the upper stripe showing. Black striping tape was carefully worked around the ends to give an attractive rounded 'nose' to the end of the styling stripe.

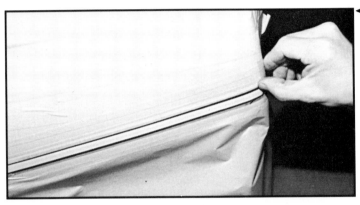

DPW17 ▶
First, Steve sprayed a 'half coat'. Then, when that had 'flashed off' (partly dried), he sprayed on a full coat of paint.

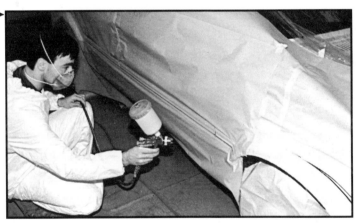

◀ **DPW18**
When the paint had been baked in the oven and was fully dry, Steve removed the masking tape, exposing the two lower styling stripes.

The sills, being covered in a slightly textured anti-chip primer, were painted in the same colour as the new wheel arches. The paint used for the sills and all of the plastic work had a Glasurit matting agent added to it which has the effect of taking the gloss finish off the paint. Not only did the matt paint look quite attractive in itself, but it also avoided a problem inherent in gloss paint; that every small undulation and blemish is clearly shown up. And all plastic finishes have undulations and blemishes in them! The sills themselves were painted separately.

Design your own colour styles

Glasurit paint is slightly more expensive than some competing brands, but it is widely recognised as being one of the best available. Glasurit is one of the paints specified by Volkswagen for use on their vehicles. Many Volkswagen owners insist that Glasurit paint is used when any refinishing work is done on their cars. You can tell a Glasurit bodyshop because of the parrot logo which is displayed there, often in the form of an inflated bird reminiscent of a living version of the one in the famous John Cleese sketch.

◄ **DPW19**
This illustrates one of the hundreds of 'in-the-know' tips that make it worth going to a highly experienced bodyshop such as Autotech. Steve rubs his hand along the back of the masking tape used for masking off the upper styling stripe ...

DPW20
... then he presses the tape down but only on each side of the newly applied strip, so as not to pull off any of the fresh paint when the tape is removed.
▼

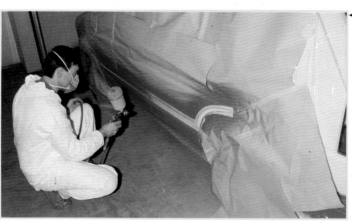

◄ **DPW21**
As shown in the earlier shots, Steve sprayed first a half coat, then a full coat, of the different shade of red required for the lower styling stripes.

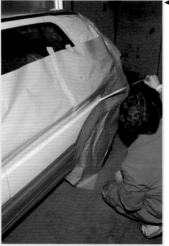

◄ **DPW22**
After the paint had been baked in the oven, the masking tape was removed with great care.

DPW23 ►
Graeme helped out again here, once again showing his skill and experience in not damaging any of the fresh paintwork.

Glasurit

DPW24
Autotech decided that the whole of the lower panels of the car should be further protected with a coat of lacquer. Steve uses a special masking-off technique to ensure that there is no hard edge of lacquer after the paint has been applied.

DPW25
Glasurit now have a new formulation of lacquer which is, to all intents and purposes, completely clear and transparent, letting the original colour show through.

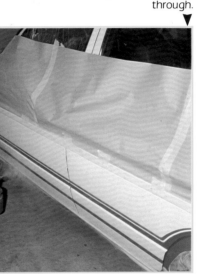

It's worth emphasizing that Autotech could spray just about any design of paintwork on to your Golf or Jetta, the example shown here just being one fairly straightforward instance of what can be done. A great deal of the work is taken up in stripping and painting plastic ware, while masking off is also highly time consuming. The end result is, as said before, totally individual and the Glasurit paint system used means that Volkswagen's extraordinarily long paintwork warranty will not be invalidated, provided it is applied by a Volkswagen-approved bodyshop.

DPW26
Refitting all of the plastic ancillaries was a reversal of the earlier procedure, with the exception of the wheel arches which were new to this car.

DPW27
Autotech's fitter offered up the wheel arches, drilled out the holes for the pop rivets and 'popped' them in place. New side rubbing strips were also fitted.

DPW28
The 'designer painted' and colour-coded Golf took on a whole new and dramatic appearance which meant that it could be confused with no other! The graduations in red looked more obvious in the flesh, and the car now made a personal statement that the owner was very proud of.

Adding styling stripes and decals

The only styling stripes that Volkswagen fit to their standard cars are the simple red strips around the grille, body rubbing strip and bumpers on the Golf and Jetta GTi models. Subtle though it is, it shouts 'GTi' and has been copied as a brand mark by other manufacturers of 'hot' hatches.

Most of us feel the need to add some individuality to our pride and joy and fitting a styling stripe is one of the simplest ways of going about it. Subtlety in this area is one of the hallmarks of Volkswagen cars and for that reason we selected relatively simple and straightforward products from the wide Branyl range of styling stripes and decals.

◄ **IA10.1**
Branyl produce a wide range of cosmetic bodywork products including the sideliners, shown elsewhere, and a wide range of decals. One of them, the 'Turbo' badge, is shown here, front left.

IA10.2
The first job before sticking on a styling stripe is to thoroughly wash the car and then wipe the area down where the stripe is to go with spirit wipe, removing every trace of grease or other contamination.
▼

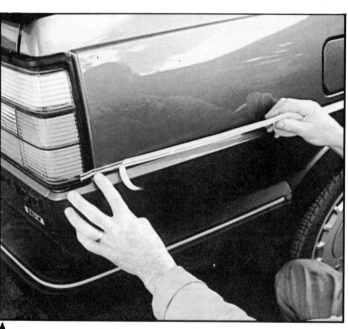

▲
IA10.3
This subtle stripe, matching the GTi's own, is protected by backing paper, front and rear. Some of the rear backing paper was removed, exposing the sticky surface, and a small part of the styling stripe affixed at the rear of the car.

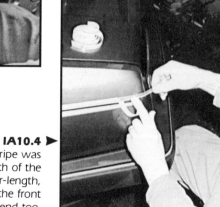

Where a stripe has been shaped to a fine point or is in such a position that possible lifting might occur, a small spot of clear nail varnish will ensure that the end of the stripe doesn't lift up.

IA10.4 ►
The Branyl styling stripe was run down the length of the car, trimmed over-length, and stuck down at the front end too.

◄ IA10.5
The backing paper was removed steadily from behind the Branyl styling stripe which was stuck down over the whole length of the car, passing right over the door gaps.

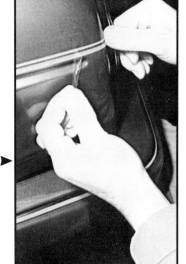

IA10.6 ▶
The Branyl styling stripe was rubbed down tight with a soft rag and then the front backing paper, like a strip of sticky tape, was peeled off leaving the styling stripe in place. Take care that the end of the stripe remains stuck down.

A badly fitted body stripe will look ridiculously wavy as it passes down the length of the car. One way of avoiding this is to align the body stripe with a bodywork moulding on the car, as we did with this Jetta, or you could draw a line with a felt pen down the length of the car. Alternatively you can ask a helper to look down the length of the body stripe as you fit it. Any waviness, which won't be apparent from a side-on view, will be obvious to an observer standing at one end of the car.

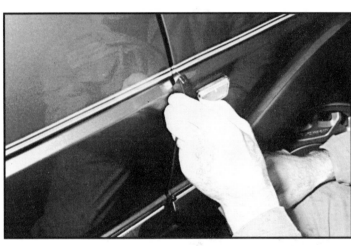

◄ IA10.7
Finally, cut the tape in the middle of each door gap and wrap the excess around the edge of doors and wings.

IA10.8 ▶
The final result, whilst subtle and elegant, added a dash of extra 'fun' to the appearance of the car and actually made it seem a little more sleek.

In years gone by the application of a coach stripe was a job for a skilled craftsman and was not something undertaken lightly. Nowadays, the addition of a stick-on styling stripe, perhaps in conjunction with a change of wheel covers, can dramatically alter a cars appearance at very low cost. Branyl produce a very wide range of styles and colours.

IA10.9 ▶
Here, the principle being the same, we combine the application of two slightly different Branyl styling stripes to give you an idea of the variations available. This one 'fades out' bottom to top.

◀ **IA10.10**
This one has stripes of a diminishing width which should again be fitted with the 'heavier' areas of shade at the bottom of the stripe. Once again, it's stuck down at the back of the car ...

IA10.11
... then carried forwards to the front of the car and stuck down there, so that the stripe can be properly aligned without any waviness.
▼

◀ **IA10.12**
Correct alignment was absolutely essential with this Branyl stripe so we adopted the following method: first the tape was stuck down with odd tags of masking tape.

IA10.13 ▶
Then other strips of masking tape were placed with the edge of the tape butting up with the edge of the styling stripe so that the position of the stripe was clearly indicated.

◄ **IA10.14**
When the styling stripe was taken away the exact position for re-locating it could clearly be seen. With this particular type of tape this was essential, as you will see.

Golf and Jetta owners are fortunate in having a body moulding which enables them to fit a Branyl styling stripe quite accurately by lining it up against the edge of the moulding which runs from front to rear of the car.

◄ **IA10.15**
The next job was to peel away the backing paper from the plastic styling stripe.

IA10.16 ►
Then the panel to which the Branyl styling stripe was to be fitted was thoroughly wetted with water containing a touch of washing up liquid.

▲ **IA10.17**
The self-adhesive surface of the styling stripe was similarly soaked.

IA10.18 ►
The stripe then slid easily into place and was aligned against the masking tape markers.

27

Adding styling stripes and decals

Any particularly wide Branyl styling stripes, or those placed a little on the high side, will run across the fuel filler opening on the right-hand side. It's essential that the styling stripe passes across the filler flap having been cut to fit the shape of the flap exactly.

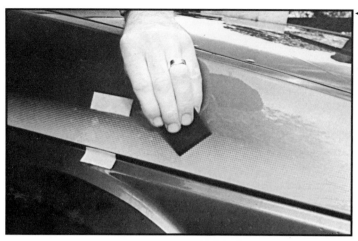

◄ IA10.19
We found that quite a lot of air bubbles were trapped behind the styling stripe and so it was necessary to use a spatula (we used a filler spreader) to squeegee out the trapped air.

IA10.20 ►
It was a warm day and after about half an hour the tape began to stick down to the panel as the water evaporated off. It was then possible to remove the masking tape.

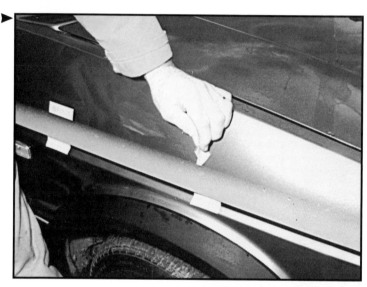

◄ IA10.21
Before it stuck down completely, the end was lifted and trimmed to shape with a pair of scissors.

IA10.22 ►
Unlike the narrow Branyl tape used earlier, this was thicker stuff and had to be trimmed exactly to the edge of the panel rather than wrapped around it.

IA10.23 ▶
Should a styling stripe become damaged and have to be removed so that the whole strip can be replaced, you can do it best by heating gently with a hot air source (we used our Black & Decker Heat Gun), easing the tape back at the start with a knife and then peeling it gently all the way back, heating as you go. Neither turn the setting up too high nor get the Heat Gun too close for longer than a fraction of a second or you'll strip the paint off too!

Several sorts of decals and badges are available from Branyl, some subtle, some amusing, and others downright vulgar! The choice really is yours!

◀ **IA10.24**
Branyl badges invariably come with backing paper over a self-adhesive pad.

IA10.25 ▶
After cleaning off with spirit wipe, marking the exact position on the panel, and peeling off the backing paper, the Branyl badge of your choice can be stuck down. Here, one is being fitted to the front left-hand wing.

IA10.26 ▶
While another is tried for size on the rear tail gate.

Bodywork styling

Body kit options

It is **very important** to note that the kits shown here are not suitable for the 16V version of the Volkswagen Jetta and Golf GTi models. A special BBS front spoiler is available for those cars from Volkswagen dealers. Any other front spoiler will run a strong risk of blowing up your expensive engine by keeping flowing air away from the oil cooler and even worse, the front brakes could deteriorate badly, as an unimpeded supply of cooling air to the front brakes is particularly essential on these models of Golf and Jetta.

Before looking at the way a specialist, Volkswagen-approved bodyshop, fits one particular type of body kit, it's interesting to take a look at some of the wide range of body styling kits available. Most of those shown here can be ordered through your local Volkswagen dealership.

◀ BK1
The BBS body kit, colour-coded black, looks mean and business-like on this Golf Cabrio. The BBS 'RO' wheels with low-profile Pirelli P7 tyres wrapped around them add to the effect.

BK2
The BBS kit, colour-coded white, takes on a totally different appearance. 'M' option factory-fit wheels are also quite distinctive. ▼

BK3
A Votex kit on a Jetta GTi and colour-coded bumpers on a Golf GTi illustrate two different ways of personalising these already highly desirable motor cars. ▼

BK4 ▶
BBS don't, at the time of writing, produce a full kit for the Jetta, so this one is fitted with a BBS front spoiler while the side skirts and rear spoiler are from Votex. Wheels are Votex again and are designated 'RS'.

BK5 ▶

This GTi is fitted with a Pfeba aerodynamic body kit which, prior to the 1988 model year, was available for three- and five-door Golfs. The kit comprises front spoiler, wheel arches, side skirts and rear valance. Wheels are 7 x 15 BBS 'RS' designation.

The range of body parts offered by Volkswagen is very wide indeed, to say nothing of those sold by other outlets. Styles and types come and go and there's nothing to say that the components shown here will still be available by the time you read this book. To check on availability, go to your local Volkswagen dealership, Hella retailer, or whichever specialist you choose, and pick up the latest edition of their catalogue.

◀ **BK6**

This Autoplas rear window spoiler is easily fitted to the window surround. It is only available for the Golf Mk II.

BK7 ▶

In March 1986, Volkswagen introduced fifty 'copies' of this limited edition Jetta GT. It was colour-coded and fitted with a Kamei body kit and a distinctive grey side stripe. Suspension was also lowered.

◀ **BK8**

Colour-coding has been carried right through the spoilers and onto the bumpers of this Votex-kitted Jetta. You can just see the Blaupunkt multi-directional speakers on the rear parcel shelf.

Body kit options

Volkswagen-approved front spoilers give a far more aggressive stance to the front end appearance of the car as well as assisting directional stability and aerodynamic efficiency at speed. However, care has to be taken with all makes of spoiler, both when driving and parking, to remember the reduced ground clearance.

◄ BK9
OTT body styling? Vic Lee's competition Golf is sponsored by Volkswagen's Parts and Service Division, whose brand name is Quantum.

BK10 ►
Body styling needn't be at all dramatic, as this subtle Hella rear window spoiler demonstrates.

◄ BK11
On the other hand, these Hella components completely transform the appearance of the front end of the Golf and add more lighting in the process.

BK12 ►
Back to the subtle elegance of a 1988 model Golf GTi four-door with full Volkswagen-supplied BBS kit and BBS wheels.

Fitting a full body kit is the ultimate way to transform the looks of your Golf. Volkswagen UK can supply several kits as approved aftermarket accessories, including the BBS product featured here. However, it is far from being an easy DIY task. Apart from the obvious skill involved, it requires a lot of space to work around the car and sufficient time to do the job properly. Steve at Continental Coachworks, who carried out the work shown here, cannot do a thorough job in less than two days, and that is not including the time in the spray booth!

All body kits mentioned here are approved VAG items, available from VW main dealerships and, as such, are top-quality items.

Painting is a highly skilled operation, much time being spent in preparation of the kit and, of course, special paint has to be used so that it does not crack as the panels bend and flex. Only VW-approved Glasurit paint should be used here, so that the paint quality matches that of the rest of the bodywork. These two-pack paints **demand** the use of a professional spray booth, for safety's sake.

◀ **FB1.**
An unsuspecting Mk II Golf GTi, parked outside Continental Coachwork's Northampton premises. CCW are Audi-Volkswagen approved bodywork dealers and this is very important with regard to preserving the Importer's anti-rust warranty. The model shown here is a three-door version although kits are also available for the five-door car. Note the fitting on this car of non-standard 'Teardrop' alloy wheels.

FB2. ▶
It makes life easier to have the car off the ground and it is seen here raised by four axle stands. The usual safety precautions should be taken when raising the car and you must **never** work beneath a car supported only by the jack. The wheels are removed and in this shot the centre caps have been taken off by using the special security Allen key.

◀ **FB3.**
It is important to position the axle stands correctly so that the underside of the car is not damaged. The position for the rear of the car is seen here, just in front of the wheel arch.

Fitting a full body kit

Steve made a special point of collecting all nuts, bolts and washers removed from the car and putting them in a small container. This way he was sure that they would be available when the time for re-assembly arrived.

◀ **FB4.**
At the front, the axle stand is positioned to the rear of the wheel arch. Note that with the wheel off, the wheel studs have been screwed back into the hub to lessen the risk of losing them.

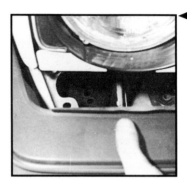

FB5.
Before the body kit can be fitted, there is much in the way of disassembly that must be done. Starting at the front, the bumper is removed by undoing the two bolts which are accessed from beneath the bracket, behind the plastic plugs in the bodywork. The only electrical connection here is the one for the indicator. This is a simple plug and socket and once unplugged, the bumper can be pulled forward and removed.

FB6. ▶
The rear bumper is removed in the same way although the indicator is mounted in the lamp cluster and thus there are no electrical connections to worry about. It pulls away from the car as shown.

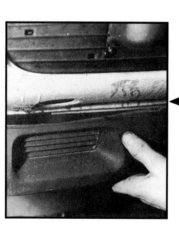

◀ **FB7.**
At the front again, the standard spoiler is removed quite simply by removing a series of 10mm bolts which pass into captive nuts in the bodywork as shown here. A second pair of hands can be useful to hold the spoiler level during removal. This is an item which will not be reused.

FB8. ▶
The small grille, which lives just below the front bumper has to be taken off. It is held by three plastic clips which yield easily to pressure from a small screwdriver.

FB9. ▶
A denuded front end, ready to receive 'the treatment'.

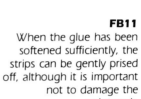

FB10.
The body rubbing strip is in three sections, the longest part being on the door itself with continuations onto the front wheel arch and rear quarter panel. The latter two have to be removed by applying heat, as shown here, to melt the glue. The DIY-er could well use a Black & Decker heat gun as shown in Chapter 5.

▼

FB11
When the glue has been softened sufficiently, the strips can be gently prised off, although it is important not to damage the paintwork.

If care is taken when removing the wheel arch extensions, it may be possible to re-sell them, particularly through a specialist publication such as the 'VW Motoring' magazine in the UK, to owners of non-GTi Golfs. (See Chapter 1, section 2.) In the same way, the spoiler is also different to that on the standard Golf and this too may have a re-sale value.

◀ **FB12.**
The GTi has black plastic wheel arch extensions as standard fittings and they must be removed. They are held by five pop rivets per arch which are drilled out.

FB13. ▶
With the wheel arch extension removed, the inner arch liner can then be taken out. Although not absolutely necessary, it gives much easier access. The liner is held by two 10mm bolts and eight cross-head self-tapping screws. The picture shows one of the lower 10mm bolts being removed.

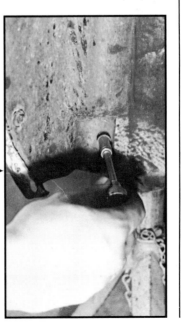

Fitting a full body kit

The thoroughness of the cleaning procedure cannot be emphasised too much. Although the new panels will be screwed into place, a silicone glue will also be used and this won't 'take' unless surfaces are totally free from contamination.

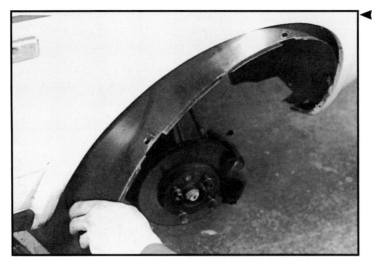

◀ FB14.
With screws and bolts removed, the liner pulls straight out as shown. The good condition of the wheel arch behind the liner shows what a good idea it is as a corrosion preventative measure.

FB15. ▶
Wherever wheel arch extensions are fitted there will also be a black plastic strip glued to the sills. This is removed in the same manner as the body rubbing strips by simply applying heat and pulling off as shown.

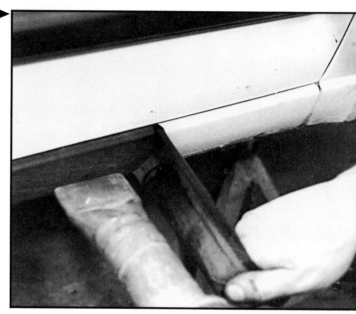

◀ FB16.
When the lower part of the car has been de-trimmed, it is important that it is meticulously cleaned. Spirit wipe or equivalent should be used to ensure that the area is free from dirt and grease.

FB17. ▶
The first of many applications of zinc paint. Here it is being applied to the rivet hole, from which the rivet was drilled out earlier on. There is a possibility that the paintwork could have been chipped while this was being carried out and as such the paint is applied to prevent any possibility of rust.

FB18 ▶

In common with many manufacturers all the hole positions were marked on the body kit but not drilled through. Shown here is one of the wheel arches which has been drilled ready for fitting. Note the letters moulded onto the inside of the arch. These are used to denote whether a particular piece is for use on the right or left hand side. It is important to check that the kit has the correct number of 'rights' and 'lefts' before commencing.

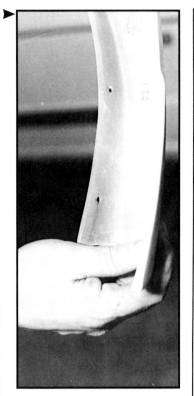

The attention to rust prevention was constant, with zinc paint and Corroless Rust Preventative spray being applied wherever there was the slightest possibility that the dreaded rust bug could get a hold.

FB19.

The wheel arches are the first to be offered up. Here the rear arch is held in place with Skyes Pickavant self-grip wrenches. Note the copious use of padding to avoid damaging either the bodywork or the body kit. The top two holes are drilled first to ensure complete accuracy of alignment with the rest of the kit. The front arch is treated in the same manner.

▼

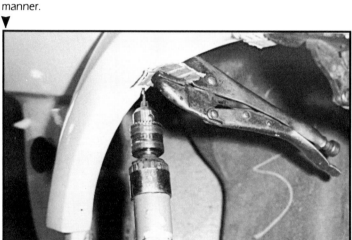

FB20. ▶

The front spoiler is held in the middle by a bolt that passes through a hole in the central bracing strut. After marking and drilling the hole accurately, the zinc paint is applied once more.

◀ **FB21.**

Every nut, bolt and self-tapping screw was treated to a liberal coating of grease as an extra anti-rust precaution. Seen here is the nut which will hold on the front spoiler.

Fitting a full body kit

It was never assumed that any part of the kit was exactly accurate. Checking and double checking was the order of the day. Steve was very aware that a small error of alignment at the front of the car would become a large error at the rear.

FB22. ▶
Having offered up the front arch and drilled the two central holes silicone glue is applied to the upper edge of the arch.

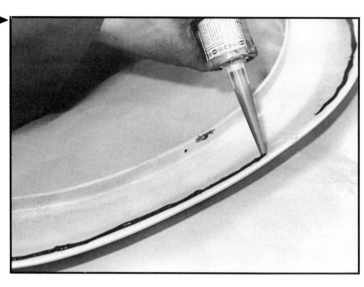

◀ **FB23.**
As the glue takes between eight and twelve hours to set and the arch has a natural tendency to spring out, masking tape is used to hold it in place. Any excess glue should be wiped away.

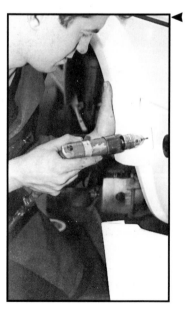

FB24. ▶
Before drilling the final holes in the wheel arch the front spoiler is held in position to ensure complete alignment. Where there is any discrepancy it may be necessary to file away small amounts from the edges of either arch or spoiler.

◀ **FB25.**
Having accurately marked the position, the lower front hole for the wheelarch is drilled. This will be covered by the bumper when re-fitted.

FB26. ▶
The spoiler is held on each side by three self-tapping screws. Two of them pass into the inner wheelarch.

FB27. ▶
This one passes through the edge of the wing. It is vital at this point that the spoiler is perfectly horizontal. This process for front wheelarch and spoiler alignment is repeated for the other side of the car.

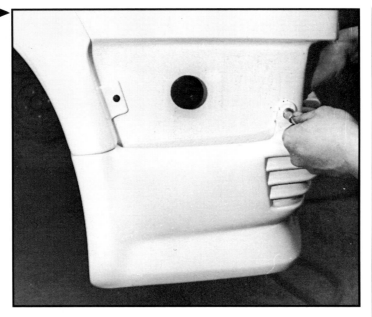

Wherever holes were drilled, the positions were carefully marked with a scriber and then pilot drilled. This is important, as it reduces the risk of the drill bit skidding and damaging the paintwork.

FB28.
Next the sill extensions can be offered up in order to check complete accuracy of alignment. As can be seen it is a two person job.
▼

FB29.
With the rear arch drilled and secured, the hole positions for the sill extensions can be drilled.
▼

◀ **FB30.**
Before the final fitting, the sill itself has to be cleaned of all dirt and grease and then lightly sandpapered in order to make a good key for the silicone glue.

Fitting a full body kit

Time and patience is required. Once the sill extension has been glued and 'wedged' in place, it is advisable to leave it for between eight and twelve hours to ensure that the glue is totally set.

FB31. ▶
As with the wheelarch extensions the glue is applied to the leading edge of the sill extension.

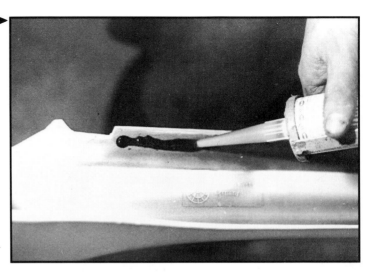

◀ **FB32.**
Curious though it looks this is what the instructions recommend. By placing thick strips of cardboard between the door and the top of the sill extension, the new section is held in place so that the glue has a chance to get a good grip.

◀ **FB33.**
The rear valance is fitted in much the same way except that no glue is used. With the rear wheel arch now totally in position the valance can be offered up, the holes drilled and self-tapping screws inserted.

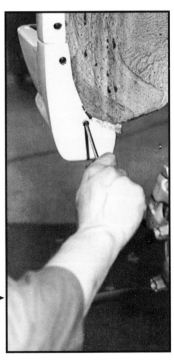

FB34. ▶
The rear valance fits around the wheel arch and is held by two self-tapping screws on each side.

◄ **FB35.**
The finished rear valance. Note that with this model, having twin exhaust pipes, there is a larger cutaway in the valance to accommodate them. (This should be specified when ordering the kit.)

Fitting the rear valance is the acid test as to whether the front and sides have been fitted correctly. In this case, the rear wheel arch and the valance were perfectly aligned.

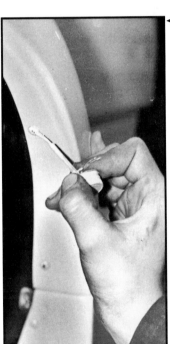

◄ **FB36.**
When the front spoiler, valance, four arches and two sill extensions have been fitted and glued in place, the self-tapping screws are all painstakingly given two coats of white paint in order to match the body kit.

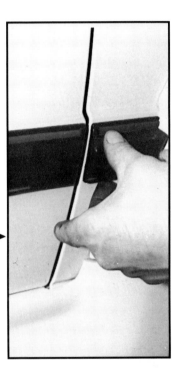

FB37. ►
The body rubbing strip which was removed earlier is carefully measured and cut to the new size, which is smaller due to the intrusion of the extended wheel arches. The new piece for the front wing is seen being replaced.

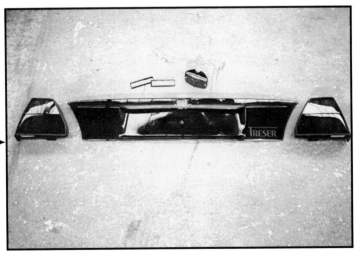

FB38. ►
In order to complete the total cosmetic package a Treser Prismatic kit was fitted. As can be seen here, it consists of a darkened centre section, two darkened lamp clusters, two stick-on reflectors and a fog lamp.

Fitting a full body kit

The Treser Prismatic lenses, available from VW dealerships, certainly add to the style of the car. However, it is very important that the fog lamp and extra reflectors be fitted as the darkened lenses prevent the internal foglamps/reflectors from meeting regulation brightness.

FB39. ▶
The old bulbs from the original clusters have to be used as new ones are not supplied with the kit. They are easily accessible by removing the centre section of the cluster simply by squeezing the plastic clips as shown.

FB40.
The clusters themselves are held in place by three nuts which require a socket and extension as shown. All electrical connections are on one simple pull-off plug.
▼

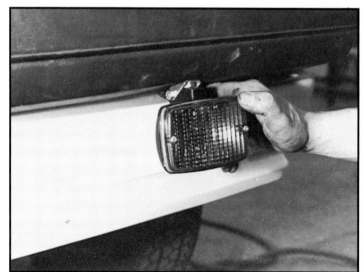

▲
FB41.
The fog lamp is fitted on the offside of the car, inboard of the towing eye. Both the bumper skin and the metal bumper itself have to be drilled for the mounting bracket. Similarly, a hole has to be drilled to allow the wiring to pass into the rear of the car, where it simply plugs into existing connections. As always where a wire passes through a metal hole, a grommet was fitted to prevent chafing.

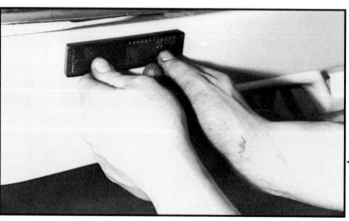

◀ **FB42.**
Two external reflectors **must** be added and these are stuck onto each side of the new rear valance.

FB43. ▶
The prismatic centre section is held by the two number plate screws and by adhesive sections shown here.

Unlike the body kit, the Treser Prismatic is very easy and quick to fit. As one would expect from this German concern, it is a high quality item, both in terms of fit and finish, and compliments the car well.

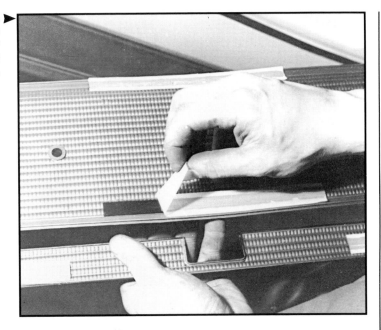

FB44.
As can be seen the effect is most stylish and it breaks up the very 'heavy' rear end look, specific to the Mk II Golf. It will be noted that the hatch lock mechanism does not have to be removed as the centre section simply slots over it.
▼

FB45.
The glue and hardener seen in this picture are all that are required to fit the Pfeba hatch spoiler. Care should be taken not to get any of it on the skin. Wear gloves or at least use an effective barrier cream on your hands.
▼

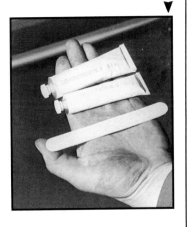

◀ **FB46.**
The lower part of the hatch should be thoroughly cleaned and then the glue applied carefully to the spoiler. This should then be offered up with some care. Note the indent in the spoiler to allow for the rear wiper.

Fitting a full body kit

Volkswagen dealers will continue to stock, for the foreseeable future, an excellent range of Volkswagen-approved, high-quality body kit components, such as those produced by BBS and Votex.

▲
FB47.
The Pfeba hatch spoiler can be obtained in a four piece version which fits along the top and sides of the hatch as well as the lower edge. It is seen here fitted to an earlier model car. (Photo courtesy of Volkswagen UK Ltd.)

FB48. ▶
Included in the BBS kit is a special adapter for the wheel jack to facilitate raising the car with the sill extensions fitted.

FB49.
The finished article. Whereas the standard car tends to be a little too softly rounded for some tastes, the BBS kit adds a touch of latent agression to the Golf, the hot hatch king. The whole kit, including the Pfeba hatch spoiler, was sprayed to match the car before fitting. According to CCW, BBS is one of the few kits that can be confidently painted before fitting without a 'mock fitting' exercise to ensure fitting accuracy.

FB50.
The car seen here is Volkswagen's demonstrator which appeared on their stand at Motorfair 1987, wearing a BBS kit. When Volkswagen dealers fit these kits modifications have to be made by them to prevent the rubbing strips getting in the way of the body kit. (Photo courtesy of Volkswagen UK Ltd).
▼

Although the BBS body kit is noted for fitting accurately straight off, without adaptation to anything but the rubbing strips, some non-Volkswagen supplied kits, particularly those in the lower price brackets, can require some fitting work to be carried out. The Black & Decker 'Powerfile', a hand-held tool with fast moving narrow sanding strip, presents a file-like surface and removes excess material rapidly. Always mark out where you want to cut to, otherwise you can easily remove too much material, and **always** wear an efficient particle mask and goggles for the sake of your health.

Bodywork accessories

Fitting an air vent cover

As with anything fitted to your car, it should really be of high quality to match the original equipment, otherwise the overall impression of the car will be lowered. Items such as this Richard Grant air vent cover blend well with the Volkswagen look and add to, rather than detract from, the appearance.

Those 'Golfers' who take an interest in the marque will no doubt have noticed that for their car's predecessor (the VW Beetle of course!) there are several manufacturers of air intake covers. These are usually produced in black plastic and, it is generally agreed, improve the look of the car. Now, they need feel deprived no more, for Richard Grant can supply a similar item to improve the look of your Golf or Jetta in much the same manner.

◀ IA17.1
The holes which accept the self-tapping screws are ready drilled but can be a little tight. We found it better to put in the screws whilst the vent cover was on the bench to alleviate any danger of the screwdriver slipping and damaging the paintwork of the car.

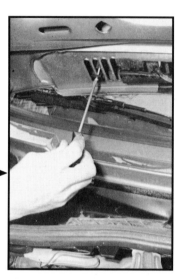

IA17.2 ▶
When the screws were an easy fit, we removed them and placed the vent cover in position over the grille. The screws tighten up against small, plastic lugs which hold the vent cover flush to the grille.

IA17.3 ▶
This was a simple item to fit and the black plastic finish of the vent cover matches the black bumpers and mirrors etc, of the Jetta.

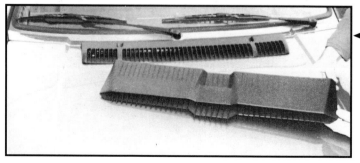

◀ IA17.4
There are two different versions of the Richard Grant vent for Mk I and Mk II cars. Alongside the vent cover we fitted to this Mk II Jetta, is the Mk I Golf/Jetta vent cover. It is interesting to note the extent to which the grille intake shapes have changed.

Fitting chromed and black 'Sideliners'

Sideliner car trims can be used both to protect the car (by using them on the edges of doors, for example) and to improve the looks when used around the wheel arches. They are available in chrome or black finish.

Branyl describe their self-adhesive trims as impossible to reposition once they are in place. From the DIY point of view, this means that much care must be taken to ensure that they are positioned correctly before pressing into place.

◀ **IA18.1**
Both black and chrome trim are shown in this shot. Note that both are supplied circular wound and, for easy fitting, it is advisable to spend some time in the warm, gently straightening them.

IA18.2
As always, the first task is to thoroughly clean the area to which they are to be fitted. This means using meths or white spirit to eliminate all traces of grease and dirt. A temperature of no less than 20 degrees C is recommended when fitting. If necessary, a hair dryer can be used to heat up both the metal and the trims. We found that the adhesive also stuck better after being placed on a radiator. ▼

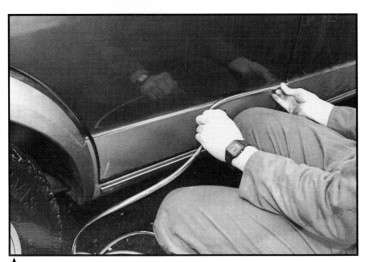

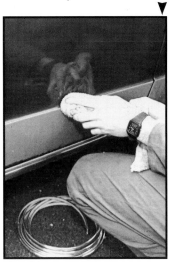

▲
IA18.3
Getting the strip straight takes some time and patience. With the backing still on, we offered the strip up into position. It was then cut to the exact length. As recommended by Branyl, we marked the position along the length of the door with a felt-tip pen as a guide to accuracy.

IA18.4 ▶
In the case of this Mk I Golf, we decided that an extra chrome body rubbing strip, under the original, would look best. The protective strip on the back of the trim has to be peeled off, after cutting to length, and then the trim carefully applied.

Fitting electric door mirrors

Keen 'Golfers' will immediately note the major '88 model year differences on the door of the car featured in this section; no quarterlight and a different mirror mounting.

Golf owners have been progressively better treated over the years when it comes to door mirrors. Early models had only one, on the driver's side. Then two were fitted and then came manual remote control. However, at the time of writing, electrically-operated door mirrors still have to be specified as an option. A 1988 model car was taken to Volkswagen's Milton Keynes HQ to see how electric mirrors were retro-fitted.

◀ **IA19.1**
The heart of the matter is the motor mounted inside the standard mirror housing.

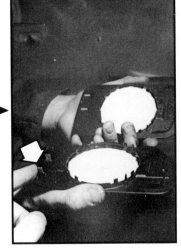

IA19.2 ▶
Similarly, the mirror heads are basically the same, but with the addition of two spade terminals as shown here. When connected into the loom, it allows not only electric adjustment, but also electric de-icing whenever the heated rear window is switched on!

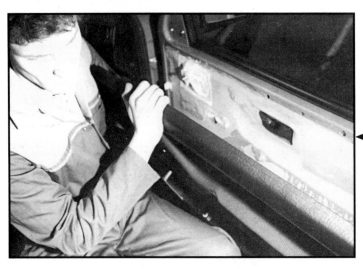

◀ **TA19.3**
The first job is to remove the trim. It is held by two screws at each end of the panel and four clips at the bottom. In addition, the armrest must be removed along with the plastic trim around the door handle and the plastic door lock catch.

IA19.4 ▶
On the outside, the mirror is held to the door by two crosshead screws. On the inside, the existing remote mechanism is held onto a bracket as shown. Removal of the retaining nut allows the mechanism and control lever to be pulled through. The original bracket is riveted to the door and these must be drilled out to allow the fitting of a new bracket which takes the electric switch.

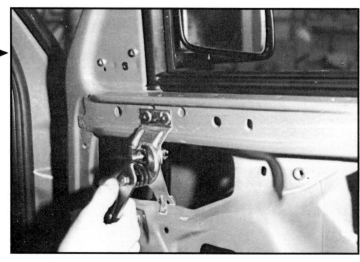

◄ IA19.5
This is the switch which will be fitted in the driver's door. By turning the centre section through 90 degrees it will operate either the driver's or the passenger's mirror.

Although far from being a cheap modification, electric mirrors are much easier and more accurate to adjust than manual remote ones, particularly for the driver trying to adjust the nearside mirror on his or her own.

IA19.6 ►
As well as the change of bracket, the hole in the trim has to be enlarged slightly to take the new switch. The hole in the passenger door has a plastic plug inserted.

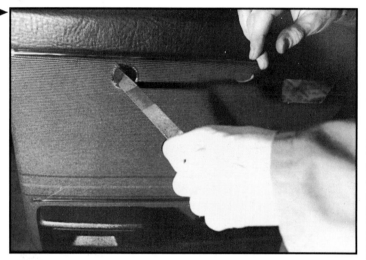

IA19.7
Not for the faint hearted!! And this is just **some** of the wiring. The loom is purpose made and fits into existing connections utilising the car's relay and fuse systems. Nevertheless, it is not an easy task.

▼

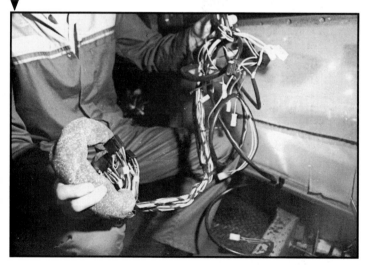

IA19.8 ►
The finished item is almost indistinguishable from the original, save for the new switch. It is possible to fit electric mirrors to any Golf. It does not have to have existing remote mirrors, nor, indeed, any mirrors at all.

Fitting a sunroof

The Britax sunroof shown here is unusual in that it is not clear, or tinted black, but white. Although a white roof on most cars would look different, when fitted to a white car it becomes, in effect, a form of colour coding. It is an option worth considering along with the rest of section 14 of this Chapter, which deals with the more conventional aspects of colour coding. It is also possible to have a coloured roof in red. The company are experimenting with other colours but the problem is producing colours which will match up with the many different paint shades on the market. The car used here had a hard moulded headlining. As the kit for cars with soft headlinings is different, it is important to specify which is required before purchase.

If you buy a new Golf and specify a sunroof, you will get a sliding steel one. However, as an after-market item, VAG (UK) Ltd, supply a range of glass roofs manufactured by Britax. The range available covers most tastes. At the top is an electronically-controlled tilt-and-slide model. The one featured here is the Sunhatch, a more modest tilt-only roof.

IA20.1 ▶
The roof comes in kit form complete with everything required to finish the job including all the trim, fastenings and sealant.

◀ IA20.2
Our fitter was a Britax expert who made the job easier by having a steel template for marking the position of the hatch. Measurements were checked and then double checked so that the template was central and straight. With the template in exactly the right place, a line was scribed around the inside.

IA20.3 ▶
In order to protect the rest of the roof paintwork, wide strips of masking tape are applied along the scribed area. Then, a hole is drilled as shown, which will be the starting point for the cutter. Four smaller holes are drilled in each corner of the marked area.

IA20.4 ▶
Before any cutting can be done, attention has to be turned to the interior of the car. The hard headlining is cut away with a craft knife using the four smaller holes, drilled earlier, as guides. With the headlining gone, the roof stiffener can be removed. This is held in position by strong glue. After using a heat gun to melt the glue, the stiffener can be pulled away at the centre. It is then cut with a pair of tin snips and pulled out.

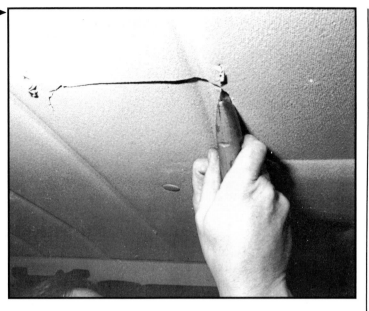

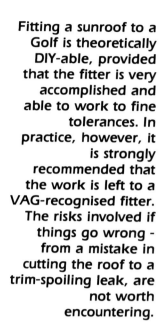

Fitting a sunroof to a Golf is theoretically DIY-able, provided that the fitter is very accomplished and able to work to fine tolerances. In practice, however, it is strongly recommended that the work is left to a VAG-recognised fitter. The risks involved if things go wrong - from a mistake in cutting the roof to a trim-spoiling leak, are not worth encountering.

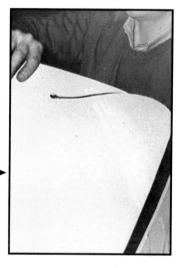

◀ **IA20.5**
The point of no return! The powerful cutter makes short work of the roof as it follows the line scribed earlier.

IA20.6 ▶
The sunhatch sized piece of roof can then be removed. Back inside the car, the headlining has to be cut back by a further ⅜ inch to allow the trim to be fitted.

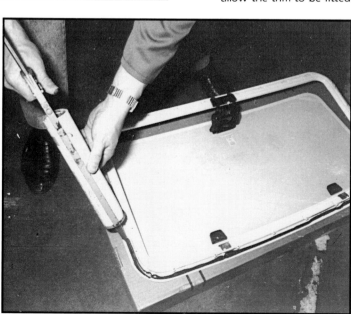

◀ **IA20.7**
With the roof upside down on the floor, sticky black silicone sealant is liberally applied to ensure that there will be no leaks.

Fitting a sunroof

The Sunhatch opens and locks in three different positions. If required, there is a similar roof available, but with a rotating control which allows infinite adjustment.

IA20.8 ▶
The Sunhatch is placed gently in position and the clamping frame offered up from inside the car. The frame holds the hatch to the roof by using no less than 24 Philips head screws. These are all tightened by hand and then given a final twist with an electronic screwdriver to ensure that the torque applied is sufficient but not excessive. At every stage, great care is taken to minimise the risk of leaks.

IA20.9
A moulded rubber surround fits under the hatch and covers the edge of the headlining and the clamping frame.
▼

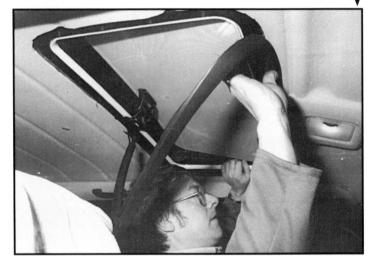

IA20.10
The last job inside is to screw on the handle trim. The roof is then ready for use.
▼

IA20.11 ▶
Back outside, the excess sealant around the hatch has to be scraped away and then the roof cleaned with a solvent.

◀ IA20.12
Seen from the outside, this shot shows the roof fully open. White on white certainly proves to be visually attractive.

Fitting a rear screen louvre

The addition of a louvre certainly makes the rear end of the Mk II Golf look different! It is not difficult to fit and, as can be seen below, the instructions are simple to follow. The design of the plastic fitting clamps is such that it can be removed in seconds but only with a special plastic 'key', which reduces the risk of theft. Although it does reduce rearward visibility, it is not as bad as may appear from the outside. The makers claim that it reduces wind turbulence and protects the glass from the effects of both snow and frost and the sun's ultraviolet rays. If it reduces the amount of road dirt that finds its way onto the rear screen of any Mk II Golf, it will surely find a strong following! It is available for both Mk I and Mk II Golfs and Jettas.

Part of the fitting of the Autoplas Louvre involves the sticking down of plastic tabs onto the rear screen. This should not be attempted where the temperature is below 8 degrees C. If it is, or even if it is close, a hair dryer could be used to warm up the area involved.

IA21.1 ▶
The plastic louvre is structurally extremely strong. The first task is to clean the rear screen for which soapy water will suffice. The louvre can then be placed onto the screen and the positions of the four fittings marked, in crayon or pencil, on the rubber surround. There are also three straight location pieces which fit under the rubber surround along the top edge of the screen. On the GTi model (with the small hatch spoiler), three areas have to be cut away from the louvre to suit.

IA21.2
The louvre is held to the fittings by means of plastic lugs which are locked in position but it can be released by using the 'key' provided. This means that it can be removed quickly, for cleaning. The lugs have a self-adhesive pad which sticks to the window. Naturally, this involves cleaning the window some more prior to fitting, this time with spirit wipe. As the other half of each lug slides under the rubber window surround, there is little danger of any of them coming adrift!

▼

◀ **IA21.3**
As can be seen, the fitting of a louvre is one way of escaping from the anonymity of owning 'just another hatchback'. The rear wiper still works underneath the louvre, although it should not be needed as often as usual.

Fitting front foglamps

Using original equipment foglamps has several advantages; not least that the bumper needs no drilling and the mounting brackets can be soundly fitted, eliminating the risk of beam 'flutter'.

Earlier on in this Chapter we showed the fitting of a front spoiler which had twin integral foglamps. Here, we visit the Milton Keynes HQ of Volkswagen UK to see how to fit foglamps without a spoiler.

◄ IA22.1
The foglamp kit comes with requisite brackets, nuts, bolts, etc.

IA22.2
A worms eye view of the nearside bumper mounting bracket. There are two bolts to undo on each side. With the indicators disconnected the bumper can then be removed.
▼

IA22.3
The oddly shaped bracket bolts onto the existing bumper. Both the bracket and the lamp should be tightened securely. With the bumper back in position, the horizontal plane of the lamp cannot be altered and so it is important to set this with the bumper off.
▼

IA22.4
Here both lamps have been mounted on the bumper. The lower grille panel baulks the back of the new lamps and has to be cut to fit as seen here.
▼

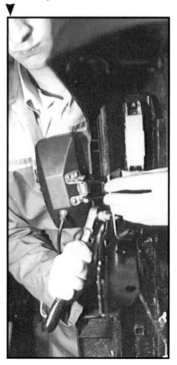

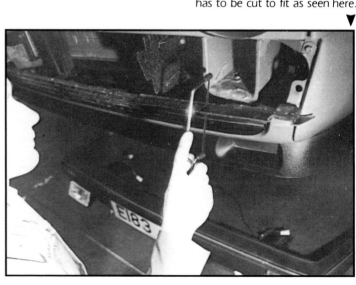

◄ IA22.5
Fitting the bumper and lamps back onto the car.

As with all front lamps, it is essential that the newly fitted foglamps are correctly adjusted so as not to dazzle oncoming traffic.

IA22.6
The connection and wiring for the lamps is already in the car. The connection point for the loom is here, alongside the nearside suspension turret. The strange-shaped box, by the way, is part of a complex alarm system; nothing to do with this section.

▼

IA22.7 ►
No lack of lighting here, with the vehicle still up on the lift. Note that the plastic cover, removed for access to the bumper mounting bolts, has yet to be refitted.

IA22.8
Back on the ground again, the foglamps add an attractive note to the look of the front end as well as making it easier to look **from** the front end. They do not just improve vision in the fog, but also in other bad weather situations such as heavy rain and/or spray. The bolt holding the lamp to the bracket allows movement for vertical adjustment.

▼

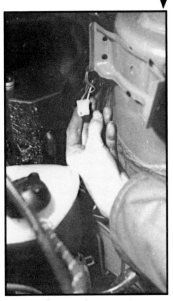

Fitting an additional rear foglamp

By fitting a replacement lamp cluster in order to obtain the extra foglamp, the look of the car is not altered at all, which is a distinct 'plus' point for those who prefer to keep the car looking standard.

As standard, both Mk I and Mk II Golfs come fitted with only one foglamp, as required by EEC regulations. It is a curious feature of the Golf, especially as Volkswagen are normally extremely safety conscious. However, fitting a second one is easy, requiring the replacement of the nearside lamp cluster and a little wiring.

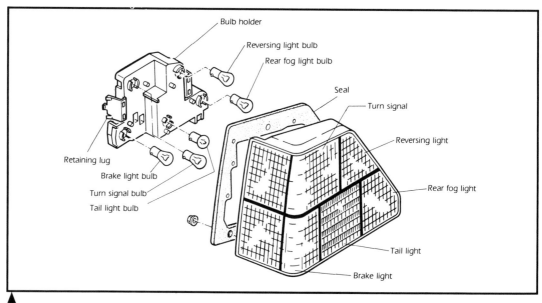

IA23.1
This diagram shows the nearside rear lamp cluster together with the multi-bulb holder and the relative positions of the bulbs. As can be seen, the foglamp section is at the lower right of the cluster and usually this is blanked off at the rear with no bulb in the holder.

◀ **IA23.3**
The bulb holder is released by squeezing the retaining lug and drawing back. With this out, the three nuts retaining the lamp cluster can be undone.

▲ **IA23.2**
Which is which? It is almost impossible to tell the old lamp cluster from the new. Although they look the same, the new one has special reflective material inside the aperture for the foglamp. Using a normal cluster and just inserting a high wattage bulb would contravene lighting regulations.

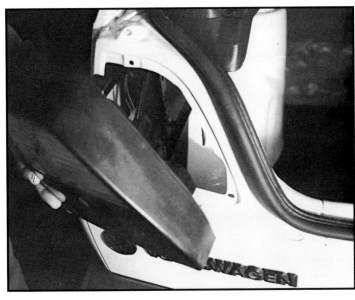

◄ IA23.4
Next, the cluster pulls straight out. The new one replaces it by reversing the previous instructions.

Fitting the foglamp as shown allows it to be wired straight into the car's electrical system; it needs no additional switching or fuses.

IA23.5
The necessary connection is already on the bulb holder board. A wire with spade connector can be fitted quite easily.
▼

▲
IA23.6
The correct degree of brightness will be achieved by using a 21W bulb, available from any accessory store.

IA23.7 ►
The finished product. Not awfully impressive in daylight, but in the fog it could well be a lifesaver. The existing foglamp switch is used.

Fitting a passenger seat storage box

The instructions for fitment supplied with the box are clear and concise with plenty of diagrammatical explanation. This exploded view shows the mounting bracket which fastens to the seat frame. It fits as comfortably as you would expect from a Volkswagen-supplied product.

The interior storage space in the Golf improved when the car evolved from Mk I to Mk II. However, even in the latter it is not especially generous. The glovebox is small and the parcel trays simply allow items to roll about when the car is cornering. The door pockets (standard on the Mk IIs but also available for Mk Is, see Chapter 2, Section 8), are very useful, but soon get full and won't take oddly shaped items. (Drawing courtesy of Volkswagen)

Volkswagen have clearly given some thought to the problem of extra storage and have come up with this ingenious solution; a German-made storage box which mounts onto the front of the passenger seat. It is able to take quite large objects and, with the lid removed, quite tall objects too, such as map books. Once the bracket and mounting plate has been fitted, it is capable of taking a fire extinguisher or a first-aid kit instead.

IA24.1 ▶
The box itself is made of extremely tough plastic and has a grained finish similar to that of the console and facia. The lid is hinged and can be removed altogether if required.

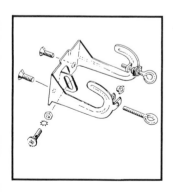

◀ IA24.2
It is not necessary to remove the seat to fit the mounting bracket; it just makes description easier. The two 'hooks' pass around the front of the seat frame and are secured to the central runner, as shown here.

IA24.3 ▶
The mounting plate can then be fixed to the bracket. Note that there are no less than ten different mounting holes. This allows the plate to be fitted to several different models. For clarity, we are showing the plate being mounted centrally, although it actually fits slightly off-centre due to the position of the seat adjustment lever.

IA24.4 ▶
The plate, when fitted, forms the basis for carrying one of three items. If either the fire extinguisher or the first-aid kit are to be installed, they are secured by this tether strap (supplied), which is threaded through the plate as shown.

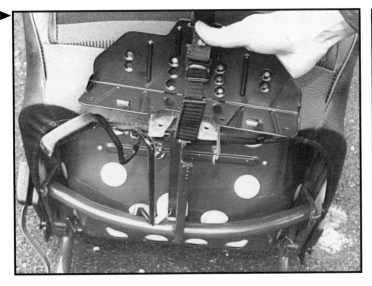

The fitment of a fire extinguisher or first-aid kit instead of the box is possible, using the tether strap supplied. With the strap in place, it is a simple task to secure either unit to the mounting plate, as shown in these diagrams.
(Drawing courtesy of Volkswagen)

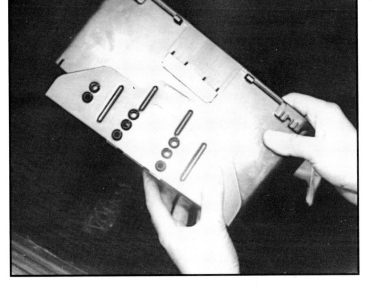

◀ **IA24.5**
When the box is to be fitted, it is held in two ways. Firstly, it slots into a lip on the mounting plate and then ...

◀ **IA24.6**
... it is secured safely by two screws which pass through the underside of the box. Again, these operations are shown out of situ for clarity.

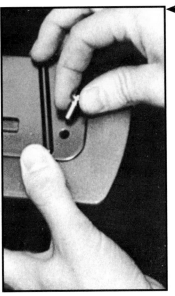

IA24.7 ▶
The storage box in position and looking, naturally enough, like original equipment. Mounted where it is, it does not cause any problem for the passenger with regard to comfort whilst travelling or when getting in and out of the car.

Fitting mudflaps

The simplest way of ensuring that VW's mudflaps are aligned properly, left and right, is to measure their position relative to the bodywork with a tape measure. Simple, but easily overlooked!

Fitting a set of mudflaps, either two or four, is always a good idea. They protect the body work against damage from stones and cut down the amount of dirt and mud which encourages rust on the bodywork. Thus, for a relatively small investment, they could conceivably add a considerable amount to your car's resale value. We fitted two different types of mudflap, both available from Volkswagen dealers. Their own is a VW universal flap which will fit any car in the range. The Votex flaps, however, are specific to the Golf and come in pairs, front and rear.

IA25.1 ▶
The VW flaps come with no markings at all. The vehicle name is available as a separate clip-on logo. The Golf badges are actually plastic and, although purchased from the main dealer, are not supplied with the flaps. They slot through small holes at the bottom of the flap and are secured by push-fit circlips at the rear.

IA25.2 ▶
Fitting the VW item is easy. It is held in place whilst the two bolts are tightened in the clamp brackets, as shown here. It is important to ensure that the small rubber inserts are placed between the bracket and the bodywork to prevent damaging the latter.

IA25.3
Seen here are a pair of Votex flaps for the rear. Both front and rear have the VW roundel moulded in, but it is only picked out in white on the rear set. They are fastened by using a set of double spring clips. With the flaps in position, the flexible mountings are folded around the edge of the wheel arch and the first spring clip placed over it to hold it in place. When all of the mountings have been secured, a second, much stronger, clip is placed over the top of the original and knocked into place with a hammer.
▼

◀ IA25.4
The nearside rear mudflap in place. It is functional, attractive and, being moulded to fit, there is no chance of fitting it at an odd angle.

Fitting exhaust pipe extensions

One thing guaranteed to spoil the look of your otherwise immaculate Golf or Jetta is a rusty tailpipe. Fitting a high quality Sedan accessory extension is a simple way to solve this problem. We tried out both the single and twin pipe options on this Jetta. If the end of the original exhaust pipe is rotten, or if the extension protrudes too far from the rear of the car, it may be necessary to cut the original pipe, even if it is sound. Extensions are available for both Mk I and Mk II cars.

Fitting an exhaust pipe extension is an easy task which should only be attempted when the exhaust system is cold. However, it is very important that it is affixed securely as it could be extremely dangerous should it fly off at speed!

◄ IA26.1
Link Sedan produce a range of extensions, some of which are seen here. There are single and twin tailpipe versions available in either chrome or chrome and black.

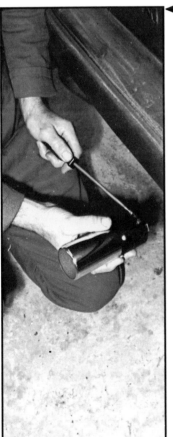

◄ IA26.2
One of the easiest things to fit, a Sedan exhaust pipe extension requires only a screwdriver, possibly a hacksaw and, of course, a cool exhaust! The screwdriver is used to tighten a clamp which holds the extension to the exhaust pipe.

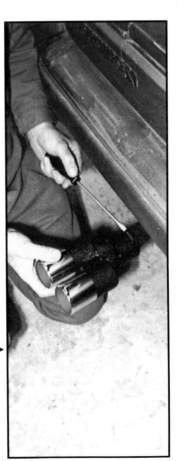

IA26.3 ►
Here, the twin pipe extension is being fitted. This is the easy way to give your car the 'Mk II GTi' look. Note that all such extensions must be mounted so that they do not protrude beyond the bumper line.

Fitting a towing bracket

As can be seen from this diagram, the Volkswagen Towing Bracket is of integral design, making it incredibly strong. As with most brackets, the electrical fitting kit seen here is a separate item. (Diagram courtesy of Volkswagen UK)

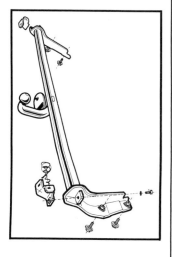

Towing brackets are now supplied by Volkswagen dealers in two kits.
1) 12N kit: 8-core cable, prewired socket, fixing parts, relay instructions, etc.
2) 12S kit: 7-core cable, prewired sockets, fixing parts, instructions, etc.

The bracket fitting is the same for all Mk II models.

The major point to consider when fitting a towbar is stress. Clearly, by harnessing a Golf to another vehicle, be it camping trailer or caravan, a whole new range of stresses and strains are placed on the car. Two things are necessary: First, the towing bracket should be strong enough to cope with the job in hand and, second, it should not place any undue strain on the car. Peka, world renowned for their expertise in towing equipment, have worked directly with VW on the design and development of a range of towing brackets to suit their cars. The result is a towing bracket which is inherently strong and which will not adversely affect the vehicle. Here, Volkswagen mechanic, Robert, is seen fitting a bracket to an '88 spec Golf GTi.

IA27.1 ▶
First job is to remove the bumper by undoing the two bolts accessible from underneath. Note that in this case, a Treser Prismatic is fitted and with it darkened rear lenses. (see Bodykit section earlier in this chapter). As such, a separate rear foglamp has been fitted which must be disconnected before the bumper can be removed. With the bumper off the original brackets have to be removed.

IA27.2
Onto the towing bracket are mounted two smaller brackets which allow it to be fitted directly to the bumper. The plastic bumper moulding has a small recess cut into its underneath to allow for fitment of a factory towing bracket.

▼

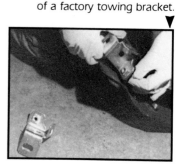

IA27.3
Volkswagen built Golfs from 1987 onwards, come complete with a hole and grommet pressed into the hatch, alongside the rear bumper mounting, to facilitate the fitting of the cable from the towbar electrics. However, as we were fitting twin sockets, a second hole was required. Here, Robert is seen filing the rough edges prior to applying zinc paint as an anti-rust measure and, of course, fitting a grommet.

IA27.4
Wiring the sockets is a matter of following the diagrams as shown. All of the necessary cabel (7 core trailer cable) and fasteners are provided in the kit. Two power feeds are required for the supplementary socket. The first, for the interior lights, has to be permanently live and was taken from the hatch courtesy light. The second, for the fridge, has to be live only with the ignition on and was taken from the rear wash-wipe system.

◄ IA27.5

When the electrical connections have been made, and the wires cut to length, the bumper, complete with towing bracket, can be replaced. The bolts should be torqued to the correct specification. As these bolts are holding the towing bracket on, this is especially important.

IA27.6 ►

The extra indicators require an uprated relay. The fuse plate has to be released from its bracket and lowered slightly for correct identification. The old relay is removed and the new one, supplied with the electrical kit, is pushed into place.

IA27.7 ►

An indicator warning light has to be fitted. The simplest method is to mount the light in one of the blank switch panels. In this case, Robert chose the one above the side/headlamp switch.

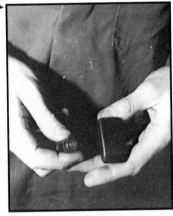

IA27.8

Fitted with the minimum of fuss, it is a compact and discrete bracket. The offset look of the sockets was mechanic Robert's personal preference. They can be mounted at several different angles. The cutaway in the plastic bumper moulding allows the towing hook to exit at a sharp angle and thus it is not a massive protruberance at the rear to trip-up unsuspecting pedestrians!

The two diagrams here show how the sockets should be wired. The supplementary socket will be required for those who use the car electrics for caravans etc, and provide power feeds for interior lights and a fridge.
(Diagrams courtesy of Volkswagen UK)

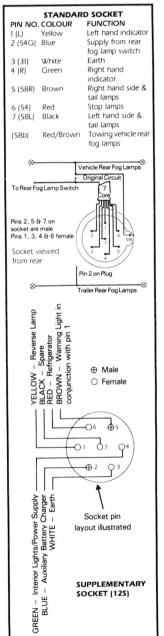

STANDARD SOCKET		
PIN NO.	COLOUR	FUNCTION
1 (L)	Yellow	Left hand indicator
2 (54G)	Blue	Supply from rear fog lamp switch
3 (31)	White	Earth
4 (R)	Green	Right hand indicator
5 (58R)	Brown	Right hand side & tail lamps
6 (54)	Red	Stop lamps
7 (58L)	Black	Left hand side & tail lamps
(58b)	Red/Brown	Towing vehicle rear fog lamps

Vehicle Rear Fog Lamps
Original Circuit
To Rear Fog Lamp Switch
7 Core
Pins 2, 5 & 7 on socket are male
Pins 1, 3, 4 & 6 female
Socket viewed from rear
Pin 2 on Plug
Trailer Rear Fog Lamps

YELLOW – Reverse Lamp
BLACK – Spare
RED – Refrigerator
BROWN – Warning Light in conjunction with pin 1

⊕ Male
○ Female

GREEN – Interior Lights/Power Supply
BLUE – Auxiliary Battery Charger
WHITE – Earth

Socket pin layout illustrated

SUPPLEMENTARY SOCKET (12S)

Fitting rear window brake lights

It is important to take note of any local regulations regarding the fitment of high level rear brake lamps.
In the UK, the **minimum** height of the lamps from the road should be 400mm. The **maximum** height should be 1500mm. The distance between lamps should not be less than 600mm. The lamps should be for brake use only and be 'E' approved for that purpose.

Link-Sedan high level brake lamps can be mounted in any Golf or Jetta, either by screws or by adhesive. When fitted correctly they can be a great safety boost, allowing drivers several cars behind you to see that you are braking and thus reduce the possibility of a multi-car pile up.

◄ IA28.1
The Link-Sedan kit comes with two lamps, brackets and various wiring and connectors. The lamp here is being mounted on a bracket prior to fitting. The wiring is a matter of 'Scotchloking' one of the cables from the new lamps into the existing brake lamp circuit and connecting the other to earth.
The bracket comes complete with a self-adhesive pad.

IA28.2 ►
When fitting to a Golf, they can be mounted either on the parcel shelf or, more practically, on the rear screen. When the lamp or lamps are to be stuck to the screen, the screen should first be thoroughly cleaned with meths and the working temperature should be around 15 degrees C. A hair dryer can be used to raise the temperature if it is a little cool. The edge of the bracket is tucked into the rubber surround for added stability.

◄ IA28.3
In this Jetta we chose to mount centrally only one of the Link-Sedan lights. The same method was used as in IA24.2, after having measured the central position carefully.

IA28.4 ►
The finished product, which leaves drivers behind in no doubt as to when the car is slowing down, even if the standard lights are very dirty. It also enables drivers two or three vehicles back to see your brake lights through the windows of the vehicles in between.

Choosing alternative wheels

The standard wheel diameter on the Mk I was 13 inch with the width of the rim varying according to the model. Usually, the more upmarket the car, the wider the wheel. Mk IIs were also fitted with 13 inch wheels, although all GTis had 14 inch rims, whether they were alloy or not.

Volkswagen fit road wheels which have been designed with specific requirements with regard to their dimensions, stresses and operating loads. Similarly, the wheel studs are engineered to very exacting tolerances and are produced to match specific wheels. It is important that they have the correct length, cone seating dimension and torque characteristics. Using an incorrect wheel bolt is potentially very dangerous indeed. Therefore, when changing wheels, great care should be taken to ensure that only the recommended wheel stud is used.

IA29.1 ▶
This diagram shows the stud configuration on the Golf, which is 4 stud on all models. PCD (Pitch Circle Diameter) is the diameter of the circle that passes through the centre of all four studs. (Diagram courtesy Volkswagen UK Ltd)

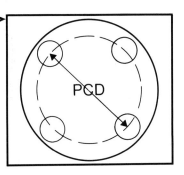

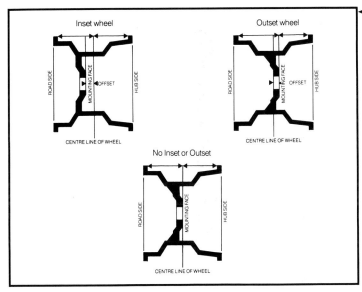

IA29.2
With Volkswagen wheels, one of the most important aspects is their negative offset geometry. In simple terms, this means that under heavy braking, the car is designed to carry on in a straight line rather than swerve around all over the place. This is a valuable safety feature and should be a major consideration when changing from a standard wheel.

Be practical when choosing wheels. For instance, you should ask yourself how difficult will they be to clean. However attractive a wheel looks when it is new, it will look somewhat different after two weeks of Winter (or Summer for that matter!). Cleaning some wheels can almost be a full time job, although it is usually the best looking wheels that take the most cleaning.

The diagrams here show offset in schematic form. (Diagram courtesy Volkswagen UK Ltd)

There are few items which will transform the look of your Golf more simply than a set of alloy wheels. Of course, some Golfs have alloy wheels as standard: Later Mk I GTis had them and so did early Mk II GTis. As the prices of the Mk II GTis rose, so the three door version was equipped with steel wheels and later, the five door also met the same fate. However, many buyers specified alloy wheels as an option before taking delivery.

IA29.3 ▶
The whole range of Volkswagen officially approved wheels for 1988. Some of them will be familiar as standard fitting to some models.

Choosing alternative wheels

When wheel manufacturers talk about 'offset', they are referring to the distance from the centre line of the wheel to its mounting surface (see Fig. 1A2.2).

When changing wheels it is very important to consider the tyres as well. Obviously, if the new wheel is a larger diameter, as is often the case, then a completely new set of tyres (and spare) will be required. Equally obviously, this will add a great deal to the overall cost. Similarly, even if the diameter of the wheel remains the same, an increase in the width of the rim may mean that the tyre is not wide enough to be safe on the new wheel.

Also, a larger wheel/tyre combination can alter the gearing of the car. This will affect acceleration, top speed and, most of all, speedometer accuracy. This is usually avoided by using a lower profile tyre with the increased diameter wheel (see Chapter 4, section 16).

Whilst these are important points, it is probable that most of the alloy wheels fitted in the UK are for good looks more than anything else. On that score, it is true that any Golf (Mk I or Mk II) looks much meaner with a set of wider wheels and tyres.

▲
IA29.4
The latest BBS offering is the RZ series. It is an attractive light alloy wheel with a removable centre cap for access to the wheel studs. Although designed to look like their three piece composite wheel counterparts, they cost considerably less.

▲
IA29.5
The Pirelli wheel, seen here on a Mk I Golf, but originally fitted to late model Mk I GTi Campaign models. Look carefully at the pattern around the edge of the wheel and you will see that it forms a circle of 'P's.

▲
IA29.6
The Volkswagen Design alloy wheel has taken little time to acquire the unofficial title of '16V wheel', due to its fitting as standard to the 16-valve version of the Golf/Jetta GTis.

▲
IA29.7
One of the best wheels around is the BBS, RS series, three part wheel. Very good and very expensive. Note the resemblance to the wheel in Fig. 1A29.4.

▲
IA29.8
The Votex wheel here is seen fitted to a bodykitted Jetta. The smooth, clean lines of the wheel suit the squarer lines of the booted car better than its hatchback brother.

▲
IA29.9
The Volkswagen 'Teardrop' alloy wheel is one of this writer's favourites, combining stylish good looks with practicality, since it is notably easy to clean. Also, it has a locking cap which requires the use of a special Allen key to gain access to the wheel studs. The wheel is seen here on the bodyfitted car shown earlier in this Chapter. Where wheels do not have lockable centre caps, we would certainly recommend the fitting of wheel locking studs.

It should be borne in mind that larger wheel and tyre combinations will also effect the handling of the car. Whilst it is true that a larger tyre area will give more grip in the dry, it is also true that the car will be more prone to aquaplaning in the wet. The same large tyres can make the already heavy steering even heavier, particularly where the massive 7J x 15 wheel is fitted.

Using a tyre dresser

IA30.1 ▶
A simple but effective way of brightening up the look of your Golf, or, as in this case, your Jetta. The Branyl Tyre Dresser itself is easy to use, being rather like an old school crayon! A steady hand is needed and ideally the wheel should be taken off altogether to allow it to be put onto a bench.

When using a tyre dresser, it is essential that the tyre is totally clean and free from grease.

Fitting locking wheel studs

Having fitted alloy wheels, and probably a new set of tyres as well, you will doubtless want to keep them. Even those who have steel wheels, may well have some very expensive tyres which would be tempting to the would-be thief. The Carflow locking wheel studs make it almost impossible for anyone to take the wheels without the special socket 'key'.

Following on from our comments in the previous section, it is vital that studs of the correct length be chosen in the interests of safety.

IA31.2
A stud is seen here being fitted to a white spoked alloy wheel. For each new stud there is a metal cover, shaped to look like a standard head. This is a nice touch for those who have wheel studs 'on show' rather than covered, as in this case.

◀ IA31.1
Carflow studs look like the originals except that they have a pattern of holes in the top. The holes correspond exactly with the prongs in the special socket provided. Without this socket, none of the wheels can be removed. Four studs are provided and are fitted one per wheel. It is obviously important to remember to keep the socket with the car in case of a puncture. Equally, it is just as important to make a note of the code number of the socket to enable you to get another should you mislay yours. A sticker is provided in the kit with this on. We found that the safest place to put it was alongside the paint code details in the hatch.

Fitting wheel clean discs

During the fitting of the wheel clean discs, all of the usual safety measures should be taken whilst the car is jacked up for wheel removal. Remember especially to chock securely one of the wheels on the ground and **never** work beneath a car supported only with a jack.

Most Golf owners know the annoyance that the fine layer of brake dust upon the front wheels can cause, especially those with complex patterned alloys! One way to help alleviate the problem is to fit a set of Carflow wheel clean discs, which fit inside the wheels and protect them. We had a natural concern about fitting these items, with regard to the effect they may have on braking efficiency. However, they are fully approved by the extremely demanding German TUV organisation. The tests insist that the discs must not cause brake fading, overheating of hubs and brakes under extreme conditions or the fouling of braking or suspension parts.

IA32.1
The wheel clean discs are sold in pairs and each disc has a metal centre with holes suitable for all 3, 4 and 5 stud applications up to 130mm PCD. Note the moulded circles around the edges of the rubber which are used as a guide should any need to be trimmed off.

IA32.2 ▶
With the wheel removed from the hub, the inside of the wheel should be brushed down to remove excess dirt. Then, the disc is offered up to the inside of the wheel. The disc must be aligned with the stud holes and then centralised. The rubber should be pushed into the contour of the wheel and if, as in this case, it is too big, it can be cut down using normal household scissors. If the right size is reached but the rubber disc fouls the braking system (disc, calipers etc), Carflow suggest that it be glued to the inside of the wheel, having cleaned it well first. They also advise that the wheel studs should be torqued up after 100 miles as a precaution.

Valeting

Cleaning and protecting bodywork

The KEW-Hobby washer is a high-pressure water pump which easily removes mud and dirt from your car. As with car washes the windows must be wound right up and the doors/hatch/boot shut tight before using.

◀ **IA33.1**
For the Golf owner who is conscientious about the appearance and condition of his or her car, the KEW-Hobby Washer is a boon. It can be used to great effect under the car, particularly around the wheel arches, where dirt and mud tend to congregate and attract the dreaded rust bug.

IA33.2 ▶
The KEW-Hobby Washer can also be used under the bonnet, something especially useful on older cars. By using the machine in this way after an application of a degreasing agent, such as Comma Hyper Clean, a sparkling clean engine bay can be yours very quickly and with remarkably little effort. For further details of engine bay valeting, see Chapter Four, Section 16.

In order to prevent marking the paintwork with any grit or harsh dirt, it is a good idea to hose down the car before shampooing.

It may sound obvious but there is a correct order to follow when washing the car - useful to tell the kids before they smear underbody mud over the windscreen with the wash sponge! Start with windows; go on to roof, bonnet and upper hatch, wash down to the body moulding and finish off with wheel arches, sills, valances and wheels.

IA33.4
Comma Car Shampoo is concentrated, which means that only two capfulls in a bucket of warm water are needed to clean a Golf/Jetta. The 300 ml plastic bottle contains enough for 18 washes. This product contains a wax which helps to protect the paintwork whereas washing up liquid (the great alternative!) contains chemicals whose job it is to cut through wax and grease. Washing up liquid also contains salt which leaves streaks on bodywork and can actively encourage rust formation.

◀ **IA33.3**
A useful feature with Comma's 300 ml plastic packs is the way in which the instructions and details are contained in a handy booklet, stuck to the back of the bottle. It is sealed down one side and can be opened, read and then resealed.

IA33.5
When the car has been rinsed and dried off, using a chamois to further help prevent 'streaking', the Comma Silicone polish can be applied.

After washing, you could give a long-lasting shine by polishing with Comma Silicone polish, which contains carnauba wax, and polishes and protects the paintwork from the elements in one application. The container should be shaken well and the polish applied sparingly with a clean damp cloth to small areas at a time. When it is dry, it should be polished lightly with a clean, dry cloth. It should not be used in direct sunlight or on hot surfaces.

Cleaning and protecting bodywork

Always take care not to get wax-based products onto the glass, particularly the windscreen, where it could smear and be potentially dangerous. From this point of view, it is usually best to make glass cleaning, with a product such as Comma's Glass Cleaner, the last job to carry out when cleaning your car.

IA33.6 ►
Comma Tar Remover is simple to apply and does not harm the paintwork. Using a soft dry cloth, it should be applied to the affected area using a gentle rubbing motion. When the tar has been dissolved, wipe with a clean cloth. The product can also be used for carpets, upholstery or clothing, although when used thus, small areas should be first tested for colour fastness.

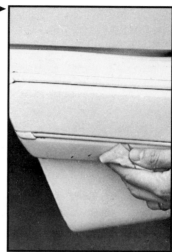

◄ **IA33.8**
There is plenty of exterior black trim on the Golf, especially later models. Here, Comma's Trim Black is being used to restore the wheel arches of this GTi to their original splendour. After shaking the bottle, it should be rubbed onto a whole area with a soft cloth in one application. Where the surface is grained, such as on the arch, the cleaner must be worked right in. When it is dry, buffing with a clean cloth will reveal a 'new look' wheelarch. It can also be used on bumpers, rubber mouldings, plastic trim, tyres and mudflaps.

IA33.7
With effect from the mid-1970s, the trend has been more and more towards the use of black exterior trim rather than chrome. It follows that the Mk I tends to have more chrome than the Mk II and on this GTi, the only exterior chrome was to be found on the wheel centre caps and this tailpipe, both non-standard items. The use of Comma Chrome Cleaner is simply a matter of applying sparingly with a soft cloth and allowing to dry for a few minutes. Polishing with a clean cloth reveals a shine that you may not have seen for years!
▼

◄ **IA33.9**
It is surprisingly easy to forget the large area of the car that isn't metal ... the glass. Comma Glass Cleaner can be used both inside and out and is particularly useful for the windscreen where it removes traffic film and squashed insects, etc, that washing alone does not. Application is simple as it is an aerosol based foam which is spread all over the window to be cleaned.

IA33.10 ▶

After a couple of minutes it can be wiped away with a soft cloth, leaving a clean, smear-free window.

IA33.11

Older cars' windscreen rubber seals may not be perfect and it is possible that after rinsing the car down, you will find that water has penetrated the interior. Comma's Seek 'n Seal is an easily applied remedy. Just ease back the rubber seal and squeeze the sealant into the affected area. It should be applied in several light coats, allowing five minutes between each one.

▼

A handy tip for the preservation of chamois leathers is to squeeze, rather than wring, them out. Also, they should not be allowed to dry out thoroughly; best achieved by putting them into a sealed container whilst still damp.

IA33.12 ▶

For those with older Golfs and Jettas which may have faded paintwork, these two Comma products could also be of use. Top Cut is a paint restorer which is wax-free and removes haze, oxidisation and surface scratches. It is applied sparingly with a damp cloth and removed when dry with a clean dry cloth or stockinette. The surface is then ready for waxing. Alternatively, Super Cut 'n Wax does both jobs in one, for paint surfaces that are not quite so badly faded. Neither of these should be used on hot surfaces or in bright sunlight. Also, if the paintwork is metallic, a small area should be tried first.

◀ **IA33.13**

The cleanest that this car has looked in a long time! The use of Comma cleaning products will certainly help to preserve paintwork and in doing so, preserve the secondhand value of your car, as well as providing you, the owner, with a Golf or Jetta you can continue to feel proud of.

Chapter Two
In-car comforts

Fitting a replacement steering wheel

◄ IC1.1
The car here is a GTi with the standard four horn button wheel. It's certainly not an unpleasant wheel but it is a little bulbous and plasticky for some. It makes life much easier later on if the steering wheel is in the central position before it is taken off. To remove, first take out the centre blank cover by prising gently with a screwdriver. It is very flexible and will not break.

Replacing the standard steering wheel is one of the most common ways of improving the look of the interior. Also, the feel of a well designed, leather wheel can make a world of difference to the pleasure derived from driving.

IC1.2 ►
Pulling out the centre blank cover reveals the retaining nut. All electrical connections are integral, so there are no problems here.

◄ IC1.3
Removal of the retaining nut requires a socket and a long extension. It can require some effort to get it to turn and a helper may be useful to hold the wheel still.

Fitting a replacement steering wheel

From a safety point of view it is important that the spring washer be refitted under the steering wheel nut and that the nut be tightened fully.

◄ IC1.4
Pull the wheel off. Although it may be necessary to ease the wheel from side to side, try to make sure that it is in the central position before pulling totally off the splines. Take care you don't hit yourself in the face if the steering wheel comes free all of a sudden!

◄ IC1.5
The wheel is held by a nut and a spring washer. Make sure that neither gets lost as the wheel comes off.

IC1.6 ►
The new wheel is held onto a boss by means of six Allen headed screws, as shown. Also shown is the spade connector from the boss to the wiring on the wheel. If you have been good during the previous steps, fitting the wheel so that it is level will correspond with the straight ahead position of the driven wheels.

IC1.7 ►
Replace the nut and washer using the socket and extension as previously. Obviously, it must be very tight and an assistant may be required to hold the wheel so that sufficient pressure can be used. It is now that the acid test comes, before fitting the final piece. A short test run will ascertain whether the wheel is exactly central on the splines. Also, check that the indicators still cancel correctly. If there are any problems, it will be necessary to remove the wheel and re-position it.

IC1.8 ▶
With the wheel straight, the centre piece can be fitted. This is held by three self-tapping screws which are inserted through from the back of the wheel.

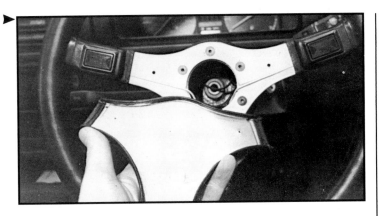

It is important to have the correct size of wheel. Sizes refer to the diameter of the wheel. Most standard wheels are a little too big, although with the inherent heavy steering common to Golfs. It is unwise to go too small unless you wish to build up your arm muscles! We would recommend no bigger than 14 inch diameter and not much less than 13 inch diameter. Cars with power steering can take a smaller sized wheel much more easily, of course.

◀ **IC1.9**
This VW-approved accessory is a much better looking wheel and is a delight to use. The horn pushes are mounted at the end of the three spokes.

Fitting replacement seats

If you think seats are just something between you and the floor, then you're wrong. Recaro have invested large amounts of time and money into car seat research. Back pain is a serious source of illness all over the world and causes many thousands of working days to be lost because of it. Bearing in mind the number of hours many of us spend in a car during the year, it is not surprising that poorly designed car seats are thought to be responsible for many back problems.

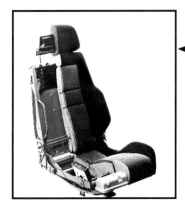

◀ **IC2.1**
No, this is not a production seat! This cutaway version of the CS model shows just how much goes into seat production. Safety, as well as comfort and ergonomics are a major consideration of Recaro design. The seat framework is stable in every direction and the whole structure absorbs shockwaves and will not splinter in the event of a crash. The upholstery is in line with recent scientific discoveries on the reduction of stress to the body muscles. Recaro seats are not too soft and give the body firm, and healthy, support.
(Photo by courtesy of Keiper Recaro GmbH & Co.)

Recaro are a German concern whose 75 years experience of car seating has made them world renowned as makers of some of the best car seats on the market. As well as making seats for all models of Golf and Jetta, available from Volkswagen dealerships, they also supply seats for fitment to airlines, trucks, buses and taxis.

Fitting replacement seats

There is a range of seven upholstery combinations which apply to all the Recaro range. In addition, they are all available in two types of leather (cow hide or water buffalo!) in a choice of six or three different colours, depending on which leather is selected.

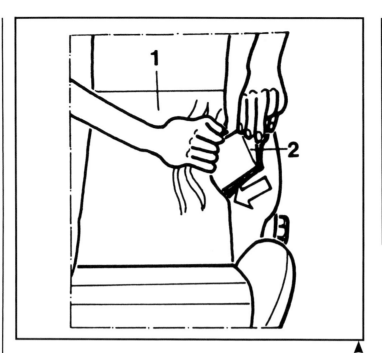

▲
IC2.3
The CSE seat shown here was redesigned from scratch and is regarded by Recaro as being the ultimate. It has electric adjustment for the height, tilt and backrest and Airmatic cushions built into the seat which can be adjusted to 'mould' the seat to its occupant. The latter is also an electronic feature and can even be used whilst the car is moving. A memory recall facility is optional which allows different drivers/passengers to programme their own requirements into the seat and thus save constant re-setting.
(Photo by courtesy of Keiper Recaro GmbH & Co.)

▲
IC2.2
A foam rubber wedge is supplied with the seat and can be inserted between the backrest cushion and backrest frame. By adjusting it to suit personal taste, as shown here, it provides excellent support for the lumbar region.
(Diagram by courtesy of Keiper Recaro GmbH & Co.)

IC2.4
The Recaro Orthapaedic has been designed for them by a team of experts including orthapaedic specialists. For those who suffer from back trouble of any description, and particularly those who have severe disorders, this seat might mean the difference between driving or not driving. It has many features including Airmatic air cushions, individually adjustable bolsters on the backrest, individual shoulder support rake and U-form fully upholstered headrest.
(Photo by courtesy of Keiper Recaro GmbH & Co.)
▼

IC2.5
The business: Firm, comfortable, practical and upholstered in leather, the C-Classic has many of the features of the CSE model and is superbly comfortable, especially on long journeys. For those not used to them Recaros can seem far too hard on first acquaintance. However, after 250 non-stop miles sitting in this seat, or any of the range, the ability to get out of the car and walk straight is something that is much appreciated!
(Photo by courtesy of Keiper Recaro GmbH & Co.)

Fitting a Recaro seat to a Golf is not difficult at all. We fitted an L model with optional electric height adjustment to a Mk II GTi. The seat fixings are the same, but they are not interchangeable.

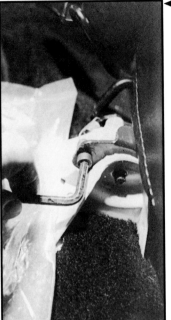

◄ IC2.6
Removing the original seat is easy. This Allen screw releases the mechanism of the seat so that it can slide backwards. Note that this area is (or should be) covered in a light grease, hence the use of a piece of plastic sheet to protect the carpet.

IC2.7
The rear of the seat is prevented from coming off its runners by a small plastic clip which is retained by a cross-head screw. On the opposite runner the trim either slides off or has a cross-head screw like this side, depending on whether you have an early or a late model vehicle.
▼

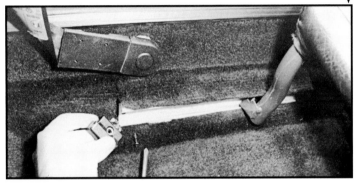

All Recaro seats are of excellent quality and are designed to give the maximum ergonomic support for your body. The main factors are that the body should be supported at the right places and to the right extent. The all important lumbar support will not 'give' when you sit in any one of the Recaro range as it is built around a well-padded metal plate. The adjustment of the backrest is made easier by the fact that there are manual controls on each side of the seat, except in cases where electronic adjustment is provided.

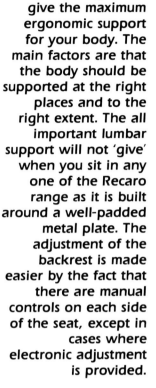

◄ IC2.8
The Recaro seat is ready mounted on a sub-frame which enables it to fit directly into the Golf. Seen here out of the car, the Recaro, on the left, appears slight and not as well padded as the original GTi bucket seat. However, appearances are deceptive!

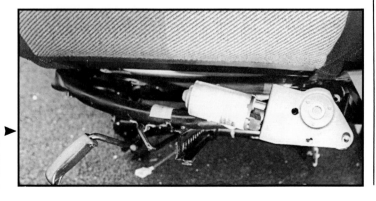

IC2.9 ▶
The electric motor used for height control is mounted at the front of the seat. This is simple to wire up.

Fitting replacement seats

Available as an option, seat heating is wired as shown here. Although regarded by some as perhaps a little too much of a luxury, it doesn't take too many winter mornings to appreciate its attractions! (Diagram courtesy of Keiper Recaro GmbH & Co.)

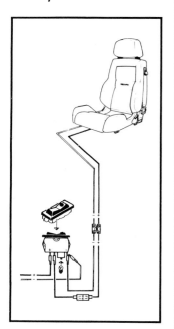

IC2.10 ▶
The height control motor cable exits under the seats and connects to the seat by the plug shown here.

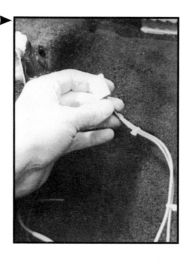

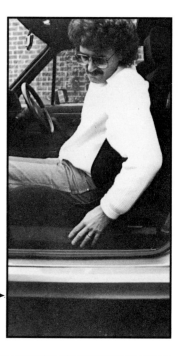

IC2.11 ▶
Co-author Dave Pollard seen here testing the electric seat height control.

IC2.12
Both seats installed; there can be no doubt as to what make they are! The backrest is very supportive with large side bolsters to hold the occupant in place.
▼

IC2.13 ▶
In this view across the car, the new seats look most attractive. Although the squab may look flat and hard, it is remarkably comfortable, particularly after a long journey. Note that the Recaro does not have an extended backrest lever for holding the seat belt in place.

IC3.1
We fitted the headrest cover first. The headrest is removed by easing out the circlips which hold it in place. The cover simply pulls over the top, being a tight and exact fit.

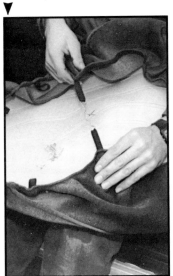

IC3.2
With the headrest still out (a necessity) the backrest cover can be pulled into place. This has to be pulled down very tight and joins front and back under the backrest by means of a strong Velcro strip.

IC3.3
The seat squab cover is secured underneath by strong elastic loops, joined by metal clips. It is shown here out of the car for clarity, although this is not necessary in practice.

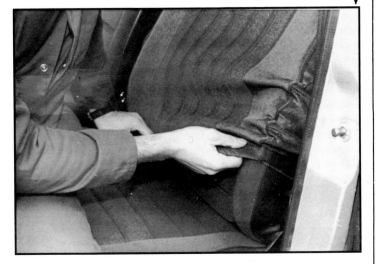

Volkswagen's own brand of seat covers have many advantages, not least the fact that they are specifically colour co-ordinated to match the interiors of their cars. They are only available in full velour cloth sets (ie, front and rear) in grey, blue or brown, and the set we fitted here included the headrest covers. They are fully washable and flame retardent. We fitted them here to a Mk I Golf, although they are available for all Golf and Jetta models. Note that it is important to state whether you have a two or a four-door car, as two-door models will have a slit in the side of the front backrest cover for the backrest lever.

IC3.4 ▶
The finished front seat is a vast improvement over the original which was looking decidedly the worse for wear. Comparison can be drawn with the driver's seat which, at this stage, had not been covered.

Fitting seat covers

When using the metal clips to secure the cover under the seat, great care should be taken, as there has to be a lot of tension in the loops. Should your fingers slip, the flying metal clip could be dangerous, especially with regard to your eyes.

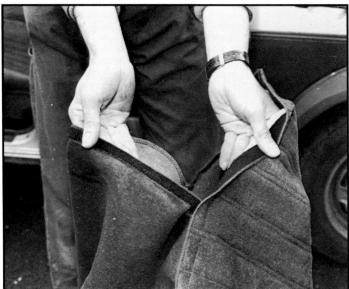

◀ **IC3.5**
At the rear, it was the work of a few moments to remove seat and squab, which made for easier access. The squab is held by two metal brackets, about which it pivots. These are held by circlips and once removed allow the whole back seat assembly to be removed. The hatch shelf has to be removed as well, which is a matter of undoing the five Philips head screws. The backrest cover fits in the same way as the front, being secured by Velcro strips, as shown here.

IC3.6 ▶
The cover has to be pulled down tight over the backrest before the Velcro strips will meet and hold.

IC3.7
As with the front squab, the rear is tensioned by connecting the various loops with metal clips.
▼

IC3.8 ▶
An excellent fit, the new covers give a really luxurious feel to the car, despite its age.

Carpet sets

IC4.1 ▶
The carpet set consists of two front and two rear mats. Note the reinforced section on the driver's side.

The advantages of using a carpet set in your Golf are many. Because they are tailored to fit exactly, they do not move around, although they can easily be taken out for thorough cleaning. They will not only make your car look better whilst it is yours, but also the protection they give to the carpeting already in the car will pay dividends when you wish to sell it.

IC4.2
The front carpets have a rather clever locating system. Two small plastic lugs are pushed through ready made holes in the carpet as shown. On the end of each lug is a sharp, corkscrew-like gripper which demands some respect if fingers are to remain intact!

▼

IC4.3 ▶
With the carpet in position, a screwdriver is inserted into the top of the lug and when turned, the gripper bites into the existing carpet with great tenacity. Thus, the carpets do not move around, as most do after a few journeys, but they can be removed for easy cleaning by simply easing them off the two lugs. The set shown here is available from Volkswagen dealers, albeit only for the Mk II Golf. The manufacturers claim that they are water, mud and fire resistant and they are guaranteed for a year or 20,000 miles.

Rubber over-mats

IC5.1 ▶
Link Sedan's mats are of good quality and, being finished in black, compliment the car's interior. The car in this case is a 16V Jetta; spot the tiny 16V badge on the glovebox! The universal mats can be fitted in the front only or in the rear as well. We would always recommend the latter, even if rear seat passengers are a rarity: it only takes one person with muddy shoes to ruin the carpet!

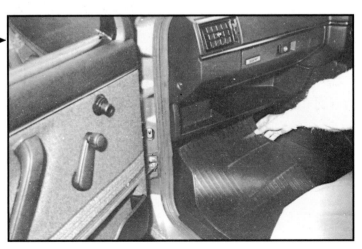

In addition to a full carpet set, rubber over-mats can also be used, and indeed, throughout the long dirty winter months, many owners use over-mats as well as a carpet set.

Fitting a sound deadening kit

We would recommend that you use some form of barrier cream before commencing this job. This will help to get your hands clean after fitting the sound deadening. The glue on some of the pieces is, of necessity, very strong, and the mastic pads are especially sticky. Comma's 'Manista' hand cleaner will be especially effective in removing the tenacious glue from your skin.

The fibrous panels used to deaden the sound also shed their 'hair' everywhere, particularly on black Golf carpets! It is almost impossible to fit sound deadening without the need for a half hour session with a vacuum cleaner afterwards (see Section 23).

Obviously, when working in the engine compartment it is important that the engine is not hot, especially if you lay the kit out like we did here!

In this Section, we are covering the fitting of the Acoustikit package for the whole car, although it is also available for underbonnet fitting only. The Golf is not an intrinsically noisy car. However, all vehicles suffer from some extraneous noise caused by the drumming of various body panels and it is this that the Acoustikit system seeks to eliminate. The kit consists of 15 fibrous panels cut to size and four 'vibrapads'. All of the panels are made from ½ inch thick double-needled Jute. Those which need it are self-adhesive with a simple peel-off backing. The 'vibrapads' are self-adhesive mastic mats, which are used to stick onto any large flat panels in the car to prevent drumming and resonance.

IC6.1
We would firmly recommend that, before starting, some time is taken to familiarise yourself with the various pieces. They are all numbered on the back. Laying them out on the ground, in a diagrammatical manner, is the easiest way to see what fits where. As you can see, you will need a lot of floor space! Dealing with one section at a time is certainly the easiest way.

IC6.2
We decided to start at the front with the underbonnet pieces. The instructions recommend that none of the self-adhesive backing strips are removed until their position has been confirmed. This makes a lot of sense and so we 'mock fitted' the bonnet sections, by holding them in place. In this way we were able to ensure that it was always the right section that was stuck down. The glue is strong and removal is almost impossible without damaging the sound deadening material (or the car's paintwork).

IC6.3
All underbonnet areas had to be thoroughly cleaned using white spirit or equivalent in order that the glue would stick properly. Clearly, the use of such flammable substances is another good reason for only working in the engine bay when the engine is cool.

IC6.4
Here, one of the panels is being stuck onto the bonnet. Before removing the protective backing, we made sure that the panel fitted exactly. In this case we had to trim a little off the edges with scissors.

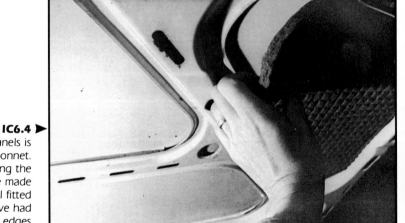

IC6.5
The underbonnet kit fitted. There were two more pieces which should have been stuck onto the bulkhead. However, on this particular car, an alarm had been fitted which prevented their being fitted.

▼

IC6.6
There are several 'lie-in-position' panels which fit on the four floor sections. The original carpet has to be lifted and then the Acoustikit panels laid underneath. Here, the four sections are seen alongside the car, the two front ones being cut to shape, whilst the rear are simply oblong pieces. As with most of the panels, some slight trimming was necessary.

▼

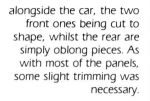

Sharp scissors and/or a sharp craft knife is essential as some of the panels have to be trimmed to the exact size. As usual, appropriate care should be taken when using either of these cutting implements as the fibrous panels are extremely tough.

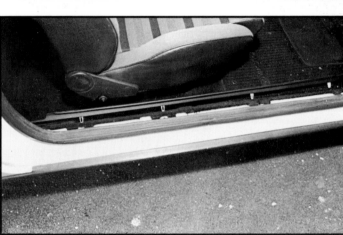

◄ **IC6.7**
The carpet is raised by unclipping the plastic rail holding it to the door sill. This is held by a Philips self-tapping screw at the rear, or at the front and rear on later model cars. The rail is further secured by plastic lugs which allow it to be prised gently off.

IC6.8 ►
The hatchback deadening, which comes in two pieces, also lies on the floor, under the carpet. The first, seen here, covers the floor area with a cutaway for the spare wheel. Note that in this case, the car is fitted with a space-saver spare.

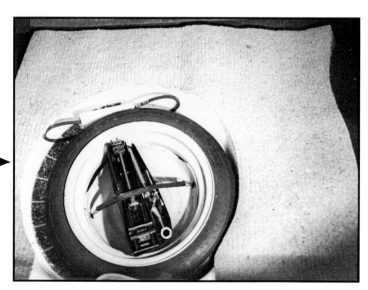

Fitting a sound deadening kit

There are two 'vibrapads' to fit to each door. The trim should first be removed and then the plastic covering. The latter should be eased away carefully so that when replaced, it is still watertight. The area should be cleaned, as previously described, and then two 'vibrapads' stuck onto the door panel. As this was a two-door car, we used the four 'vibrapads' remaining to stick onto the inside of the rear three-quarter panels. It should be noted that the 'vibrapads' are extremely brittle, especially as the temperature drops, and we found that it was necessary to warm them (on a radiator as it happens) in order to prevent them from breaking up.

After fitting the full Acoustikit, we noticed a reduction in noise almost straight away, although the improvement was most prominent at higher speeds. Anyone will be able to notice the difference but those who do particularly high mileages will be in a position to appreciate the improvement in comfort and reduction in noise most of all.

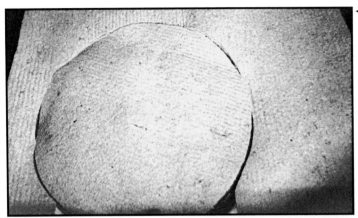

◄ IC6.9
This is the separate circular section which fits over the spare wheel. This will also fit the standard wheel, despite its raised position.

IC6.10
Still at the rear, there are two Acoustikit panels to fit around the suspension units, shown here on top of the carpet for clarity. These, too, are self-adhesive.
▼

IC6.11
At the lower edge of the hatch, two more self-adhesive pieces are fitted. This area is usually fairly clean and so sticking should not be a problem. However, there are plenty of wires around and care should be taken to stick the panel **under** the wires, as has been done here. Something else to bear in mind is that they fit over the factory fitted sticker giving details of paint codes etc. In this case we noted these and included them in the handbook for safe keeping.
▼

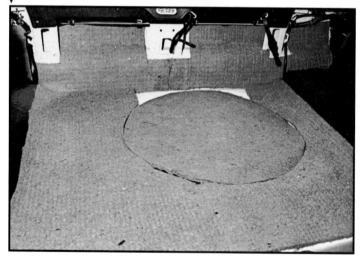

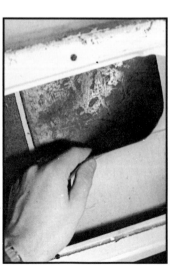

IC6.12 ►
The mastic 'vibrapads' are designed to fit to the inside of the outer door panels to reduce any drumming effect.

Fitting a centre console

Fitting Volkswagen's own console, whether as a new fit or as a replacement for the original, makes a lot of sense. Not only is it of excellent quality and fits exactly, but also it has two DIN-size apertures to facilitate the fitting of extra in-car audio equipment (See Chapter 3) and/or instruments and switches. It should be noted that the top aperture is DIN width but not **depth,** as the lower part of the facia intrudes.

As can be seen from the diagrams within the text, the first of VW's Twin-DIN consoles were supplied as an add-on front to the original which had to be hacksawed through. Later versions were complete consoles. Although the latter is slightly dearer, it is easier to fit.

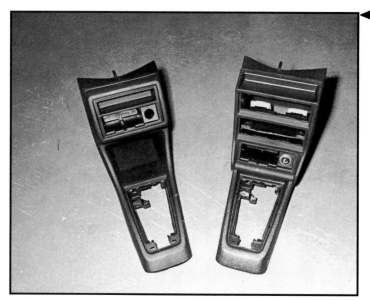

◀ IC7.1
The old (left) and the new, complete console (right). The new version permits easy fitting of extra audio, but the space beneath the ashtray is lost and this was ideal for cassette storage. (See section 10 of this Chapter.)

IC7.2
The console is held by a self-tapping screw near the gear lever and two more which pass into the lower half of the dashboard. Here the gaiter and coin holder is being removed, which is achieved by gently prising the coin holder until a firm grip can be obtained and then pulling upwards.
▼

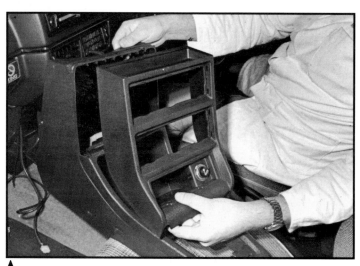

▲
IC7.3
With the front of the original console cut off, the new one can be offered up. The only electrical connection is the one for the cigar lighter which is simply unplugged and then plugged in when the new front is fitted.

IC7.4 ▶
A The front of the old console is carefully cut away with a panel saw ...
B ... and the replacement front-piece clipped into place. (Courtesy of Volkswagen UK)

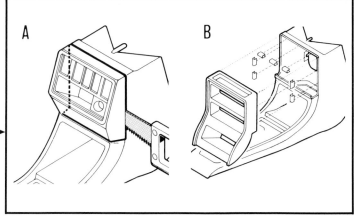

A   B

Fitting door pockets

The map pocket shown here is a dual purpose unit, having also the facility to mount an elliptical speaker which saves having to make holes in the door trim.

Storage space in the interior of the early Mk I Golf and Jetta is not a strong point. However, this was given a boost with some later Mk Is which had a combined map pocket/speaker housing fitted as standard. This is available from Volkswagen dealers as an 'aftermarket' item and here we show one being fitted to a Golf GLS.

◄ IC8.1
The two pockets, with removable speaker grilles. As can be seen, there are several bags of self-tapping screws supplied with the kit.

IC8.2
First job was to remove the trim panel. This involves prior removal of the window winder (prise up the plastic cover and remove the Philips head screw), the armrest and the door handle trim.
▼

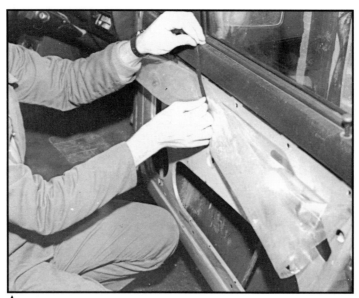

▲
IC8.3
Always try to keep the plastic sheet in one piece. In this case we did, and to hold it out of the way, we taped it to the top of the door.

IC8.4 ►
With the panel out of the car, the holes can be marked from the outside by using a sharp bradawl or similar.

◀ IC8.5
The self-tapping screws pass through from the inside of the trim into the relevant holes in the pocket.

Although the unit fitted here was black, they are also available in blue or brown, to match the colour of your car's interior trim.

IC8.6 ▶
When all the holes have been made and the self-tapping screws inserted, this should be the end result. The chrome strip on this GLS ensured that the new door pocket was fitted perfectly level.

◀ IC8.7
When the pocket has been attached to the trim, the grille simply slots into place. It clips in first at the rear and then at the front.

IC8.8 ▶
A final self-tapping screw is used to secure the speaker grille at the front.

Fitting wooden dash and door trim

If the sombre interior of your beloved Golf or Jetta is just too much for you, then a splash of polished, veneered woodwork could be just the ticket. The Rokee products featured here are available in various finishes, the one shown here being a rather attractive ash grey.

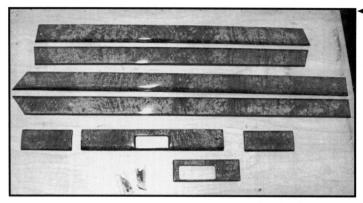

◀ IC9.1
The Rokee kit consists of four side trim pieces: two for the tops of the front doors and two more for rear doors or rear quarter panels, depending on whether the car is two- or four-door. Four more sections fit on the dash and on the ashtray lid.

IC9.2 ▶
The various sections of Rokee trim should first be held in place, each in turn, to ensure that they are the correct pieces. With something like this ashtray section, it is quite obvious, although the door pieces could be confusing. The holes for the fixing screws are pre-drilled and with the trim in place, their positions should be marked through the holes onto the plastic dash/door using a bradawl. It is best to start the screw in the hole before fitting the wooden trim in order to avoid the possibility of the screwdriver slipping and damaging the veneer.

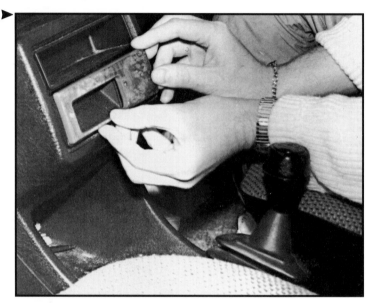

◀ IC9.3
This picture shows the passenger side facia, ashtray and glovebox trim in position. The operation of the glovebox and the ashtray are unaffected.

Rokee recommend, when marking the position of their trim sections through the pre-drilled holes onto the car trim, that a piece of masking tape is used to identify the position of the hole.

IC9.4 ▶
The trims for the top of the door do not fit along the whole length otherwise they would foul on the dashboard. All in all, the natural finish of the wood rests well in the artificial plastic interior of the Golf and fulfills the function of adding a little 'English' luxury.

Cassette storage

The in-car cassette player (more usually a radio/cassette player) is a boon to those of us who regularly have to make long, tedious journeys. It does mean, however, that cassettes have to be carried and as most of us like to have a reasonable selection at hand, this poses a storage problem. Fischer C-Box have acquired a reputation as being **the** people when it comes to in-car cassette storage and so we took a look at what the German company could provide.

Apart from making your car considerably tidier, the use of some form of cassette storage will help to preserve your tapes. It should protect them from excesses of heat and cold and prevent damage to both case and mechanism.

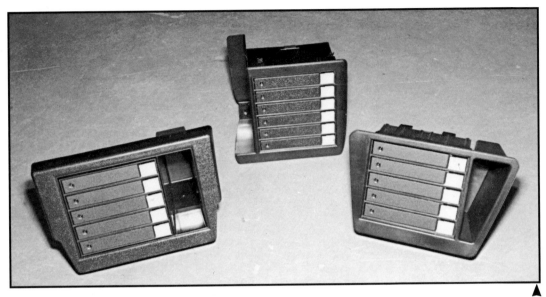

▲
IC10.1
Fischer can offer a fitted unit for all models of Golf and Jetta. As can be seen from these three units, they are shaped to fit the exact aperture. They also have a tell-tale indicator in each drawer which shows whether a tape is in or not. All console models have a space at the side of the cassette holder for odds and ends (petrol receipts, opera tickets, car park tickets, etc).

▲
IC10.2
As an alternative, Fischer make a number of units which do not fit in the console. The one shown here is designed for dash or under-dash mounting. Note that this model does not have the drawer indicators.

IC10.3 ▶
The basic mechanism is shown here, out of the car. The cassette is placed, without its box, on these two spindles and then the drawer is closed. It is then held flush until the button is pressed, at which point it springs out allowing the cassette to be taken out. The whole unit is made of shatter-resistant plastic.

Cassette storage

The tailor-made units for the Volkswagen cars are available from Volkswagen dealerships as part of their wide range of aftermarket accessories. The universal units are available from all good accessory shops.

◀ IC10.4
As can be seen here, the unit fits exactly into the console and is of a high quality construction which matches the car's interior. This is a Mk II car, although the fitting is similar in all models. It is held in position by strong spring clips which press against the inside of the console.

IC10.5 ▶
Fischer also produce this C-Box Carry Case which can be clipped into the brackets provided, once they have been screwed into a suitable position in the car, but lifted right out for use in the home.

Fitting rear seat belts

The fitting of Britax seat belts, as supplied to Volkswagen UK, into the rear of your Golf is certainly an excellent idea, particularly where children are passengers. Volkswagen fitted all Mk II models and some later Mk Is with rear belts but early Mk Is did not fare so well. We fitted Britax belts to a 1978 Golf 1500. It should be noted that mounting points for the lap belt are not fitted to the car in this instance.

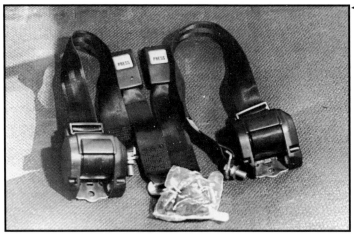

◀ IC11.1
This is what you get. To prevent the mechanism unravelling the webbing, a small plastic insert or polystyrene wedge is used to prevent the belt unwinding during transit. This can be released by gentle pressure from a screwdriver, but only **after** the inertia reel has been fitted.

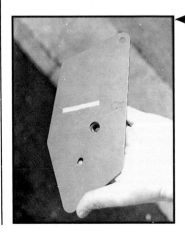

◀ IC11.2
Not part of the kit, but a necessity, is this reinforced mounting bracket required in order to mount the mechanism itself. It's available from your VW dealership.

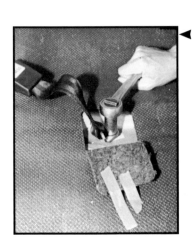

IC11.4 ▶
The rear speaker shelf should be removed by undoing the five self-tapping screws holding it to the car. The trim underneath it should also be taken off. This is held by plastic lugs and pulls away with a few sharp tugs. When this has been removed, the positioning for the separate mounting bracket can be seen. The bracket should be bolted securely in place and the trim replaced. The hole positions for the mechanism are clearly marked on the trim. They can be pushed through and the mechanism mounted.

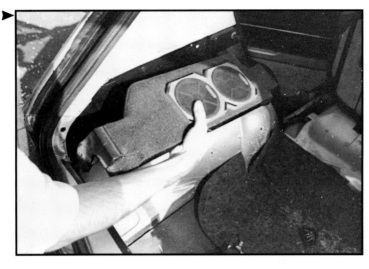

Although this is a fairly simple DIY fitment, it is a safety item and as such great care should be taken to ensure that all anchorages are securely fastened and that the webbing is not twisted in any way. The position and order of the washers and bushes in relation to the anchor plate, should be noted and retained. Have a VW dealer check the installation when it is complete. (Illustration courtesy of Britax)

IC11.5 ▶
The underside of the speaker shelf is a solid plastic moulding except for the strip shown here. By using a craft knife, this oblong section of carpet can be cut away.

IC11.6
The webbing and all of the attachments should be passed carefully through the newly made slot in the ▶ speaker shelf and the shelf repositioned. The centre anchor plate can then be screwed into place. The hole for this is found by running your fingers along the headlining, half way up the 'C' pillar. When it has been located, a hole can be cut and the bolt, supplied with the Britax kit, inserted. This anchorage should allow the mounting to move, even when fully tightened.

IC11.3
The rear seat and squab should be pushed forward all the way. The holes for the anchor plates are already there, built into the floor of the car on the production line. The felt carpet has two squares marked into it and when these are lifted the captive nuts are accessible under a strip of tape (used to prevent the ingress of dirt). Make sure that the threads are totally clean. The anchor plates can then be fastened using the bolts supplied in the Britax kit.

IC11.7 ▶
The lower anchorage point is located just to the front of the rear wheel arch. The carpeting has to be pulled back and, once again, the captive nut should be uncovered by removing a piece of tape. Tighten the mounting, making sure that the webbing and buckle are correctly positioned and not twisted.

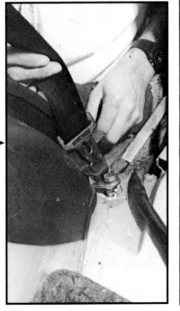

Finally, with a passenger sitting in the rear, the belt should be worn as normal. The mechanism should allow easy movement of the webbing when pulled gently, but the ratchet should stop it quickly when the webbing is jerked.

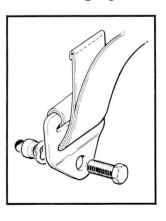

Child safety seats

Fitting some form of child safety seat is a wise move, although Cabriolet owners should check before purchase as many seats are not suitable for open top Golfs.

Volkswagen have an excellent record when it comes to the safety of those who occupy their cars. Their 'safety cell' car design, whereby the front and the rear of the car are designed to crumple when in an accident, is one aspect of this. Inside the vehicle, they have been leaders in providing safety items as standard, being among the first to fit front seat belts as standard and likewise with the rear. During 1987, the company strongly backed the 'Belt up in the back' child safety campaign, aimed at reducing injuries to children in cars involved in accidents. All Golfs, except early models, have adult rear seat belts fitted and so it comes as no surprise that, for those with children, there is a range of high quality child safety seats available.

◀ IC12.1
We were able to try out four different types of child seat available from Volkswagen UK. From left to right they are: The Bobby, the Babysure, the Booster Cushion and the Recliner.

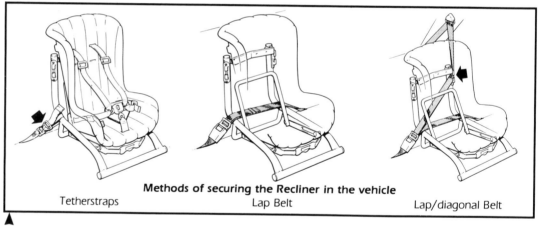

Methods of securing the Recliner in the vehicle

Tetherstraps   Lap Belt   Lap/diagonal Belt

▲
IC12.2
The Recliner looks like everyone's idea of a child seat, being rather akin to a scaled down racing car seat. It is fitted with a full harness to hold the child securely in position. As can be seen from these diagrams, fitting can be by using the tether straps, a lap belt or a lap/diagonal belt. (Diagrams courtesy of Britax Ltd)

It is recommended in the instructions of all the seats shown here, that children are carried in the back of the car wherever possible. We must agree wholeheartedly with this, and indeed, in some countries this is a legal requirement. It is also often a legal requirement that children are 'belted-up' in the back.

◀ IC12.3
Seen here in a 5-door Golf, the seat has been mounted by using the lap/diagonal belt. Safe as she is, Lucy appears non too impressed by it! The Recliner is suitable for children aged approx 6 months to 4 years and weighing between 9 kg - 18 kg.

IC12.4 ▶

The Booster Cushion is as simple as the Recliner is complex. It is for use by older children and effectively raises them to a height whereby the ordinary lap/diagonal belts can be used safely. There is only one strap adjustment to be made, which is the one which passes from the Booster Cushion behind the child. This clips onto the diagonal part of the seat belt at shoulder height. It is designed for use by children aged approx 4-11 years and weighing between 15-36 kg. This belt is too loose - see Margin Note

IC12.5

The Bobby is a non-adjustable seat which can be fixed in either front or rear seats. It is seen here being used on the front seat of a 3-door Golf. It should only be used with a lap/diagonal belt (ie not a lap belt). With the seat in position and the child in the seat, the belt should be fitted as normal. The adjustable guide strap can then be used to ensure that the seat belt is comfortable and does not touch the neck area or the stomach. It is designed for use by children aged approx 8 months - 7 years and weighing between 9-25 kg.

▼

It is important to ensure that safety seats have approval, either from the EEC or the British Standards Authority. All of the seats featured in this section have such approval viz:

Recliner	BS 3254
Booster Cushion	BS AU185
Bobby	ECE 44-02
Babysure	BS AU202

The lap section of a seat belt should always be adjusted so that it fits snugly across the bony part of the hip.

IC12.6

The Babysure is one of the new generation of child seats, as it is designed to be used facing rearwards. The manufacturers state very clearly that it should not be used facing forwards. Once again, it uses the standard lap/diagonal belts which thread through the seat at various points as shown in the diagram. (Diagram courtesy of Britax Ltd)

▼

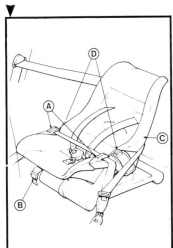

Method of securing the Babysure in the vehicle

A - Webbing guide hooks
B - Crutch strap adjuster
C - Removable cover
D - Recliner buttons

IC12.7 ▶

The seat can be used on either the front or the back seats (but NOT with a lap only belt), although for clarity it is shown here in the front of this three-door car. The Babysure is a strong and comfortable item and can quite easily be removed for use in the home. However, it should not be used in the car in any other manner than that prescribed here. It is designed for use by children aged up to approx 9 months and weighing up to 10 kg.

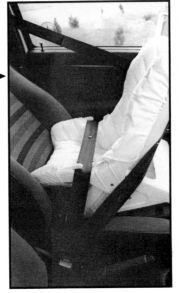

BELT UP IN THE BACK
SPONSORED BY VOLKSWAGEN

Electrical accessories

Fitting electric windows

When fitting electric window mechanisms, it is very important that they are not bent in any way as this could damage them or at least prevent smooth operation.

The kit fitted here is the one fitted by Volkswagen as standard, or as an optional extra on some models. It is available as a two- or four-door kit, although this is the two-door set-up. It will fit all models except the Cabriolet.

◄ IC13.1
This is what you get. This shot shows the two new sets of electric mechanism. Also supplied are comprehensive instructions and all relevant wires and connectors.

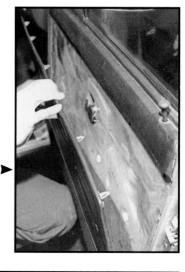

IC13.2 ►
Removal of trim panel is necessary, after also removing the window winder, the armrest and the door handle trim. Carefully ease up the plastic sheet.

IC13.3 ►
Removal of the existing mechanism is surprisingly simple. It is held by two 10mm nuts at the winder, one at the top of the mechanism and one which is reached from underneath the door. The latter is almost certain to be rusty, so some penetrating fluid may be called for. The window itself is held by two 10mm nuts, which can be reached if it is wound down approximately half way, as shown.

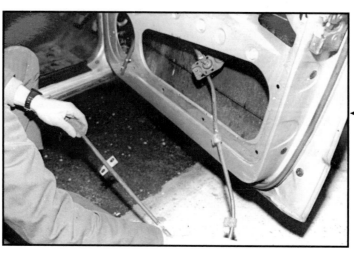

◄ IC13.4
With these nuts removed, the mechanism can be wiggled out of the door. It is wise to take note of the routing so as to make fitting the electric mechanism simpler. Do not discard altogether until you are sure that you have got the new ones working!

IC13.5 ▶
The two power wires connect into the Bosch motor as shown. The plug has to be pressed hard into the socket to ensure that it is a waterproof fit.

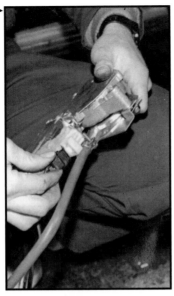

IC13.7
Mounting the switches is a question of deciding where they are to be placed and marking the exact position by using the template supplied. There must be enough room behind or beneath them to make the necessary connections. Ideally they should be able to be reached by the driver and passenger. In the centre console is the most common position. There is a kit available which contains three separate switches. One switch is mounted in each door and an extra one for the passenger door is mounted in the console, for use by the driver.
▼

IC13.6
Fitting the new unit is a matter of threading it **carefully** through the inner door. Do not bend the mechanism or it will not work smoothly. It is wise to leave the door trims off until the wiring has been completed, to ensure that the units work smoothly. The glass should slide up and down without 'snagging' anywhere.
▼

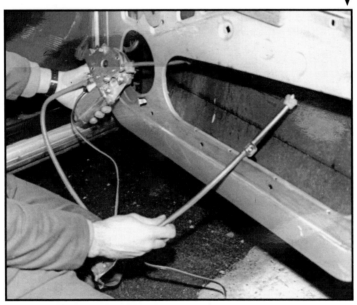

As can be seen from the diagram, the wiring is not especially complex. (Diagram courtesy of Volkswagen UK Ltd)

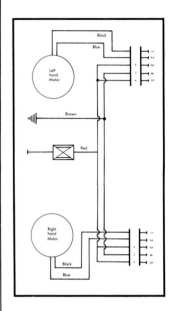

IC13.8 ▶
You can tell the car has something extra by what is missing! The winder is replaced by a black plastic blanking plug. The panel now looks much neater and allows taller maps, etc, to be placed in the map pocket. In cases where a door speaker is fitted, the manual winder can catch on the speaker trim and so this could be another advantage of electric windows.

Fitting a cruise control

When fitting this cruise control unit, it is essential to check that the brake lamp switch is in good condition and is adjusted so that the lights come on at the start of the pedal movement. Also, the connectors need to be totally secure as a touch on the brake pedal is the primary method of turning off the cruise control when in use.

DRIVING

The Econocruise is an excellent accessory for those who have to make long tedious journeys. The electronic 'brain' of the system checks the speed several times per second and adjusts the throttle setting accordingly, making the car much more economical. Another advantage is that it could help you to hang onto your driving licence! As most of us know, over a period of time on a motorway, there is a tendency to increase speed, no matter how hard we try not to. The Econocruise has no such tendencies and keeps to the legal speed. Some owners imagine the throttle sticking open and the car going out of control. Because of the various safety precautions incorporated in the kit there is absolutely no danger of this.

The Econocruise kit is so named as to highlight its two main advantages: it allows a constant cruising speed to be maintained easily and in so doing, allows a higher mpg figure to be returned. Fitting is not overly difficult, although some time and patience is required to do it right and for safety's sake it **must** be done right! (Seek professional assistance if you are not fully competent to carry out the work.) It would certainly pay the average DIY 'Golfer' to make sure that the comprehensive instructions are fully understood before venturing from the fireside. There are kits available for both carburettor and fuel injection models.

◀ IC14.1
Fitting the throttle operating mechanism in the already crowded 16V underbonnet area. It is important that in routing the cable there are no tight bends or snags. Each model of Golf and Jetta has its own fitting kit, supplied by Econocruise.

IC14.2 ▶
The Econocruise can be activated in one of two ways, either by a pair of switches on the dash or by a dash-mounted stalk. However, we favoured the self-adhesive stalk, shown here, which sticks onto the wiper stalk and is easy to use and unobtrusive.

◀ IC14.3
Dash switches, on the other hand, could be fitted to drilled switch 'blanks'.

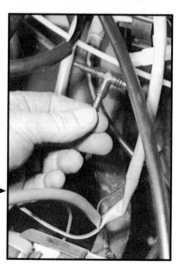

IC14.4 ▶
The throttle is operated by vacuum power. Tap the T-piece supplied into a suitable underbonnet vacuum pipe.

Central locking is now common on many Golfs and Jettas, and is usually specified as an extra fitted when the car is new. (Unless, of course, the car has it fitted as standard.) We take a look at how to fit a Moss Security Central Locking system to a 4-door Jetta. The kit is available for 2- or 4-door cars and offers good value for money. It includes electric drive motors, a relay switching unit, cable looms and linking rods to attach to existing door lock mechanisms. When installed, all doors can be locked from **either** the driver's door or the passenger's door. Golf owners may, quite rightly, be pondering where they fit in, as Golfs are either 3- or 5-door. The answer is that a separate unit has to be purchased to fit to the hatch (Ref MS723).

The fitting of central locking may sound a little daunting, but this kit should pose few problems for the keen DIY 'Golfer'. The wiring diagram seen here is, fortunately, nowhere near as difficult to wire as it looks! (Diagram courtesy of Harry Moss International Ltd)

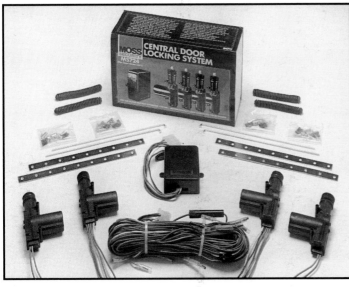

◄ IC15.1
The Moss Security kit comes complete with everything required to do the job; and there's a lot of it, particularly as this one is for a 4-door car. The kit includes detailed instructions designed for the amateur car mechanic.

IC15.2
The door trim has to be removed from all four doors including the stick-on plastic sheet. If removed carefully, this will come off without ripping and the glue is such that it should stick back in position when the job is completed.

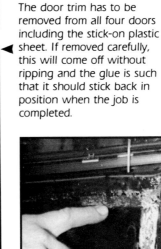

IC15.3
As with any job of this nature, it is always wise to offer everything up in position before fixing. A lot of unwanted holes are saved this way! Here, the solenoid and rod operating mechanism is being tried for size.

▼

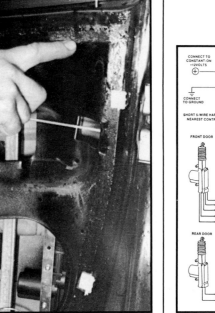

IC15.4 ▶
The solenoid and rod operating mechanism is fixed to a mounting strap which in turn is fastened to the door by means of self-tapping screws.

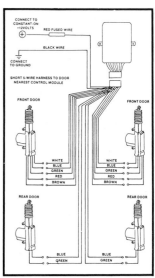

Fitting a central locking system

This particular central locking system is compatible with the Moss Security alarm, which allows all the doors to be locked and the alarm set with just a push of a single button on the key fob.

IC15.5 ▶
This is the operating mechanism being screwed into place on the rear door. The operating rod has been bent to allow it to clear obstructions.

IC15.6
The wiring is profuse, and requires some thought before starting. First thing to do, as always, is disconnect the battery. Obviously, the mechanisms inside the door have to be wired up and it is important that the wires are sleeved properly where they pass from the door into the 'A' position to protect them from chafing. The main connections are made into the fuse box which, in the case of this Mk II Jetta, hides behind a plastic cover under the right-hand side of the dash.

▼

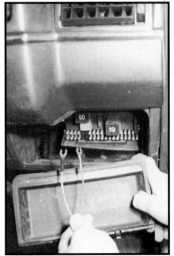

▲
IC15.7
The loom itself exits into the scuttle and connects to the control box.

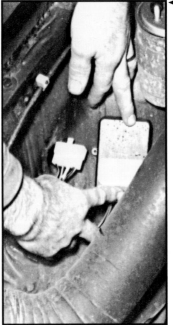

◀**IC15.8**
The brain of the whole operation is this control box which mounts inside the engine compartment, but away from sources of extreme heat. Two small holes have to be drilled and should be zinc painted. Note the multi-pin connector which patches into the wiring loom. Having checked all the connections, re-connect the battery and try it out. We found the system to be both quick and quiet and much easier than going round checking the doors, especially useful if you have children. It does not operate on the boot, but, for Golf owners, a single Moss Security pack can be purchased to include the tailgate lock if required.

Fitting extra instruments and switches

EI16.1 ▶
There's no question of having to cut into the Golf or Jetta dash because Sedan produce a wide range of instrument and switch mounting pods and brackets.

Many of the functions offered on the Sedan instruments shown here are covered by the Golf and Jetta's warning light system. However, while a warning light is perfect for drawing your attention quickly to a fault, and perfect also for the uninformed driver, the addition of extra instruments will provide further information to the driver. They will constantly monitor and measure the engine's functions and provide the intelligent Golf or Jetta owner with a picture of exactly what is going on in the engine bay and elsewhere.

◀ **EI16.2**
The three instrument mounting pod looks as if it was made to fit to this part of the Golf's dash and angles the instruments up towards the driver's eye-line for better visibility.

EI16.3 ▶
Push-in pegs locate the front of the mounting pod to the rear of the case. The two are easily separated ...

◀ **EI16.4**
... allowing the instruments to be pushed home into the front panel, the front panel to be fitted to the car, and the rear casing to be slid and pegged back into place.

Fitting extra instruments

In addition to the Sedan instruments and switches shown here, there is a wide range of Sedan warning lights, illuminated switches and other instruments, such as voltmeters, water and oil temperature gauges, oil pressure gauges, tachometers, ammeters, an econometer and an outside temperature thermometer, as well as two different styles of three-in-one gauge sets. Many Sedan gauges are available in different sizes and styles.

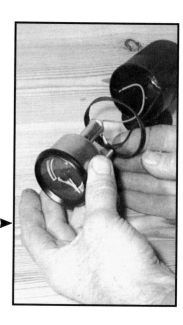

◄ EI16.5
An alternative mounting position, particularly suitable for the tachometer or econometer, is this mounting cup suitable for fitting gauges either on top of or beneath the dash.

EI16.6 ►
A rubber grommet which comes with the mounting cup kit, is pushed onto the gauge which then forms a tight fit inside the mounting cup casing.

◄ EI16.7
Alternatively, if you are fitting a single instrument such as an econometer, you could use a conventional mounting pod beneath the dash. These are available in one, two, three and four hole varieties.

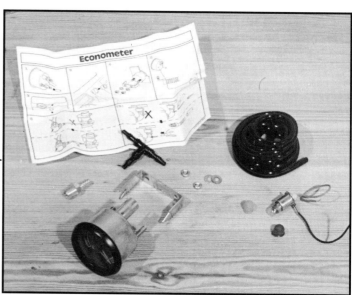

EI16.8 ►
Sedan pride themselves on producing accessories suitable for the DIY enthusiast. The kit of parts which comes with the Sedan Econometer, just as with all the other instruments in the range, contains a very clear set of diagrammatical instructions.

EI16.9
The Sedan oil pressure gauge is one of the best indicators as to whether an engine is wearing out or not. It can also provide advance warning, ahead of the warning light, of an imminent engine-wrecking oil pressure drop.

Where electrical connections have to be made, the Sykes-Pickavant crimping tool used in conjunction with Sedan's own range of connectors is ideal. See page 195 for some wiring hints and tips.

EI16.10 ▶
The Sedan sender unit must be screwed into the block in place of the Golf's own oil pressure warning sender unit. You must ensure that the oil pressure warning light can still be connected up (consult your local Volkswagen main dealership) and you **must** never carry out this modification to a Golf or Jetta still under a Volkswagen warranty period.

◀ **EI16.11**
Sedan switch mounting brackets are available for both rectangular and round switches. The latter can be removed from their panels by pushing in the spring clips on the rear of the switches from the back of the panel.

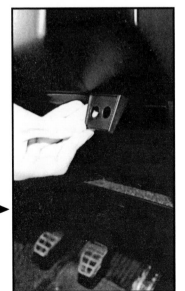

EI16.12 ▶
These switch panels can be mounted in any suitable place, preferably beneath the dash, using self-tapping screws and after drilling a small pilot hole.

Fitting an overhead console

The wiring diagram supplied with the kit shows the straightforward connections for the three switches for the integral lights.

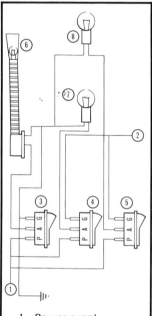

1. Power supply
2. Supply from existing courtesy light
3. Rocker switch
4. Rocker switch
5. Rocker switch
6. Map light
7. Console light
8. Console light
P. Power
A. Accessory
G. Ground (earth)

The overhead console featured here is another Autoplas product and is constructed in well finished and very strong plastic. It is in self-coloured black, which suits most Golfs. It is relatively easy to fit, both sections fastening to the roof by utilising existing holes and screws. The section which fits along the roof between the doors houses two speakers and tweeters and the 'T' piece, which joins it from the driver's mirror, houses a map light and three switches. The latter can be used to operate the map light/twin overhead lights or, by rewiring, other accessories. The console cannot be fitted to a car with a sunroof and is available for only Mk I Golfs.

IC17.1 ▶

The console comes in two sections with holes pre-drilled and all the necessary wire and connectors required. It is wise to measure all cable and fit all connectors before offering the console up. As far as possible, it should be totally wired before fitting. At the front, the sun blind fixings near to the interior mirror have to be removed. The front edge of the console is placed underneath and then the fitting is replaced. It helps to have an assistant hold the section at the back to prevent any unnecessary strain on it. This part of the console is shaped to fit exactly around the interior mirror fitting.

◀ IC17.2

The 'T' piece goes across the roof lining and mounts in a similar manner by utilising the grab handle mountings. Note that the small 'tweeter' housing was temporarily undone to allow better access to the mounting. Again, your assistant can support both sections whilst fitting is being carried out.

IC17.3 ▶

Sitting in the back seat, this is the view. The illustration supplied with the console shows a radio mounted in the unit. However, we would suggest that it would have to be a fairly light one to be safe there. All told we found this a very easy item to fit and most useful too, giving a map light and more general illumination in the front and a separate, switchable light in the rear.

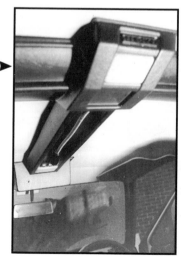

Fitting a map reading lamp

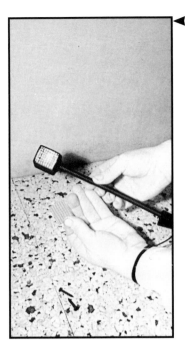

◀ IC18.1
Since Hella parts are no strangers to the insides of Volkswagens, it seems appropriate to choose a Hella accessory lamp here.

IC18.2 ▶
The Reading Lamp must be mounted in a position where it can be folded neatly and safely out of the way, but where it is still capable of shining onto a map without dazzling the driver. The black wire goes to 'earth', while the brown wire is connected into the lighting circuit behind the sidelight switch. Refer to your Haynes manual for wire identification.

It can be difficult for a passenger to read a map or instructions during darkness without turning on the interior lamp and distracting the driver.

The Hella Reading Lamp has the advantage of having a powerful 5W halogen bulb, a tough glass-reinforced plastic body and base, and a long-lasting flexible metal arm. There is also an alternative red lens.

Fitting a 'lights on' warning buzzer

Driving with lights on in daylight when visibility is poor is now a legal necessity, and that is certainly no bad thing. The problem comes at the end of the journey when the driver gets out and forgets about the lights. Volkswagen, in their wisdom, have made their cars so that the headlights go off with the ignition, but that still leaves the sidelights to remember. With the addition of the Hella 'lights on' warning buzzer it is unlikely that you will ever leave your lights on again. It is **loud!** The buzzer is suitable for all Mk I and Mk II models, and we fitted this unit to a Mk II Golf.

IC19.1
This is what you get. The buzzer is connected into the side light/courtesy circuits. Because of the way they are wired, Golfs and Jettas require an additional door contact switch (part no 6ZF

003 592 001). As the diagram shows, the Hella buzzer simply needs 'Scotchloking' in between the courtesy light and the sidelight circuit.

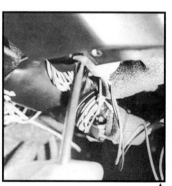

The diagram shows how simple this device is to fit, requiring the attachment of only two Scotchloks to complete.
(Diagram courtesy of Hella Ltd)

▲ IC19.2
With the lower dash removed we found a self-tapping screw just under the steering column which was almost purpose made for holding the bracket. Mounted thus, it is not only handy from a wiring point of view, but also tucked neatly out of the way from an aesthetic viewpoint.

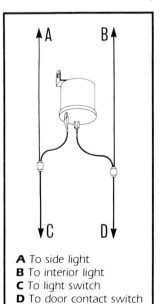

A To side light
B To interior light
C To light switch
D To door contact switch

Fitting an intermittent wiper control

As can be seen from IC20.4 the wiring is simple and all necessary Scotchloks, etc, are provided in the kit. However, a test lamp is almost essential for establishing which lead is which. (Diagram courtesy of Hella Ltd)

This is a useful device which is relatively easy to fit and most apt in those lands where the windscreen wiper may well be the most used part of a Golf! The device can be fitted, as the makers intended, to the front wipers or, with the addition of a small relay, to the rear wash/wipe system. Many owners may well prefer the latter, as the standard set-up allows only three sweeps at a time. The Hella unit fitted here allows intermittent operation between two and twenty sweeps per minute. We fitted it to a Mk II Golf but it can be fitted to Mk I and Jettas also.

IC20.1 ▶
A comprehensive package, including full instructions, which should be studied carefully before starting to fit. The system is manufactured by Hella for the front wiper system and thus a small relay, shown here, is also required to allow its fitment to the rear wiper.

IC20.2
Access to the relevant wiring is gained by removing the under dash section. This is held by five self-tapping screws. Once removed, the dash section drops down and can be set aside for easier working. The wiring is clearly visible and the correct wires to tap into can be located by using the Sykes-Pickavant test lamp.
▼

IC20.3
As usual, the biggest problem is where to fit the switch. It must be easily accessible by the driver, but similarly it must be reasonably unobtrusive so as not to detract from the interior style. A small bracket is supplied with the kit and we decided to use this to mount the switch at the top of the centre console, just underneath the ashtray, to the driver's left.
▼

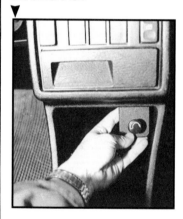

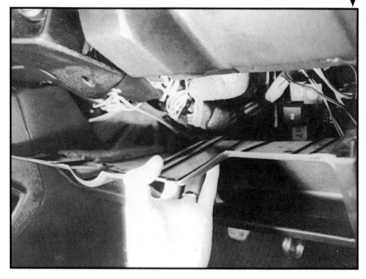

IC20.4 ▶
The wiring diagram supplied with the Hella kit is straightforward and relates to VW's own numbering system.

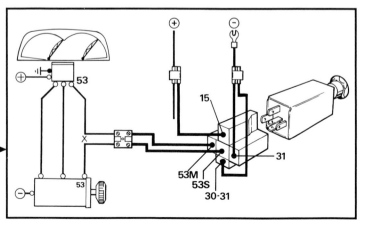

If you have fitted just a few of the items featured in this book then you will have a very desirable Volkswagen indeed. The problem is that those with less than honest intentions may also admire your handiwork and taste! With the statistics for car theft (and theft **from** cars) rising at an appalling rate, it makes sense to try to protect your 'pride and joy' by fitting an alarm system. There are many makes and types on the market, but we fitted one of VWs own, a remote control system shown here with the optional ultrasonic detector. This is suitable for all Golfs and Jettas and can be linked to a central locking set-up if fitted, although the latter was not present on the three-door GTi shown here. If triggered, the very powerful siren will sound and all four indicators flash simultaneously. It will also immobilise the ignition system. If no further disturbance occur, it will switch off after 60 seconds and prevent your battery running flat. Should there be any problem in using the remote 'key' (flat battery, loss of 'key' etc) then an emergency key is provided which can be used in the back of the siren to switch off the system manually.

As this Volkswagen system is activated by means of a small remote control 'key', it is quite possible that it could be pressed accidentally whilst in the car. A special safety circuit prevents the alarm from being switched on whilst the engine is running.

IC21.1 ▶
This is the basic alarm system. All wires and connectors, Scotchloks, brackets and screws are supplied. The two small boxes are the remote 'keys' with which the alarm is activated. The large siren is pre-wired to two looms and sockets (one being for the central locking interface). When triggered it pulsates at 120 decibels, which is louder than a road drill!

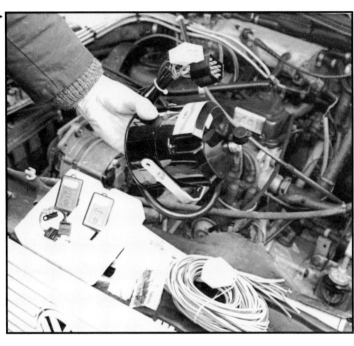

IC21.2
This is the optional quartz-controlled ultrasonic detector. This wonderful device triggers the alarm when it detects any movement in the car, such as, for example, if a window were broken and someone reached inside. Although officially an option, many owners regard it as being essential to any comprehensive alarm system.

▼

IC21.3 ▶
There are several points to consider when mounting the siren. It must not be exposed to water or be too close to any heat generated by the engine or exhaust system. We chose the left-hand upper bulkhead as being suitable. There must also be access to the back of the unit so that the emergency key can be inserted if required. The bracket has to be mounted separately, as shown. We drilled two holes to suit the self-tapping screws included in the kit. Zinc paint was used to prevent any rust forming around the holes. Here, the header tank has been removed from its mounting to facilitate the fixing.

Fitting an alarm system

When routing the wiring, great care should be taken to keep all cables away from the exhaust and cooling systems and any moving parts. By using the cable clips used for the existing loom, the alarm wiring can be held well out of harm's way.

◄ IC21.4
Once the bracket was secure, the siren could then be re-attached to it. Note that the back of it is facing inwards so that the emergency socket is accessible. Shakeproof washers were used to prevent vibration loosening the unit.

◄ IC21.5
The wiring is not complex, as can be seen from the diagram on facing page. Here, the alarm is being connected into the indicator circuit by means of a Scotchlok.

IC21.6 ►
A microswitch has to be fitted to the bonnet. The hole used for the body of the switch was already there and so it was only the two small holes for the self-tapping screws that had to be drilled. Again, these received the zinc treatment.

IC21.7 ►
The two usual mounting positions for the ultrasonic detector are either the roof at the rear of the car or on top of the dashboard. The former is aesthetically best but is far more difficult to wire. Thus, we chose the latter! Mounted as shown here, it does not obstruct forward vision and is well placed to function correctly. As well as two small holes for the self-tapping screws which hold it in place, another hole has to be drilled to pass the control cable through.

IC21.8 ▶

Some would say that these stickers are the most important part of any alarm system. By giving a visual warning, they may well prevent a thief from even attempting to break into your car. Should they not be convinced, a glance through the window will show a small red LED light on the ultrasonic detector confirming that an alarm is fitted and is switched on.

The ultrasonic detector has a sensitivity control which should be set carefully before using the alarm in public. Too sensitive a setting could result in the siren going off everytime there was a slight wind or someone walked by the car, which is not to be recommended! Similarly the sunroof should not be left open when the alarm is turned on.

◀ **IC21.9**

The system is switched on and off simply by pressing on the soft pad of the remote control 'key'. To confirm that it is set, the indicators flash twice. When the unit is switched off, they flash once. When central locking is fitted and wired into the system, all of the doors/hatch will lock when the alarm is activated. Several checks have to be made to ensure that it is functioning correctly and is not, for example, too sensitive. Of necessity, this involves deliberately setting off the siren and is not likely to make you 'neighbour of the year'! Once activated, the ignition is immobilised straight away and the rest of the system 'arms' after about 60 seconds.

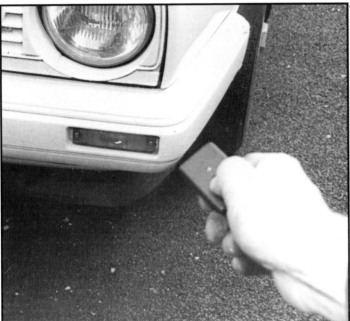

IC21.10 ▶

The wiring is no real problem and the use of this schematic diagram helps enormously. Before wiring commences, the battery should be disconnected. (Diagram by courtesy of Volkswagen Ltd)

Fitting air horns

The wiring should present few problems, as can be seen from the diagram here. The shaded area represents wiring/equipment which will not be required with the new set-up. (Diagram courtesy of Hella Ltd)

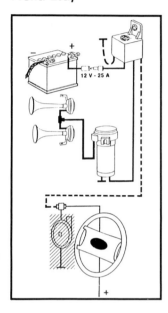

IC22.1 ▶
The Hella kit consists of twin horn trumpets, a small compressor, a relay, plastic hose with 'Y' piece and various fixings. You may need to make up a small bracket for the trumpets, as we did when we fitted them to a Mk II GTi. You will also need a couple of 'Scotchlok' connectors and some 28/0.30 mm wire. As ever, the first task is to remove the earth connection from the battery.

◀ **IC22.2**
In this case, the original horn lives behind the front grille. Mounting the new trumpets in the same, or a similar, position as the standard horn is a fairly good idea, not least because there will be some form of mounting already there. The trumpets should be facing downwards to prevent them from becoming full of debris! Wherever possible, we prefer to use existing holes/fixings rather than start drilling more as it may invalidate the bodywork warranty, where the car is still within the warranty period.

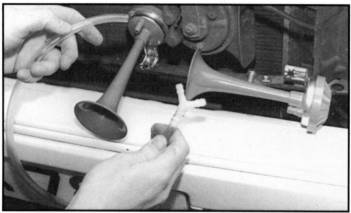

◀ **IC22.3**
The relay has to be mounted quite near to the compressor and horns in order to save running miles of wire all around the car. Here, we utilised an existing hole to position the relay just in front of the battery, which meant that the short length of wiring could be passed through the rear of the grille.

◀ **IC22.4**
The bracket for the horns is here being placed in position. The plastic hose will need to be checked for exact length so that it can be routed properly, without kinks, and all connections must be checked and tightened. Note the alignment of the compressor, which must be mounted in an upright position. If required, the Hella air horns can be wired so that the existing horn remains and all three are sounded at once!

Cleaning interior trim and surfaces

Cleaning the inside of many owners' cars is one of those tasks that always seems to go to the bottom of a priority list. Usually, by the time that three weeks mud and dirt have been removed from the outside of the car, there is not the time (or energy) left to do the interior. By doing the job regularly however, it does not have to take long and as the saying goes, 'an inch is a cinch, but a yard is hard'. Also, it means that you can keep a check on the general condition of the trim and if any new stains have appeared, there may be some chance of removing them before they become too ingrained.

Cleaning the interior of your Golf is made much simpler by emptying the car before you start. Take out any mats or additional carpets, rubbish, loose cassettes, pieces of paper, maps, sweets, scrapers, pens, parking tickets, etc, and you're halfway there!

IC23.1 ▶
The dashboard is a place where the dirt accumulates slowly and is usually not noticed until disturbed, as on the glove box of this Mk I Golf. Here, a paintbrush (dry of course!) is being used to remove the dust in those tricky-to-get-at places such as the heater controls. Another good idea is to use an air brush, as used by photographers for lens cleaning.

◀ IC23.2
Comma Cockpit Spray interior trim cleaner is being used on the plastic dash of this Mk II Golf. This will clean off the various marks and stains that accumulate, but without putting a harsh 'shine' on the surface. It is sprayed on, as shown here, and then ...

IC23.3 ▶
... spread along the surface by using a cloth. A final polish after five minutes will finish the task. The Comma product also restores that aromatic 'new car' smell. The finish is anti-static, which will doubltess be good news to many who frequently suffer from 'shocks' in the car.

Cleaning interior trim and surfaces

By using high quality products, such as the Comma range featured here, the appearance of your Golf will remain much as it was when it left the factory. And don't forget that an 'as-new' interior is one of the greatest factors in maintaining the re-sale value of your car.

IC23.4 ▶
Replacing a full set of original carpets in a Golf is an expensive business, so it pays to take care of them. The easiest way to clean them is to use a vacuum cleaner. The Link-Sedan vacuum seen here, operated from the cigar lighter socket, makes light work of the carpets in this Jetta. Mats - rubber or otherwise - should be taken out and shaken before being vacuumed.

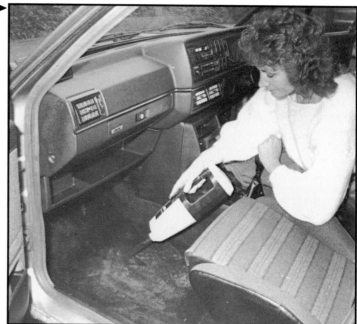

IC23.5
For stain removing, Comma have two products which will clean deep down: Interior Clean and, in aerosol form, Upholstery Cleaner. Both are suitable for various cleaning purposes including fabric, vinyl, leather and, of course, carpets.
▼

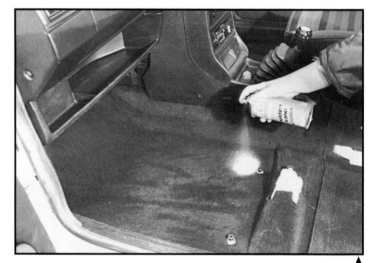

▲
IC23.6
Upholstery Cleaner is a dry foam shampoo which has to be shaken well before spraying onto the carpet, as shown here.

◀ **IC23.7**
The foam will lift out the dirt from the fabric. After 30 seconds, foam and dirt can be wiped away with a damp sponge.

◄ IC23.8
Don't forget the insides of the windows. The constant misting and demisting of the glass inside the car will cause a film to form. This is most noticeable as you clean it off and look through clear windows at your filthy cloth!

IC23.9 ►
At some point, the heated rear window may cease to function because of a broken element. Replacements are not exactly cheap! Enter Comma Electrocure, which is a metallic liquid, painted onto the rear screen and which effectively re-makes the electrical connection between the broken elements. It is simple to apply and most effective.

On this Golf, Comma Glass Cleaner is being used on a dry window. The whole window should be covered with the foam which should then be spread around using a cloth. After a couple of minutes it can be wiped off using a soft, dry cloth to reveal a sparkling, clean window.

Motorsport Mod - fitting a roll cage

Drivers of Golf Cabriolets can turn the page here, as their cars come with a roll cage fitted as standard. However, fixed head cars do not. John Aley Racing Limited have been making roll cages since 1964 and so their experience is considerable. Whilst most cages are supplied for motorsport applications, more and more are being sold for use on standard, road going cars. The statistic quoted alongside gives food for thought ...

IC24.1
The cage here is shown out of the car for clarity, its various components laid out prior to assembly. The tubes are clamped together with the fittings that come with the John Aley kit and then the whole thing is welded up, once in place, into a solid entity.
▼

IC24.2
Inside the motorsport Golf, the John Aley cage forms an incredibly strong safety zone around the passenger compartment. They are FIA approved, naturally.
▼

It is a terrifying fact, but statistics show that in 15 per cent of all 'real' accidents (ie, more than just a car park 'ding'), the car actually overturns. It is believed by some that legislation to include a compulsory roll cage of some description in all cars is on the cards.

MICHELIN

Chapter Three
In-car entertainment

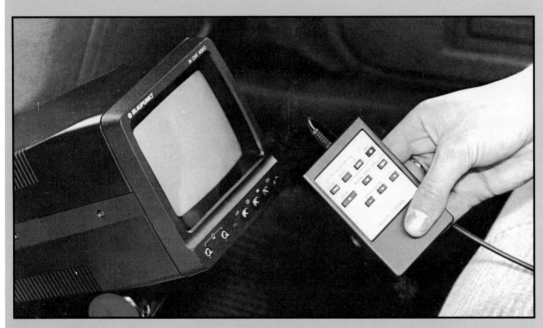
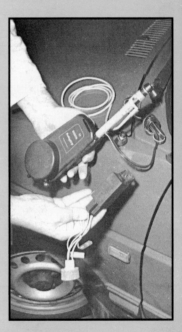

Some details about the Company

Volkswagen, as a Company, supply Blaupunkt equipment and have been doing so for a good many years.

The origins of the Blaupunkt Company date back to 1923 when, trading in Berlin as the Ideal Radio Company, they manufactured detector devices, headphones and radio accessories. The name 'Blaupunkt' became a trademark a year later although the famous 'Blue Spot' had already come into being, as the headphones were actually marked with a blue spot as they were passed through quality control.

Their first car radio was produced as long ago as 1932 and even that had remote control! Since then, the Company has followed a path of continual development, producing their first FM radio in 1950 and the first push button car radio (called the Omnimat) in Europe, in 1953. In 1969, the 'Frankfurt' model was the first stereo car radio in the world with the electronic car radio being introduced in 1973.

In 1974, Blaupunkt introduced their ARI traffic information and warning system for which they were awarded the ADAC (the German equivalent of the AA) safety prize. Such a record of technological achievement reflects an unwillingness to accept that a peak has been reached and this clearly shows in the products.

In choosing your ICE you should bear in mind that both the Golf and the Jetta are high quality vehicles and to fit anything less than high quality audio equipment is doing an injustice to both yourself and your car.

Over the years since the Golf's inception, it has been equipped with an ever improving level of in-car audio equipment as standard. In 1987, all Golfs and Jettas were equipped with a radio/cassette player and this reflects the rise in popularity of 'music on the move'. A glance through any brochure will confirm that the days when this meant slotting any old radio into the dash have long gone. Advising which equipment to fit to your Golf is difficult, almost to the point of being impossible. Everyone has different opinions as to what constitutes a good in-car audio system, from the simple and straightforward to the incredibly sophisticated.

There are a number of limiting factors, not least of which is the amount you can spend, and good quality sound does not come cheaply at any level. There is also useage. If the car is only driven four miles a day throughout the year, it makes little sense to load it up with the latest high-tech stereo system. Another major point is to judge which is best for your personal listening. Although most car fitments are combined radio/cassette units, some people like to listen to the radio and seldom use the cassette player. Thus, a set with particularly advanced radio features but with less sophisticated cassette facilities will appeal. Those who prefer cassette listening will be looking for features such as Dolby B and C noice reduction, metal tape facility, track search, etc. It is worth noting that, by and large, in most combination units, the radio is more advanced than the tape deck and thus a high performance cassette player will usually be accompanied by a high quality radio.

The advent of Compact Disc players has added another facet to the various permutations. Whilst initially an expensive item, the CD player is rapidly becoming more affordable. Although being more limited than tape in some respects (you can't record on a Compact Disc of course) its superb clarity of sound and dynamic range have lead to increasing popularity. Whatever the personal choice, it is worth sitting down for a while and deciding exactly what **you** need from a car audio system.

Bear in mind that when improving your in-car audio, uprating one item will almost always mean that another link in the chain has also to be uprated. For example, an uprated radio/cassette deck may require uprated speakers.

In this section we will be looking at some of the options offered by Blaupunkt from their wide range of radio/cassettes. The German company have a well deserved reputation for producing high quality equipment, achieved over more than 60 years in the business. The standard of fit and finish is always high and it is pleasing to note that this applies uniformly to the whole range and not just to the top models. Their attention to detail and, in particular, to the ergonomics of their sets matches Volkswagens own production standards. Because of this, Blaupunkt equipment will not look out of place in any Golf or Jetta, being as subtle and understated, yet stylish, as the cars themselves.

Golfs and Jettas have DIN sized apertures for fitting in-car audio. All of the Blaupunkt range will fit as they too are DIN specification.

In this Chapter many technical terms and abbreviations are used. In order to save repetitious explanations, we have included a Glossary on page 126.

It pays to try to understand some of the jargon attached to the in-car audio market. Although advertisers love to load their copy with impressive-sounding terminology, it doesn't actually mean a thing unless you know what the jargon means! A much more comprehensive glossary of terms appears in the full Blaupunkt catalogue.

(Our thanks are due to Senior Blaupunkt Engineer, George Richardson, for his help in the preparation of this entire Chapter.)

Choosing your in-car entertainment

When buying a radio/cassette unit, one should always remember that at some time in the future, an upgrade of some kind may be desired. The sets featured on this page are all capable 'front end' units for utilising additional amplification, speakers, etc.

◀ **ICE1.1**
Part of the range lined up along the bonnet of a Jetta. All of the models suit the subdued and subtle black interiors of the VW range.

ICE1.2 ▶
The Porto is a lower range model which would go nicely with the standard speaker system in the Golf. It has manual tuning with three wavebands (FM Stereo/AM/LW) and 2 x 12W output (music power). The cassette deck is a basic unit offering no form of noise reduction although it boasts a hard permalloy head.

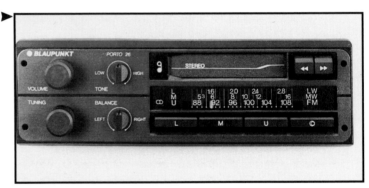

◀ **ICE1.3**
The Stockholm is visually very similar to the Porto, but has several improved features on the cassette deck. The frequency response has been increased and autoreverse fitted. The output is the same as that of the Porto.

ICE1.4 ▶
Moving to the London is quite a leap, particularly with the tuner which is the phase-locked-loop type and has a digital readout to display the frequency. Up to five stations can be preset on each of the three wavebands and it has manual tune or automatic search facility. As is usual in any manufacturers range, it is usually the tuner which benefits first and so it is here, for the cassette deck has no noise reduction or autoreverse. However, the power output is 4 x 6W (music power).

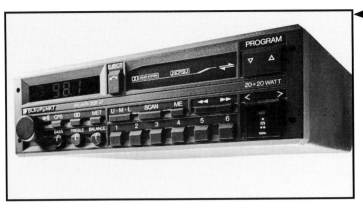

ICE1.5

The Atlanta is a well equipped unit as well as being suitable for adding on a whole host of further equipment. Power output is 2 x 21W or 4 x 7W (music power) with a DIN socket pre-amp out. The highly specified tape deck features Metal tape, Dolby NR, Autoreverse, CPS (track search) and scan. The tuner is similar to that on the London except that there are now six preset stations available on the three wavebands.

ICE1.6

The Toronto is extremely popular and justifiably so. It takes the high specification of the Atlanta a stage further. It is one of only two sets in the Blaupunkt range to have short wave as well as the usual three and it has a preset facility of five stations on each waveband. As well as Dolby NR, it also has Blaupunkt's own noise reduction system, DNR, which operates on the radio as well as the cassette deck.

One of the major points about this set is that it has its own built-in form of theft prevention in that it is code protected. Once the power supply has been interrupted, the code (known only to the owner) has to be entered before it will work again.

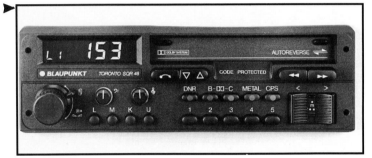

ICE1.7

BLAUPUNKT BERLIN IQR 85
The Berlin is very much a top of the range set with advanced features abounding and reflected in its price tag. Not surprisingly, it is code protected. It comes complete with a 4 x 20W (music power) amplifier and a high specification tape deck. The latter features autoreverse, scan and CPS (track search) and has an excellent frequency range of 35-18,000 Hz. (The latter represents the sound range the tape deck is capable of dealing with. The wider the range, the better the deck.)

The radio, however, is the cherry on the cake. Once switched on, a microprocessor compares any station received with those stored in its memory and when identified, the name (rather than just the frequency) is displayed. It also has two PLL tuners which operate independently of each other.

One of the Berlin's tuners picks up the station, the other searches for alternatives. The display shows the actual **names** of the four nearest alternatives (four more are shown on touching the 'PCI' key) and the set switches inaudibly to a 'stronger' transmission of the station tuned to, if one becomes available. The database of frequencies/station names are fed into the Berlin via a cassette and thus travelling in another country requires only a simple (two minutes) update to make the set fully operable there. The AVC control is a useful device which measures the amount of noise in the car and increases or decreases the volume of the set as appropriate.

It is not possible to cover every aspect of the Berlin, but, as mentioned earlier, this really is **the** set for the radio enthusiast as well as providing a superb radio/cassette. The illustrations show the dual function of the lower range of controls, making the facia simpler and clearer to use. When 'MOD' is pressed, the four lower function controls light up.

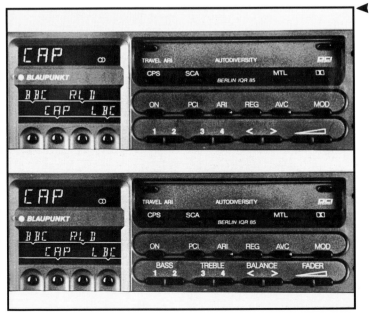

Fitting a radio/cassette player

This part of the book is not primarily about DIY (although the fitting of a basic set plus speakers and aerial is certainly a DIY proposition). Anything more complex should be left to a qualified engineer, but here is an overview of how Blaupunkt's Chief Engineer, George Richardson, goes about fitting a variety of sets to a Golf or Jetta ...

Remember! Always disconnect the battery before starting to fit a radio/cassette player, for although all Blaupunkt and many other sets are internally fused, it is still possible to cause damage to the set and/or to other electrical fitments through just a moment's inattention.

Fitting a radio/cassette can be easy or difficult, depending on a number of factors, not least of which is the DIY Golfer's 'electrical' ability and the complexity of the set being fitted. By and large the average owner should be able to fit an average set with few problems. However, as one progresses towards the top of the Blaupunkt range, the wiring can become somewhat tricky and home fitting cannot really be recommended. For that reason, in this section we are presenting an overview of the sort of work that may typically be required. The car featured here is a Mk II Golf, although the basic principles apply to Mk I models also.

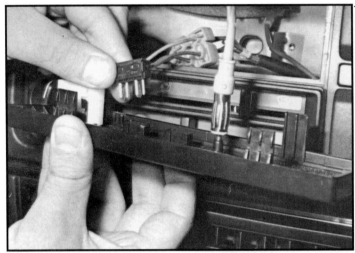

◄ ICE2.1
The back of the blanking plate, fitted to any Golf that comes without ICE, has sockets which retain the various plugs used for installation. Most of the relevant wires are available directly through the hole in the dash, known as the DIN aperture. However, it is sometimes necessary to have access from underneath which could mean removing one or both of the lower dash panels and/or the centre console.

ICE2.2 ►
Blaupunkt sets all work on a simple plug-in system. Here, the power feed plug has been 'Scotchloked' into the existing wiring.

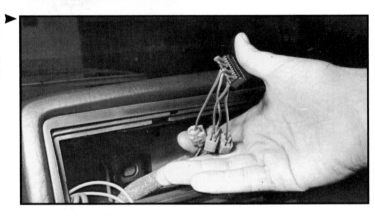

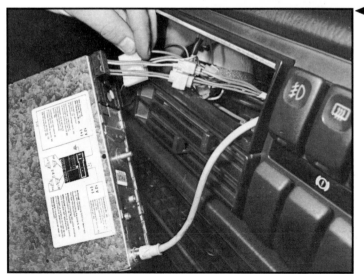

◄ ICE2.3
The Volkswagen plugs connect straight into the back of the Blaupunkt set, as shown here. It is very important not to trap the wiring as the set is being pushed into the DIN aperture. The same basic wiring system is kept for most of the sets in the range meaning that, for the most part, sets are interchangeable. The most notable difference is where a replacement set has a security code. Then, a permanent fused feed has to be connected.

◄ ICE2.4
Before the unit can be fitted into the DIN aperture, this metal housing has to be inserted. Note the locating pegs being bent upwards here for illustration purposes, but actually bent into position **after** the housing has been inserted.

If your car has been fitted with an 'odd' set at some time and the power and speaker plugs have been changed, you'll have to obtain new ones from your Blaupunkt or Volkswagen dealer. They clip onto the wire in an ingenious manner which requires no soldering; just a pair of pliers. Wiring in a new DIN plug (one of the round, multi-pin plugs) ought to be entrusted to experts, however. As indicated in the text, fitting one of the more exotic sets ought to be left to your Blaupunkt or VW dealership too. How important is a fitting charge compared with the cost of replacing a ruined Toronto or Berlin?

ICE2.5 ►
The housing allows the set to be slotted neatly into place. When pushed fully home, the set locks itself into position with a 'click'. Note the two holes at each side of the radio/cassette.

◄ ICE2.6
These holes accommodate the releasing tools, which look suspiciously like pieces of bent coathanger but, in fact, have specially-shaped ends. When inserted as shown here, they connect with lugs on the metal frame which enable the set to be pulled out; a simple but most convenient and effective idea. Clearly, this means that changing up from one set to another presents very few problems; simply pull out the old set, remove the plugs from the back and insert them into the new set and push the set home into the housing.

Fitting a radio/cassette player

Good quality in-car audio products are not cheap and we would recommend that, having installed the equipment, serious attention is paid to the problem of theft prevention. Security of the set itself is allied to the security of the car, which is dealt with in Chapter 2, Section 21.

Perhaps the simplest way to keep your radio/cassette actually **in** your car, is to use the Blaupunkt safety cassette. This is a cassette shaped device which slots into the cassette aperture in the normal way. Once in position, it is locked and a metal pin projects from the cassette at right angles through the radio/cassette unit, through its special fitting frame and into the dashboard. The special slotted housing (see ICE2.4) comes supplied with the safety cassette.

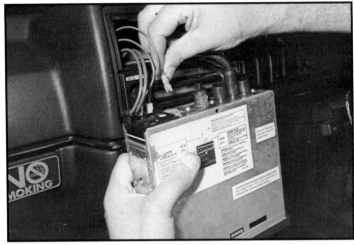

◀ **ICE2.7**
The more complex sets use seven-pin DIN plugs for interfacing with other parts of the audio system, such as amplifier, graphic equalizer, CD player, etc. Unlike many manufacturers, Blaupunkt provide a spade connector for the all-important earth terminal. Bad earth connections are responsible for many of the problems associated with radio/cassette fitting.

ICE2.8 ▶
The ultimate in high specification in-car Hi-Fi is the Blaupunkt Berlin, described elsewhere in this Chapter in some detail. An amazing piece of Blaupunkt technology, its installation is definitely not a DIY task! Despite being a top-line set, it still blends well into the Golf interior.

◀ **ICE2.9**
The lockable cassette requires the fitting of a standard 1.5V (AA) battery which powers the red warning light. When in use, this light flashes constantly as a visible warning to potential thieves. The battery lasts for months of normal use.

ICE2.10 ▶
The safety cassette fits into the player as a normal audio-cassette would and once locked into place, renders the unit 'immobile'. In this case it is being shown in the Berlin which also has security coding; doubly a safe set!

ICE2.11 ▶

When installing the Detachable Plug-in unit, the special backing plate is fitted onto the rear of the radio/cassette as shown. There are two versions, one for mechanically tuned radios and one for radios electronically tuned. The latter contains a nicad battery which means that pre-set stations on digital units will be retained. The battery has a life of 20 hours continuous use and when the set is replaced in the bracket it is automatically recharged.

The only certain way to ensure your precious audio equipment is not stolen is to take it with you. The Blaupunkt transportable fitting kit allows instant removal of the radio/cassette for storage in the boot/hatch or even safer keeping in the home.

◀ **ICE2.12**

With the panel pushed into place, it is secured by this nut. The plate houses a multi-pin interconnecting block which, when the radio/cassette player is pushed fully home ...

ICE2.13 ▶

... connects with the female multi-pin connector in the back of the special housing fitted in place of the one shown in ICE2.4. Once in position, the unit operates normally. Note the carrying handle which folds flat when the set is installed and mates with lugs on the frame which prevent the unit from being released unless the handle is raised again. This is a sensible safety measure which prevents the set flying about should the car be involved in a crash; typical Blaupunkt thoroughness!

Speaker selection and fitting

On no account should speaker leads be connected together. To do so could ruin both speakers and amplifiers.
In order to make things reasonably clear, the table below should help to understand some aspects of this and later sections:

Speaker	Frequency response
Bass (Woofer)	35/4,000 Hz
Mid range	300/12,000 Hz
Treble (Tweeter)	2,000/25,000 Hz

The loudspeaker could possibly be regarded as the cinderella of in-car audio. Time and again we see (and hear!) impressive systems with expensive radio/cassette units, amplifiers and graphic equalizers which are drastically let down by using standard speakers. This is the audio equivalent of turbocharging your Golf and then running it on 4½ inch wheels and 155 section tyres: not to be advised! Essentially, a speaker is a device for converting the electrical impulses emanating from the radio/cassette into sound waves, capable of being picked up by the human ear. Very simply, the amplifier causes the speaker cone to move in or out and thus create sound waves.

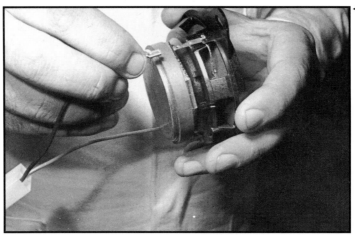

◀ **ICE3.1**
All speakers have a + and a - terminal and it is important that all speakers be connected in the same way so as to prevent 'phasing'; one speaker moving in as another is moving out; the sound waves created by the two speakers thus partly counteracting each other. Blaupunkt speakers have different sized terminals to prevent this from happening.

ICE3.2 ▶
Two multiple-cone speakers awaiting fitting in a Golf Mk II rear parcel shelf. The large outer speaker is a mid-range and the small one in the centre is a tweeter (treble).

ICE3.3
The diagram shows a cross section through a typical single-cone speaker, with a single diaphragm for the reproduction of the entire frequency range.
(Figure courtesy of Blaupunkt)

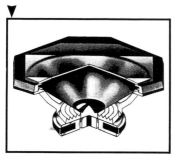

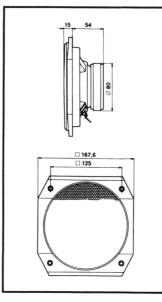

◀ **ICE3.4**
All Blaupunkt speakers come complete with fitting instructions. Seen here are part of those for a 'Blue Magic' speaker where the measurements given are comprehensive. Probably the most important is the depth of speaker which should be checked carefully before the cutting of any panels is considered.
(Diagram courtesy of Robert Bosch Limited)

ICE3.5 ▶

Speakers are simple enough to uprate if you are carrying out a minor uprate. On this Mk II Golf, the dash mounted speakers are accessed by gently prying out the plastic cap and undoing the Philips head screw. As can be seen here, the cover lifts off, and the speaker can be removed.

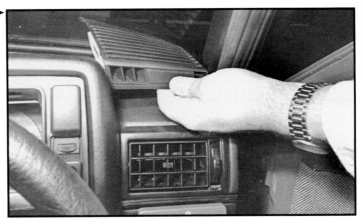

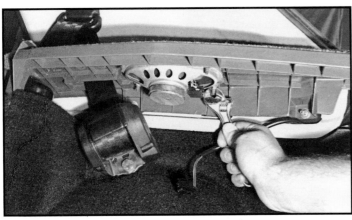

◀ **ICE3.6**

At the rear, the speakers live in the very edge of the parcel shelf, just behind the shock absorber mountings. They are held by four nuts, unscrewed as shown.

ICE3.7 ▶

The speaker can be removed and its replacement fitted. This is a twin-cone type which should give an improved response. The main problems with the standard speaker apertures are twofold: first, the size, which isn't really big enough to hold a speaker of any real consequence and second, a reasonably high powered system will require more than four speakers, which means that you will have to look beyond the standard mountings in any case.

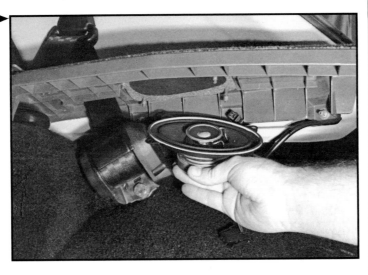

Speaker Types

There are three basic speaker types plus a new Blaupunkt innovation.

The Broadband speaker is the one most usually fitted as standard. As its name suggests, it is something of a compromise and handles frequencies from the bass, middle and treble ranges. The next step up is the dual cone speaker and almost any improvement in the car-audio system will require at least an upgrade to this type.

The speaker is, in fact, two speakers in one, with either a bass or mid-range speaker having a tweeter in the middle. (See ICE3.2.) A component speaker is one designed to handle just one set of frequencies, either bass, mid-range or treble.

Ever improving on existing technology Blaupunkt have introduced their Honeycombe Speaker range. These speakers radiate all frequencies from an equal, flat surface, regardless of where they are positioned.

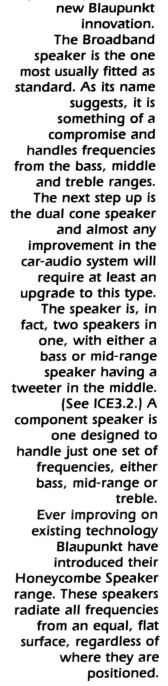

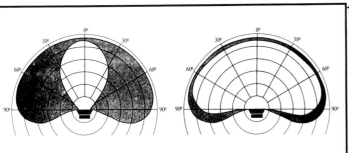

◀ **ICE3.8**

The diagram clearly shows the advantages of the Blaupunkt Honeycombe design speaker (right). The sound is radiated over a much wider area than the conventional speaker shown here on the left. (Diagram courtesy of Robert Bosch Limited)

Speaker selection and fitting

Wiring speakers in a car is something of an art. Not only must the connections be correct, but also the routing of the wires must be considered very carefully, so as to avoid using hundreds of yards of speaker cable! The basic rule is that the power handling capacity of the speakers must at least equal the output. In the two diagrams here the output is 4 ohms.

Fig. ICE.A
Two speakers have to be wired in series, as shown.

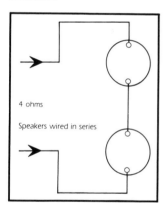

Fig. ICE.B
However, with four speakers, a parallel wiring arrangement is called for, in order to stay within the output level (4 ohms) of the amp.

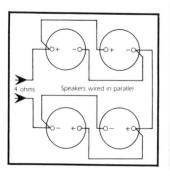

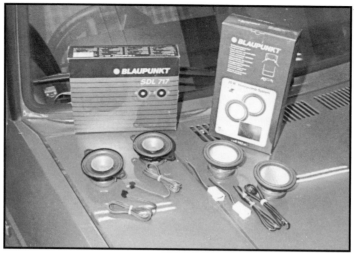

◀ ICE3.9
Blaupunkt speakers usually come in pairs. Here a pair of the new type Honeycombe speakers (on the right) are seen alongside a pair of the more conventional twin cone SDL 717 speakers. As can be seen, all come complete with cable and fittings.

ICE3.10 ▶
On our visit to Blaupunkt, speakers were being fitted to a high-powered system in this Jetta. Honeycombe speakers were being used which meant that, because of their unique design, they could be fitted in the door panel **behind** the map pocket.

◀ ICE3.11
Obviously, the door trim had to be removed and measurements had to be very accurate, particularly as this car had manual rather than electric windows. (Clearance for the window winder was needed.) Not only was this important for the positioning of the speakers, but also the routing of the cables.

ICE3.12 ▶
The result was that four speakers were fitted behind the map pocket, avoiding the structure of the door frame. Whilst the actual pocket itself would not affect the sound, the placement of large objects directly in front of them would make clarity a problem.

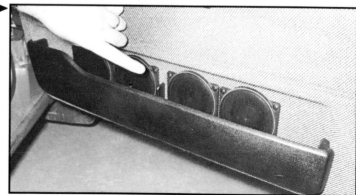

Sub-Woofing

Despite its strange name, a Sub-Woofing speaker system is a highly desirable piece of car audio equipment. It is designed for use mainly with uprated systems, particularly where high output amplifiers are used and/or where a CD player demands much of the speakers in order to maximise its incredible dynamic range. The Sub-Woofer boosts the bass frequencies and pushes them out through two 130mm speakers.

◄ ICE3.13
In addition, a further speaker was added in front of the window winder and a tweeter just above it.

ICE3.14
The parcel shelf of a Jetta provides an excellent base to mount speakers, as can be seen here. These are component speakers ranging from deep bass to high tweeters. Golf owners lose out slightly because although the hinged rear shelf can be used for extra speakers, it somewhat hampers the practicality of the hatchback. ▼

ICE3.15
A Blaupunkt Sub-Woofing system comes complete with the BXN-SUB 07 crossover network which sorts out the various frequencies, sending the bass (between 50-350 Hz) to the sub-woofer box and the other frequencies to their relative speakers. ▼

▲ ICE3.16
The usual place for mounting a Sub-Woofer system in the Golf is the nearside corner of the hatch.

Always keep tapes away from the speakers; the magnet could damage them irreparably.

Amplifiers, graphic equalizers and crossover units

With certain radio/cassette and CD players a separate amplifier is a necessity; they will not work without one. However, there is nothing to stop the enthusiast from boosting the power of his existing system. The principle of in-car amplification is not to reduce your neighbours to tears as you pull onto your drive or to enable the whole of the High Street to listen to your latest choice of music. It is the same principle as building an engine that produces 150 bhp and can achieve speeds well above the legal limit. It is being able to listen at reasonable volume levels with an amplifier working well within its capability. It is quality, not quantity, that is the keynote.

The graphic equalizer is best described as a more versatile tone control switch. Effectively, your car is its own tone control and because it modifies the sounds at random because of the effects of engine noise, wind noise, tyre noise, etc, the chances of getting the sound you would really like are minimal. By using a graphic, you can tune out the problems more accurately. A crossover unit does as its name implies, and separates the different frequencies into treble, mid-range and bass. Having done so, it passes them onto the correct speakers, thus giving a much cleaner sound.

There are two important points to note when considering any of the improvements mentioned in this section. The first is that none of them can make a bad basic unit good. In fact, if you have a poor quality radio/cassette, adding a graphic or amplifier will only serve to make its shortcomings worse.

Secondly, all of the products should be matched, preferably by make, but certainly by technical specification. Uprating the whole system except the speakers, for example, will at best give you very little extra performance for your money and at worst, ruin your speakers!

◄ ICE4.1
As with most manufacturers, Blaupunkt amplifiers and other accessories are designed to connect to each other simply by using standard 7-pin DIN plugs. Thus, the wiring is relatively easy and the main problem is where to fit the amplifier. In the Golf/Jetta, the two main choices are under the front passenger seat or ...

ICE4.2
... in the nearside hatchback as seen here. In the Jetta, the large boot means there is lots of space for mounting audio equipment. The large fins on the edge of the unit form a heat sink. This particular amp is a BSA 107, a stereo version producing 2 x 45W music power. **▼**

ICE4.3
Blaupunkt produce a full range of connection cables to allow the add-ons shown in this section to be connected up. This is the connection set for tweeters in conjunction with active diplexer SC-XN-A and separate amplifiers. So there! **▼**

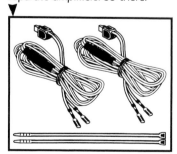

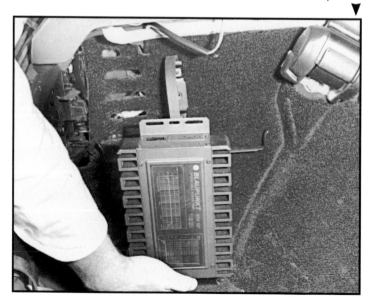

ICE4.4 ▶
For a real taste of power, how about the BSA 247. It produces an amazing 2 x 120W! (Photo courtesy of Robert Bosch Limited)

Much thought has to be given to the mounting of extra audio equipment. Not only does it have to be secure, in most cases there has to be some room available for cooling air to circulate. Also, if holes are drilled in the bodywork, it is important that they are correctly rustproofed.

◀ **ICE4.5**
There is a wide range of graphic equalizers but this remote version has a lot going for it. Apart from the obvious improvement in sound quality by tuning the tone controls precisely, it allows fitment without the need for another DIN aperture. It is flexibly mounted near to the driver and can be adjusted to personal preference. When the car is left for any length of time, the stalk can be bent down along the edge of the seat where it cannot be seen. The control unit is mounted out of sight and is thus no temptation to a thief.

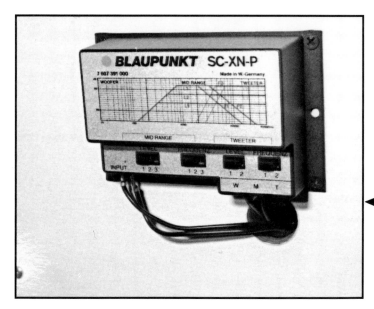

◀ **ICE4.6**
The Blaupunkt passive crossover unit. The input and output for mid-range and treble are adjustable meaning that the effective crossover points can be altered.

Amplifiers, graphic equalizers and crossover units

When mounting a crossover, amplifier or graphic, you must always ensure that there is no possibility of the unit getting wet, even from water dripping off the boot lid, for example. Seen here in Blaupunkt's demonstration Jetta is an active crossover unit. Similar in operation to the passive unit, it adds even more to the sound by strengthening the separated signals by separate amplifiers.

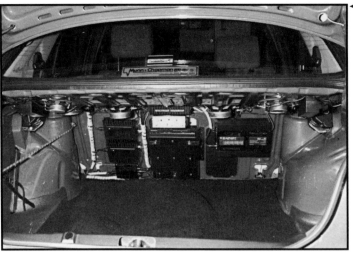

◄ ICE4.7
The demonstration Jetta, showing the amazing extent of the audio modifications! What you see are; two bass speakers, two mid-range, three amplifiers, and four crossover units. Despite the bulky nature of much of the equipment, it says much for the boot space in the car that there is still plenty of luggage space. The black, steel box in the centre is the video recorder, no less! (see section 6). This car provides the most incredible depth and clarity of sound imaginable!

GLOSSARY OF TERMS

With the help of Blaupunkt, we have listed here some of the most frequently used words and phrases which may prove useful.

AUTOMATIC LOUDNESS — Adapts sound reproduction to the human ear by boosting trebles and bass at low volume.

AUTOMATIC MUTING — Circuit which silences the sound 'between stations' during the tuning search process.

AUTOREVERSE — Automatic reversal of tape direction and track changeover at end of the cassette. The track can be changed manually at any time.

BASS — Sounds in the low frequency range (up to approx 600 Hz).

CPS — The Blaupunkt name for their track search function. When pressed the tape will fast forward or reverse until it comes to the next track when it will stop automatically and play it. Particularly useful in a car environment where most attention should be concentrated on driving.

CHROME DIOXIDE TAPE — Tape with a magnetic coating of chrome dioxide (CrO_2).

CROSSOVER NETWORK — Electronic device for distributing the output of sounds in such a way that different frequencies are handled by different loudspeakers.

DOLBY* NOISE REDUCTION — A system developed by Ray Dolby as a means of reducing tape hiss.

DNR — Dynamic noise reduction. Another system of reducing tape hiss.

FADER — A control enabling the sound to be distributed between the front and rear speakers in a four-speaker set-up.

FERRIC TAPE — A tape with a magnetic coating of iron oxide particles (Fe_2O_3).

HARD PERMALLOY TAPE HEAD — Tape head that provides extremely high quality sound reproduction and long service life.

HERTZ (Hz) — A unit of measurement for frequency. It measures the number of cycles per second.

MUSIC POWER — The maximum (peak) power available from an amplifier for a short period of time. See also Rated Power.

NR — Abbreviation of 'Noise reduction'; that is, any system for reducing tape hiss (for example, Dolby NR).

NOMINAL POWER RATING — The maximum electric power (in watts) which a loudspeaker can handle continuously.

PLL CIRCUIT (Phase locked loop) — An electronic circuit with a quartz stabilised frequency scanning system, into which station frequencies exactly 'lock' and are held with high stability.

RATED POWER (RMS) — The average continuous maximum output of an amplifier. See Music Power.

SCAN — A helpful feature if you cannot remember what is on a particular tape. When pressed, the SCAN function will seach out the beginning of each track and play ten seconds before progressing to the next track and repeating the operation.

TREBLE — Sounds in the high audio frequency range, approx 4,000-20,000 Hz.

TWEETER — A loudspeaker for the reproduction of higher frequencies, approx 4,000-20,000 Hz.

TWO WAY LOUDSPEAKER — Loudspeaker with two different systems in a common housing, eg, woofer/mid-range and a tweeter.

WIDE BAND LOUDSPEAKER — A single system loudspeaker which reproduces the whole audio frequency range.

WOW AND FLUTTER — Unpleasant howling sounds caused by speed variations in the tape transport system.

*DOLBY IS THE TRADE MARK OF DOLBY LABORATORIES.

ICE4.8 ▶

This system of Blaupunkt add-ons even **they** call the 'creme de la creme'. It comprises the Berlin radio/cassette and CDP 05 compact disc player, BEQ-F/R Equalizer and the BQA 160 amplifier. This little lot drive an army of speakers through appropriate crossovers. Ah well, we can all dream! And the sound quality produced by this arrangement really is a dream.

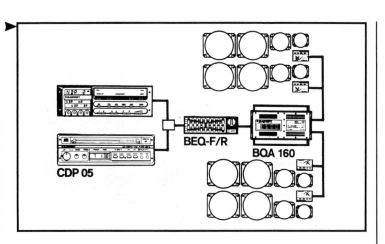

BEQ-F/R

CDP 05

BQA 160

Aerials

Radio waves are electro-magnetic and move through the air somewhat rapidly: at 300,000,000 metres per second, to be precise! A well designed aerial, such as all of those in the Bosch range, is essential to collect them and provide the good reception required. (All diagrams in this section courtesy of Blaupunkt)

The car aerial has specific problems because the radio is constantly moving around in relation to the signal. This can lead to poor reception, not only if the transmitter is too far away, but also if it is too close. If the set is too close to a strong signal but is tuned into a more distant one, then it may become confused and mix up the two. The resultant audio melange is called **cross modulation.** Conversely, if the set is already tuned into the near, strong signal, there is a danger of overloading. If the signal required is too far away there is an opposite problem. (This is particularly noticeable with FM, where the signal travels in 'sight' lines and therefore is easily

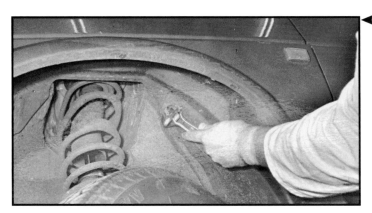

◀ **ICE5.1**
Remove the wheelarch liner (when fitted) before fitting a wing mounted aerial.

ICE5.2
Standard fitting point is the left-hand front wing.

▼

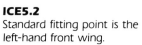

ICE5.3 ▶
Most models either have an aerial fitted as standard or have the hole pre-drilled and covered by a blanking plug. If no hole is present, one must be drilled and it is important to make sure that the positioning is correct and that the length of aerial below the wing will not foul in any way. The Sykes-Pickavant 'Unicut' variable hole cutter comes in two sizes, cutting holes from 6mm-30mm between them. It's shown being used in the 'use-anywhere' Black & Decker cordless re-chargeable drill.

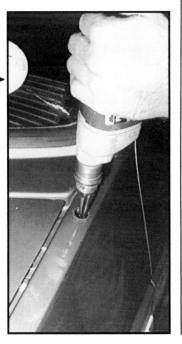

Continued overleaf

Aerials

Continued from previous page

interrupted by the horizon or tall buildings.) The volume will fall but interference will increase. The difficulties associated with all of these phenomena can be largely overcome by having both a good tuner and aerial. For this section we have looked at four types of aerial; a standard telescopic, an Autoflex flexible, a windscreen mounted aerial and an electrically retractable unit.

A light coating of grease on the outside of a chrome telescopic aerial helps to keep the rust at bay and also prevents it from sticking. Most of the drawings are used courtesy of Bosch and Blaupunkt.

ICE5.4 ▶
When the hole is complete it should be de-burred (all of the rough edges removed) and then the underside of the wing should be scraped clean. This is vital as you **must** ensure a good earth. (Bad earthing accounts for most car radio reception troubles.) To prevent any rust problems, the scraped area should be treated with an acid-free grease, preferably one which includes particles of copper, to improve conductivity.

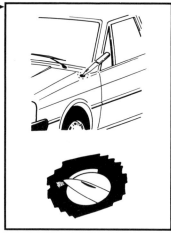

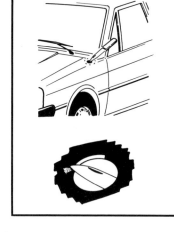

◀ ICE5.6
Once in position, the washers can be added and the top nut tightened. Ideally, the aerial should lean back slightly, almost parallel with the line of the 'A' pillar. The high quality of the Bosch aerial becomes most apparent when you begin to appreciate the neat way it all comes together.

ICE5.5 ▲
The aerial can then be inserted into the hole from underneath, after having removed the top nut and various washers.

ICE5.7 ▶
To hold the aerial steady, a metal bracket is provided which can be bent to suit. This should be fitted, using a self-tapping screw, as shown in this diagram for the Autojet II electric aerial, where the extra weight involved makes the use of the support strap even more vital.

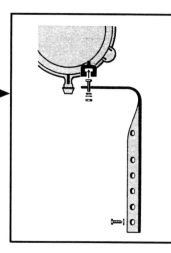

ICE5.8 ▶
The Bosch Autoflex aerial shows how advances in technology have been of use to the motorist. It is noticeably shorter than most at 45cm long. Despite this, in FM it's helically wound coil makes electronic amplification unnecessary. In LW and MW an impedance matching circuit ensures a better adaptation of the aerial to the car radio.

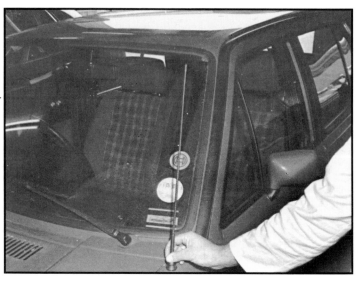

ICE5.9

The Bosch Autoflex fits in a similar way to the standard VW/Bosch telescopic unit alongside which it is viewed in this photograph. The Autoflex is essentially a glass fibre rod and this makes it extremely tough so that for example, it does not need to be removed for a car wash. It is removable if necessary and simply unscrews from the base unit, as can be seen here.

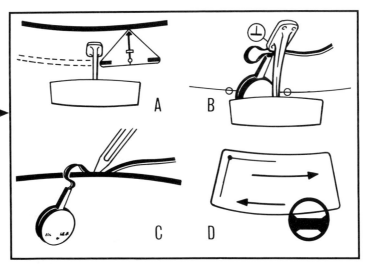

ICE5.10

The Autojet II is in the middle of the Bosch three model electric aerial range. An electric aerial always costs more but it is certainly worth it if the radio is used to any great extent. For example, there is nothing more frustrating than to join a motorway, and turn the radio on, only to find that the aerial is down! As with most others, the Autojet extends automatically when the radio is switched on. This feature also makes it vandal (and car washer!) proof. Again, fitting is very similar to the previous two, although, there must be extra room for the motor at the bottom of the aerial and the control box featured here must be fitted in a dry place.

Aerials, like speakers, tend to be the poor relations in the field of in-car audio. When fitting a radio, especially if it is an upgraded set, it is always wise to seek professional advice as to which aerial would best suit the characteristics of the set in question.

ICE5.11

The wiring is fairly simple, as can be seen from this diagram.

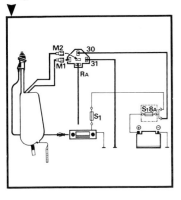

ICE5.12 ▶

A novel Bosch idea is the Autofun. windscreen mounted aerial. This involves no drilling or complex fitting and is, of course, totally vandal proof, being inside the car. Ideally it should be fitted at the top of the windscreen, in the centre.

A. However, there must be sufficient room to mount the amplifier box and reception elements (a marking jig is supplied to enable this to be ascertained easily).

B. There must also be a good earth nearby, which can usually be supplied by the interior mirror mounting screws.

C. When mounted in this way, the cable should be pressed between the rubber surround and the windscreen frame.

D. If it cannot be mounted centrally, it should be mounted in the corner of the screen, preferably on the passenger side.
In all cases the aerial kits come complete with a front wing installation. Where fitting at the back of the car (on a Jetta) is required, a Bosch aerial extension cable will be needed.

Advanced equipment

As with many of the items covered earlier in this Chapter, the equipment featured here is not at all well suited to DIY fitment. It would be silly to spend money on sophisticated ICE equipment and then to ruin it, just to save the cost of main dealer installation ...

Compact Disc

In-car Compact Disc players are becoming more and more widely used nowadays. Initial low sales were due largely to the high cost of the machines and of the discs themselves. However, the costs of both have dropped quite dramatically and a CD player can now cost a lot less than some radio/cassette units. Compact Disc has two main assets; first the sound quality is excellent and second, given a reasonable degree of care, the discs will continue to provide this high quality sound almost literally for as long as you want to listen. The latter is because the disc is 'played' by a laser beam bouncing off the tracks and therefore the disc is not physically worn during every play in the same way as a conventional record. In terms of quality, the best comparison of tape performance is D.A.T. (Digital Audio Tape). However, like records and existing tapes, they will, quite simply, start to wear out and thus clarity will suffer. Early CD players were plagued by 'jumping', which was caused by the beam being unsettled by uneven road surfaces. However, this has been eradicated on all except the bumpiest of roads. Because of its extraordinarily wide dynamic range, a CD player will normally require quite a high-powered amplifier and also matched speakers. Fitting a CD player is also a very good reason for adding a graphic equaliser, again for the same reason.

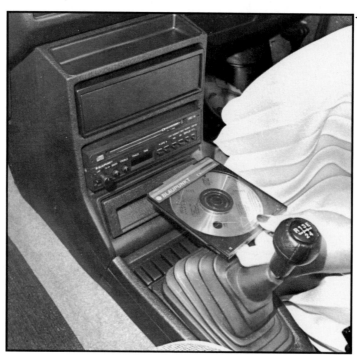

◀ **ICE6.1**
The Blaupunkt CDP 05 Compact Disc player shown fitted in a Jetta. Note the cartridge in which the disc is held and protected. By using this, the life of the disc is prolonged extensively, not only from scratches and other marks but also from the distortion which can effect standard CD covers at temperatures of over 50 degrees C. The cartridge can withstand temperatures of up to 70 degrees for 24 hours. The player is seen here in the twin DIN aperture console.

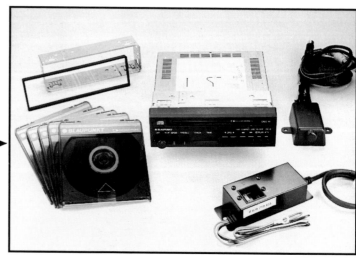

ICE6.2 ▶
The CDP 05 in its entirety. As well as the usual CD attributes (skip a track, fast forward etc) it is also fitted with an adjustable pre-amplifier and is, therefore, independent of car radios not fitted with a CD input.

In-car TV and video

Although having a TV and/or Video system fitted to your Golf may sound a little far fetched, in reality, it is far from it. Blaupunkt have designed a TV with a 4½ in screen suitable for in-car use, mounted between the rear seats. It could also be fixed on a moveable mount allowing easy access for the back seat passengers. TV reception is always delicate although the colour pictures are reasonable and when the car is immobile, they are perfect. An interface box can be fitted which allows a video machine to be linked with the TV. It is based on the Blaupunkt RTX 260 portable video deck and as such can be removed from its special car mounting bracket and used for its original purpose if required.

Make a note of the law; it is illegal to position a TV so that it can be seen by (and therefore possibly distract) the driver.

ICE6.3 ▶

The ultimate luxury for back seat passengers? The small TV is mounted on an adjustable bracket in this Jetta. Obviously, a third passenger may be a little uncomfortable! The remote control unit being used is for the video, although an infrared control is available for the TV. Should the rear seat passengers want to listen to something that the driver doesn't, twin headphone sockets are provided. On some models, the in-car audio system is so wired that when the headphones on the TV are in use, the rear speakers cut out.

ICE6.4

The RTX 260-C Video is based on Blaupunkt's portable deck and is mounted at the front of the boot so that the controls can be reached via the armrest. Again this is seen in a Jetta and the installation in a Golf could pose a few headaches. Note that the cassette is inserted vertically.

▼

ICE6.5

It would be fair to expect that it won't be long before your Golf leaves the factory already fitted with your choice of mobile phone. Volkswagen already offer them as an after market accessory. The Bosch system seen here, has been discreetly mounted in the Jetta so as not to impinge too much upon available space. It requires, of course, the fitting of a special aerial to the car. This is usually mounted in the rear screen or arranged so that it receives through the glass in the rear hatch of the Golf. As well as 'phones actually mounted in the car, there are portable models available which can be removed from the car to give even more freedom. The convenience of having a car phone has to be experienced to be believed, especially where there is a business use. Whether or not a carphone comes under the heading of 'In car entertainment' depends, I suppose, on who you are talking to ...

▼

Chapter Four
Mechanical uprating

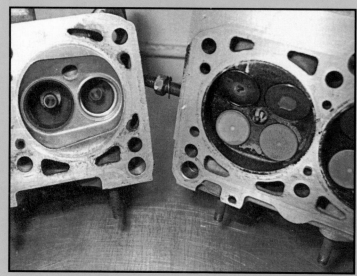

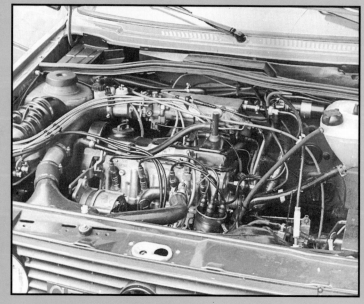

Fitting a free-flow air filter

The main aim of fitting a non-standard air filter is to improve the air flow into the carburettor and let the engine 'breathe' more freely. Small power increases can be obtained, typically of two to five bhp, although the main benefit is usually better engine response. This particular filter has no provision for connecting up VW's system of hoses for supplying hot air to the carb, which may be a problem in severe weather, as Volkswagen carbs are notorious for icing up. It is important to make sure that you get the correct filter for your engine. Always quote the reference number of the carburettor which, in the case of the standard Solex, is found on the side of the float chamber.

The Ram-Flo filter featured here has a removable, washable filter element. It is important that it should be washed only in soapy water and not with petrol, as with some filters. Thanks are due to BR Motorsport for demonstrating how the Ram-Flo is fitted.

MU1.1 ▶
The filter has an attractive chrome finish and comes complete with Jubilee clip for fixing filter to carburettor, washable element and breather spout.

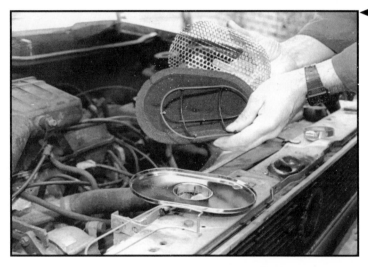

◀ MU1.2
The clip over the top of the filter comes off giving access to the element which is held in place by a strong, plastic grid. It is washable, which obviously saves on the cost of replacement filters. It should be fully dried before refitting after washing.

MU1.3 ▶
With the Ram-Flo filter in place, the underbonnet area certainly looks much less cluttered, and the chrome adds a touch of sparkle which shows up the rest of this dirty engine bay.

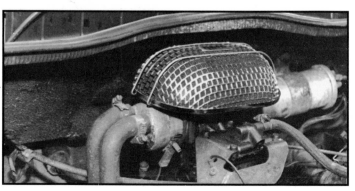

Fitting a free-flow exhaust system

Fitting a less restrictive exhaust system is usually regarded as a fairly simple way to extract more power from a standard engine. However, it is often a way to create a lot more noise in the process. The Jetex system shown here not only gives a quite substantial increase in power but it also makes the car **quieter!** It is just as noteworthy that it weighs much more than the original system which bodes well for its longevity, as does the fact that the boxes are aluminised. Encouragingly, it is guaranteed for a year.

The system shown here was fitted at the Leamington Spa workshops of BR Motorsport. In order to check the effect of the exhaust on performance, the car was connected to the BRM diagnostic equipment and fine tuned so that the car with standard exhaust was giving of its best. There then followed a rolling road session to check the bhp at the wheels. After the fitting, this process was repeated in order to ascertain the power increase. The results are shown in the tables on the opposite page. Thanks are due to VW Motoring magazine for their permission to use the photographs shown here.

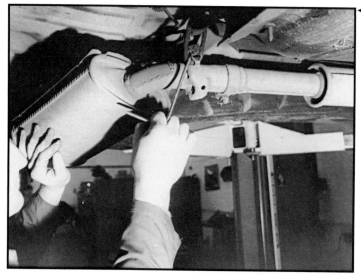

◀ **MU2.1**
For ease of removal and fitting, the car was placed on ramps. With all the mounting clamps undone, the mounting rubbers can be removed. The tool that BRM's mechanic, Ross, is using here is one he made up especially to make the job easier.

MU2.2 ▶
Removing the first two sections in one piece requires a second pair of hands.

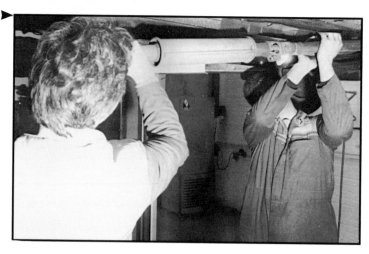

The graph below shows the effect that the Jetex system had.

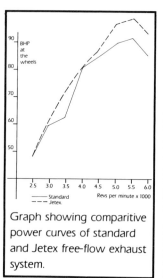

Graph showing comparitive power curves of standard and Jetex free-flow exhaust system.

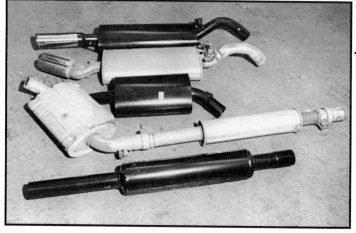

◀ **MU2.3**
The new and the old, side by side. The new system still has its dark paint on it! Note that the Jetex has only one tailpipe instead of two and that it is made of stainless steel. The original system was about two and a half years and 30,000 miles old. Although not leaking in any way, it is unlikely that it would have carried on for much longer.

MU2.4 ▶
Because the new system is much heavier than the original, it needs uprated mounting rubbers. The new rubbers are so strong that BR Motorsport use them on the Rally Golfs they prepare!

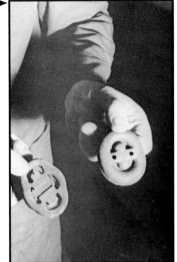

MU2.6
With everything fitted, Ross checked for loose bolts while ensuring that the exhaust was not too close to any part of the bodywork. This was performed again with the engine running in order to listen for leaks. ▼

MU2.5
By using a transmission jack (seen here supporting the front box), Ross was able to fit the new system without assistance. Exhaust paste was used on all joints to ensure that there were no leaks. All three sections were loosely placed in position before the clamps were tightened up. ▼

The tables below show 'before' and 'after' power outputs in bhp, measured at the wheels on the BR Motorsport rolling road. As with all such reliable figures, they have been adjusted to take into account the ambient humidity, temperature and barometer readings at the time and place of the test.

STANDARD SYSTEM

RPM	BHP
2500	48.9
3000	59.1
3500	65.2
4000	82.5
4500	84.5
5000	89.6
5500	91.7
6000	85.5

JETEX SYSTEM

RPM	BHP	NET GAIN
2500	48.9	0
3000	61.1	2
3500	73.4	8
4000	82.5	0
4500	87.6	3.1
5000	98.9	9.3
5500	99.8	8.4
6000	94.8	9.5

◀ **MU2.7**
Listening to your car (and this particular car was co-author, Dave Pollard's **own** vehicle!) being revved around the clock is not for those of a nervous disposition! Note that two free-standing fans are being used. The one at the front directs air into the radiator to prevent over-heating. At the side, an immensely powerful, and noisy, fan cools the underside of the car to prevent things like underseal wax, mounting rubbers, cables, etc, from melting.

As can be seen from the graph on the opposite page, around 18 per cent of gross power disappears into the transmission, etc. Despite this, the Jetex exhaust improves the power of the otherwise standard 1800 cc GTi from 112 to almost 122 bhp.

Fitting electronic ignition

Electronic ignition has been around for some time, although many still regard it with some suspicion. This should be dispelled by the fact that in 1987, Volkswagen fitted all their Golfs with electronic ignition systems. BR Motorsport fit the Bosch system, shown here, to earlier non-electronic ignition Golfs and Jettas.

Fitting the breakerless system is a fairly simple DIY project with the only tools required being a crimping tool, a screwdriver, an open jaw wrench and a drill with 5.5 mm bit. It is important that the heat sink is mounted correctly and away from sources of heat. The left-hand bulkhead is the position recommended by BR Motorsport. Similarly, the wiring diagram should be carefully studied before making any connections, as there are a great many to make.

Adjusting the system once installed requires the use of a conventional timing light. The dwell angle is electronically controlled and cannot be reset. Noise suppression is similar to that of a standard system.

When correctly set up, the benefits of an electronic ignition system are: much better fuel consumption, improved performance and a smoother engine response.

The Bosch system shown here is certainly not the cheapest, but it is of excellent quality and the firm has a long history of providing VW with equipment, including fuel injection systems for the GTi models.

Perhaps the most vital point to make is that the massively increased voltages can produce a safety hazard. It is extremely important that the battery be disconnected before fitting commences and that once fitted, care is taken whenever you are working in the engine compartment. Bosch take the trouble to supply a large sticker warning of the high voltage, which BR Motorsport stick in a prominent place under the bonnet.

MU3.1 ▶
The breakerless system, as the name implies, does not use the contact breakers at all. This means that there can be no contact point wear, with the ignition timing remaining exact for several years. Improved fuel economy is just one advantage of having an increase in voltage of 40 per cent over the whole speed range and up to a 90 per cent increase at high speeds.

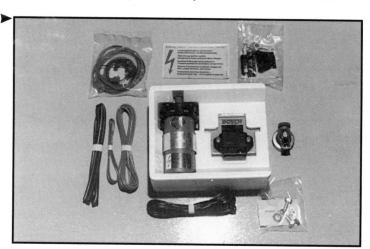

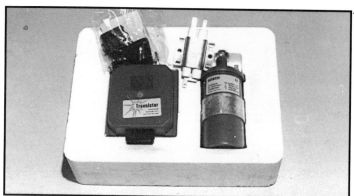

◀ MU3.2
The inductive semiconductor ignition system works on a similar principle but retains the contact points. For many people, the fact that there are still points gives more peace of mind. However, if fitting is done correctly, there will be no need to adjust either points or dwell angle as there is no burn-off of the contact points.

MU3.3 ▶
(Left) An exploded view of the distributor before fitting breakerless ignition. The parts crossed through will not be used again.
(Right) The same diagram but with the new system fitted. Parts 9 and 10 are the new distributor rotor and the trigger wheel, which effectively replace the points. (Diagram courtesy of Robert Bosch GmbH)

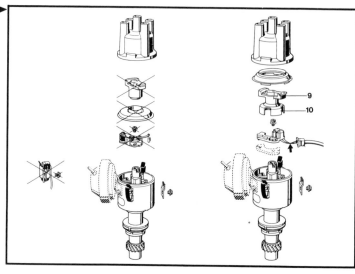

Fitting a manual choke conversion

When Volkswagen fitted some Golfs with automatic chokes, it was with admirable motives; it would help the engine to be more efficient, as the choke would only be applied when necessary and would thus save fuel. However, for a variety of reasons, the auto-choke is far from being universally popular and in any group of Golf owners there will always be someone who would prefer to have a manual system. At BR Motorsport a Pacet choke conversion is shown being fitted to one such customer's 1979, Mk I Golf GLS, with the 1457cc engine. The carburettor on this particular model is the standard Solex 34 PCT, although the principle of fitting is the same for all cars.

MU4.1 ▶
The bubble packed kit, as supplied by Pacet, comes complete with all necessary parts to effect the swap. The instructions for this fairly easy DIY project are on the back of the card.

MU4.2
The first task is to actually get at the carburettor, which is at the back of the engine under the large air cleaner assembly. The front part is held by three clips. The hot air inlet is connected to this, so take care. The second half of the air filter housing is attached to the top of the carburettor by a ring clamp. Note that there are several pipes which must be disconnected and tagged for easier re-connection.
▼

The new choke is supplied ready to operate in a clockwise direction. However, as the Golf/Jetta carburettor choke mechanism operates in an anti-clockwise manner, it had to be dismantled and reassembled, as per the concise instructions supplied as part of the Pacet choke conversion kit.

◀ MU4.3
A close up shot of the ring clamp and securing screw on the second part of the air filter housing after removal. BR Motorsport warn that removal of this screw can be tricky as access is awkward.

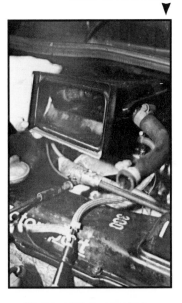

MU4.4 ▶
Next, remove the auto choke assembly. This is the canister-shaped object on the left-hand side of the carburettor. It is held in by a securing ring attached by three screws. They require a long screwdriver for easy access. With all three screws removed, the auto choke assembly simply pulls off. Note the two water pipes attached to the rear. These are responsible for the 'auto' part of the choke.

Fitting a manual choke conversion

The screws holding the auto choke unit to the carburettor are usually very tight and so some caution is required as it is all too easy to damage the screw heads.

◄ MU4.5
The two water pipes have to be removed from the auto choke by undoing the Jubilee clips. These pipes should **never** be removed when the engine is hot. To do so would run the risk of serious scalding. Similarly, the next task of easing the pressure in the water system by removing the radiator cap, is equally dangerous with anything but a cold engine. Pacet supply a piece of aluminium tube which is pushed into the pipes and then the Jubilee clips retightened, as shown.

MU4.6
There is only one electrical connection involved, which attaches by means of a spade connector to the side of the auto choke unit. This should be pulled off. With this car, the wire leads to the sensor unit where it ends in another spade connector. As such, this too was pulled off and the complete wire removed. On later models, where the wire disappears into the complex wiring loom, it is sufficient to insulate the terminal and tape the wire safely back.
▼

MU4.7
There is no need to remove the original choke clamp from the now discarded unit as the Pacet unit uses three small indented lugs to do the job. They should be screwed in loosely and then the unit can be positioned before tightening.
▼

MU4.8 ▶
With the new choke mounted, the cable can be fitted. From its approximate position inside the car, it should be routed through the bulkhead making sure that there are no kinks in the cable. Here, an existing grommet was used and the cable simply pushed through the centre. If a new hole is required, it should be zinc painted afterwards to prevent rust. Also, a grommet should be used to prevent the cable chafing.

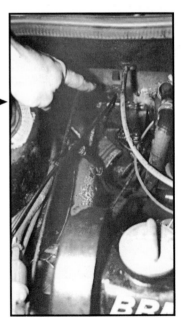

◀ **MU4.9**
Although the cable looks far too long, it isn't, and should be routed as shown so that there is no danger of it sticking. Once in position, it is held by a small clamp onto the new choke. Replacement of the air filter assembly is a reversal of previous instructions.

It is vitally important to ensure that the installation is correctly set up and the cable routed without snags, before driving the car. Driving the car with, for example, a sticking cable, could be extremely dangerous.

MU4.10 ▶
Inside the car, the cable has to be mounted within easy reach of the driver, but not so that it is in the way. Here, it was mounted under the dash on the driver's left. The choke pull is held in a bracket which is mounted by means of two self-tapping screws.

Fitting an engine pre-heater (in cooling system)

Basically, the Kenlowe pre-heater is a pump and heater element which is mounted underbonnet. Approximately ten minutes before the car is required, a lead is connected from a mains power supply to a socket on the pre-heater. The water in the engine is then heated to the correct temperature. When you are ready to leave, the cable can be removed and the car is ready to go, with a ready warmed-up engine. The screen clearing and comfort benefits in really cold weather are obvious. However, one not quite so obvious benefit is that, with the engine warm, the choke will not need to come on. Thus the usual early morning petrol 'washing' of the bores, causing severe wear, will not take place. Used regularly, it could make a massive difference to engine life.

The Kenlowe engine pre-heater is an ingenious device which could save you a lot of trouble during the icy winter months and also save wear on the engine throughout the year.

MU5.1
The Kenlowe kit complete, with pump assembly in the centre.
▼

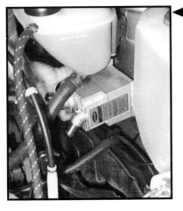

◀ **MU5.2**
Here the pump assembly is being offered up by a BR Motorsport mechanic for mounting inside the engine compartment of a Jetta, and connection into the heater system pipework. Note that it must be below the level of the car's top hoses to avoid airlocks. Similarly, for correct operation, the car heater must be in the 'on' position when the pre-heater is being used.

Fitting an oil cooler

Fitting an oil cooler can be very advantageous if your driving requirements mean that your engine is working hard for long periods of time. It's an especially good idea if you intend towing with your Golf or Jetta.

Pacet produce two types of cooler: One, which has a remote mounted cooling radiator and is shown here being fitted by BR Motorsport to a 1978, Mk I 1500 GLS and the other, which is an oil/water model, similar to that fitted by Volkswagen to some models. With the latter system the car's cooling water disperses excess heat from the oil and also imparts heat into the oil in very cold conditions, therefore aiding oil warm up.

◄ **MU6.1**
Here is the complete kit, plus the oil/water cooler that Pacet manufacture. All brackets, pipes, nuts and bolts are supplied.

MU6.2 ►
Seen in close up, the oil/water version is very similar to Volkswagen's own product and works on the same principle, using a thermostat inside the unit.

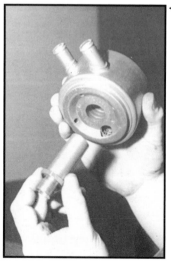

◄ **MU6.3**
When fitted, it needs a special extension to allow it to be fitted to the oil filter.

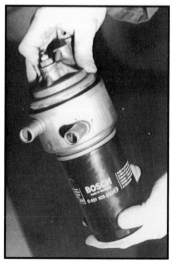

MU6.4 ►
This is how it would be fitted, shown here out of a car for the sake of clarity.

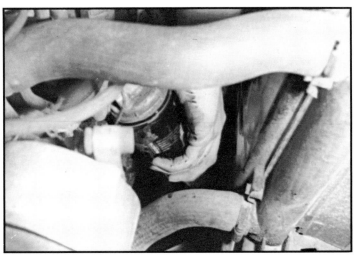

◀MU6.5
The first job is to remove the oil filter. It should be hand tight, but if not a special tool may be needed to twist it off. It is wise to have a can underneath to catch any oil spillage.

In order to fit the remote mounted cooler, a thermostatic adaptor block has to be placed between the oil filter and housing. By connecting pipes to this spacer, the new cooler is integrated into the car's oil system when the car requires extra cooling.

◀ MU6.6
The underside of the spacer showing the rubber sealing ring. BR Motorsport emphasize that it is important that this is in place and seating correctly, otherwise the system will leak.

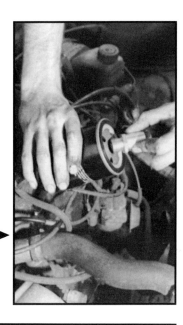

MU6.7 ▶
Fitting the extension supplied into the oil filter. This is then fitted as normal, but with the spacer between it and the oil filter housing.

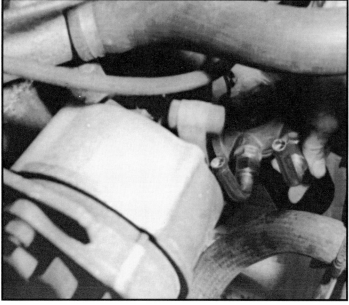

MU6.8 ▶
The two compression joints can then be screwed finger tight onto the spacer, making sure that they are pointing in the direction of the soon to be fitted cooler.

Fitting an oil cooler

If you are considering this as a DIY project, you should remember that the cooling fan on the Golf does not switch off with the engine and that working on a warm engine, in close proximity to the radiator could be dangerous. Also, of course, you could burn your hands!

MU6.9
Here is the cooler itself, with one compression joint already connected. It is important to ensure that no foreign bodies get into the cooler.

MU6.10
BR Motorsport recommend fitting the cooler alongside the radiator in order to get the correct flow of air. Here, two existing holes in the top crossmember were used to fasten the cooler at the top. At the bottom, a small hole was drilled and the cooler held with a self-tapping screw. The small amount of bracketry required is provided in the kit and only needs bending into shape.

MU6.11
With the cooler in position and the compression joints all fitted, the rubber oil pipe can be measured and cut to length. It is important that the pipe is routed with no sharp bends. Also, it must not foul other equipment, such as in this case the alternator. The pipes simply push over the ends of the joints and are held by Jubilee clips.

MU6.12
With the pipes routed correctly and all the joints checked for tightness, the oil level should be checked and topped up if necessary. Despite their long experience and high level of skill, BR Motorsport always run the car for a while in their well ventilated workshop to ensure that the system is functioning correctly before making a road test. Bear in mind that the Golf oil pressure can run as high as 110 psi when cold! This incredible amount of pressure will very quickly highlight any joints which have not quite been tightened up to the correct poundage.

Uprating the braking system

Braking system conversion

◄ MU7.1
The new BRM system, is shown here as it will be fitted. On this prototype disc, the cooling holes are round. In production versions the slots are elliptical as on the originals.

MU7.2 ►
In this photo, the new disc on the right is clearly larger than standard, giving better heat dissipation. However, the discs are the same thickness.

Braking is an area in which the Mk II Golf owner scores quite heavily. The braking system was much improved over its predecessor, especially when the four disc set-up on the GTi was introduced. Brian Ricketts, of BR Motorsport, has devised a braking conversion whereby Mk I owners can have their braking systems improved quite dramatically. Mk I GTi drivers in particular will find this most comforting.

MU7.3 ►
The car was raised and the front wheels removed. The caliper housing has to be pulled away from the hub by undoing the two bolts. These are accessed from the back of the hub by using a ratchet and extension.

Brian Ricketts at BR Motorsport went to some pains to point out the absolute necessity for keeping any kind of oil or grease well away from the brake pads, for self-evident and crucially important safety reasons.

Braking system conversion

The BR Motorsport conversion has been designed to fit all Mk I Golfs and Jettas, with the exception of early models fitted with Dunlop or ATE calipers. It can only be used, however, if 14 inch diameter wheels are fitted. BRM supply a kit consisting of two new discs, two revised caliper brackets and new brake pads. The standard brake disc is 239mm in diameter whereas the new one is 258mm. The thickness of the disc remains the same at 19mm.

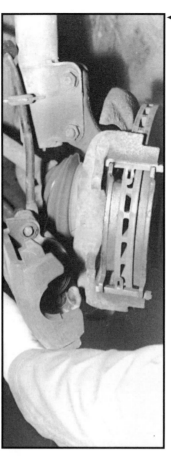

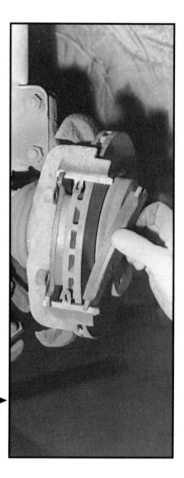

◄ **MU7.4**
With the bolts removed, the caliper housing can be pulled away easily. It is still connected to the braking system by the flexible brake pipe and care should be taken not to place undue strain on this, to prevent the possibility of a leak or stretching of the hose. Note old disc pads still in position.

MU7.5 ►
At this point, removing the old disc pads is simply a matter of withdrawing them from the caliper.

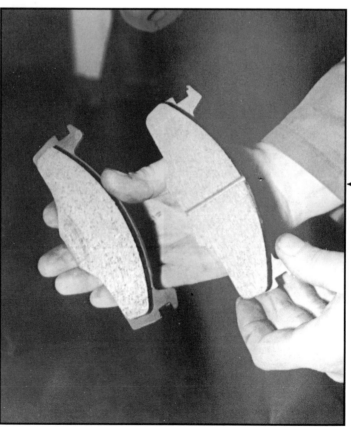

◄ **MU7.6**
New Volkswagen brake pads against the old. Mintex Don D171 pads give greatly improved initial retardation which makes them ideal for braking systems of average or below-average efficiency. However, the BR Motorsport conversion inherently improves the Golf/Jetta's basic braking efficiency enormously, so D171s should **not** be used with this conversion. Otherwise, they could lead to brake lock-up, which could be disastrous at high speed or on a slippery road surface.

◄ MU7.7
The disc is removed by undoing the crosshead setscrew as shown. It is very likely that it will be rusty and some patience and penetrating fluid may be called for. Use of a Sykes-Pickavant impact screwdriver would speed the job up considerably and could save the need to drill out a rounded-off screw.

Extreme caution should be used when working under any vehicle, however it is supported. It should never be supported only by a jack. Axle stands or ramps should be used and the remaining wheels chocked.

MU7.8 ►
Like the housing, the caliper is held by two bolts which are reached around the back of the hub.

MU7.9
With everything removed, all that remains is a very bare 'front hub'.

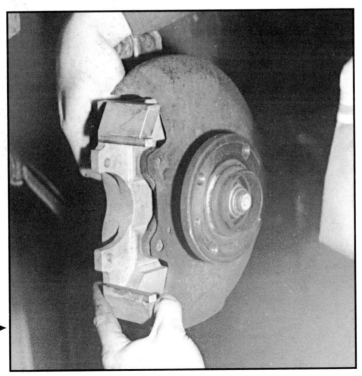

MU7.10 ►
Fitting the new calipers is a reversal of the removal procedure.

Braking system conversion

Whilst working on the braking system under the car, BR Motorsport automatically check to make sure that all of the brake pipes and connectors are in good condition.

◄ MU7.11
Similarly, fitting the new disc just requires the replacement of the crosshead setscrew. It is a good idea to dip this into a dab of Duckhams grease, so that any future removal will be somewhat easier. Be careful not to get any on the brake pads.

MU7.12
With the new pads and caliper housing in place the job is complete. At this stage, the surrounding pipes should be checked to ensure that there are no leaks.
▼

MU7.13
As mentioned earlier, the round ventilation holes seen on this rear view, mark the disc as a prototype model.
▼

MU7.14 ►
Mintex Don D171 brake pads are available for all Golf and Jetta models and, in themselves, offer a small but noticeable improvement to the stopping power of any Golf. This is a particularly welcome, low-cost way of improving early Golf GTi brakes, although the scale of improvement can't be expected to come near that of the comprehensive BR Motorsport modifications. As stated earlier, D171 pads should **never** be used in conjunction with the BR Motorsport conversion; only with standard disc.

MU7.15 ▶
The pipes are all circular wound, and labelled clearly as to where on the car they fit. It is best to lay them out on the floor in a schematic representation of the car. This way it is easier to plan.

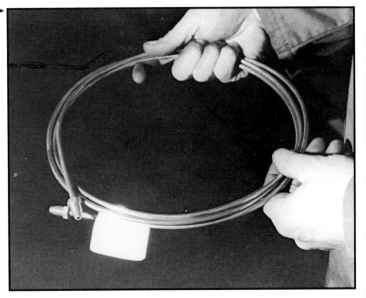

This is another task which requires the car to be lifted from the ground, or raised on ramps. The usual safety precautions apply. Also, beware of dirt and rust falling from the car into your eyes as you disturb it.

◀ MU7.16
This Sykes-Pickavant hydraulic hose clamp makes the job much easier. It clamps onto the flexible pipe and prevents any leakage of brake fluid. Note that it should be attached before the pipe union nuts are undone. Once it is clamped on, it can be locked and left whilst the rigid brake pipe is changed. It is seen here in the front left-hand side position for clarity.

Fitting new pipes is not a difficult task and should be a morning's work for a competent DIY enthusiast. The Automec pipes shown here come in a kit, clearly labelled and with all union nuts ready fitted. What we show in this sequence is the fitting of one section, the rear offside. Fitting the other sections follows the same principle. BR Motorsport kindly carried out the work shown here.

MU7.17 ▶
With the hose clamp in place, the union at the wheel can be undone. These are usually well rusted and may take some persuading. A little penetrating oil should do the trick. A Sykes-Pickavant brake pipe nut spanner, which is effectively a ring spanner with a piece cut out, is best as it gives a much better grip on the nut.

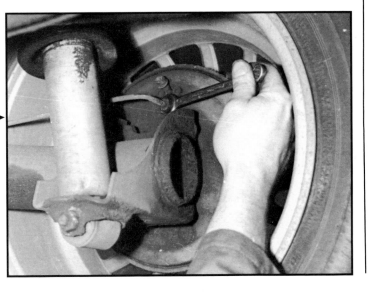

Have any work you carry out on the braking system checked over by a qualified mechanic before using the car on the road.

Fitting new brake pipes

Brake pipes are a sadly neglected area of car maintenance and, Brian Ricketts at BR Motorsport claims, that they are largely a case of 'out of sight, out of mind'. This is sad, to say the least, of course, because a damaged or corroded brake pipe could lead to tragic consequences, even given the Golf's diagonally split braking system. Braking two wheels is no substitute for braking four. The permanent solution to the risk of brake pipe corrosion is to fit copper brake pipes such as the Automec pipes shown here. Never do so within the Volkswagen warranty period. Consult your Volkswagen dealership if in any doubt.

◄ **MU7.18**
Hard to see, but this is the BR Motorsport mechanic undoing the other end of this particular section where it joins a flexible pipe (arrowed). Once uncoupled, the section can be pulled clear and held alongside the new pipe as a template.

MU7.19 ▶
The Automec copper pipes are especially easy to work, but even so, bends very close to the pipe ends can be tricky to form. By using a special Sykes-Pickavant pipe bending tool you can ensure that any bends are smooth and accurate. If using steel pipes, the S-P tool will almost be a 'must'. A little time taken here to get the shapes of the new pipes identical to those of the old ones, will pay dividends when you're trying to fit the replacement pipes back under the car.

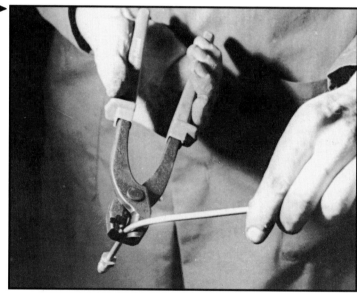

◄ **MU7.20**
The Automec copper brake pipe kit comes complete with plastic clips which hold the rigid pipes to the bodywork. These are necessary as it is often the case that the originals are damaged whilst removing the pipes.

MU7.21 ►
Installing the shiny new copper brake pipe, bent exactly to fit. This is the easiest part of the task. Brian Ricketts emphasises that a great deal of care must be taken to ensure that the unions are not cross-threaded on replacement. This is particularly important at the wheel cylinder.

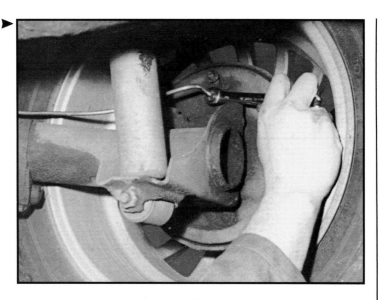

One advantage of Automec Silicone Brake Fluid is that it is non-hygroscopic; that is, it does not attract or absorb water. In effect this means that, unlike conventional fluids which have to be changed every two years to prevent water causing internal corrosion and the risk of water in the fluid turning to steam (you then lose your brakes), Silicone Fluid is in there for life. One other advantage is that it is non-corrosive and does not harm paintwork. The makers claim that it is compatible with conventional fluids, although, once the system has been drained and refilled with Silicone Fluid, topping up with anything else negates the plus-points of the Silicone Fluid. You will only reap the benefits if all of the old brake fluid is pumped out and replaced with Silicone Fluid, possibly when the brake pipes themselves are changed. You may be competent enough to 'bleed' air from the brakes yourself after refilling with fresh fluid, following the instructions in the Haynes Manual for your car. It may be best to leave the job to your main dealer.

◄ **MU7.22**
When the job is finished it is a wise move to check the brake fluid reservoir. It is doubtful that there will have been any leakage, but it's worth looking just the same. Here, the level is being topped up using Automec Silicone Fluid.

MU7.23 ►
This diagram should help to understand the braking system better. This is an exploded view of a Mk II Golf pedal, servo and master cylinder assembly. Note that, unlike the Mk I, the servo is directly behind the pedal, rather than remotely mounted with a pressure sapping linkage.

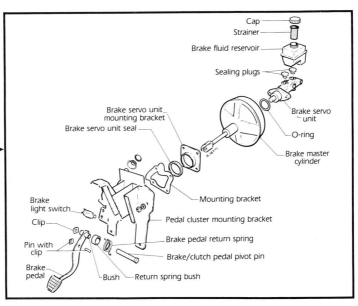

Cap
Strainer
Brake fluid reservoir
Sealing plugs
Brake servo unit mounting bracket
Brake servo unit seal
Brake servo unit
O-ring
Brake master cylinder
Mounting bracket
Brake light switch
Clip
Pin with clip
Brake pedal
Bush
Pedal cluster mounting bracket
Brake pedal return spring
Brake/clutch pedal pivot pin
Return spring bush

Fitting new brake pipes

Don't even **consider** working on your own braking system unless you are qualified and able to do so, in which case a copy of the appropriate Haynes manual by your side will be invaluable.
Otherwise, leave such a crucial area to the specialists! Also see margin note on page 147.

◄ MU7.24
By the time this book was almost complete, BR Motorsport had developed yet another method of slowing down the Mk I Golf/Jetta owner. This servo looks ordinary enough, but it is a special, made to the exacting specifications set by BRM which enables the Mk I Golf to stop considerably better than standard. It fits all models with the torturous right-hand drive's cross-over brake linkage and when combined with the conversion described earlier, provides incredible stopping power.

MU7.25
BR Motorsport can also fit Mocal flexible brake hoses with braided stainless steel coverings. They have not, however, been approved by the Department of Transport for use on road vehicles (the specification is said to cover only conventional hoses) and can only be recommended for competition use. Their resistance to damage and improved pedal response - the pipes don't expand marginally as non-braided pipes do - gives better braking from a firmer feeling pedal.
▼

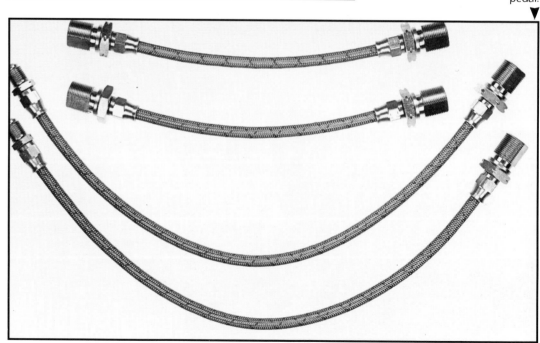

Engine conversion

Weber carburettor replacement

Although dealing mainly with fuel injected cars, BR Motorsport can also tune 'conventional' Golf and Jetta engines. Possibly one of the easiest methods of tuning an engine is to replace the carburettor. Weber have a long history of manufacturing performance carburettors to the extent that their twin 40 DCOE kit (as mentioned later) has become almost a motoring legend. Not all of their products, however, are aimed at producing masses of extra power and performance, and there are several models which will simply replace a worn out or faulty standard carb.

By their very nature, carburettors need to be kept clean and on no account should anything other than fresh air be allowed to pass into them. **Always** use an air filter. It is easy to ruin not only the carb, but possibly the whole engine! Run without an air filter, the engine **might** run better (although not necessarily), it may sound better, but its working life will be cut dramatically.

MU8.1 ▶
At the bottom end of the scale is the Weber 34ICH carb, which is suitable for the 1100, 1300 and 1500 engines. Any power increase will be small, but the main benefits will be better breathing characteristics and engine response. This particular carb is suitable for models dating from 1974 to 1979, as can be seen by the two stud mounting.

MU8.2
Fitting the same carburettor to cars with the later, four stud mounting, requires a different adaptor. This one, on the base of a 34ICH Weber carb, will suit 1100 models from 1979 to 1984.

◀ MU8.3
For those with a 1600cc or 1800cc Golf, BR Motorsport do a conversion in which both the original carb **and** manifold is replaced. The Weber carburettor is a 34DMTR model and the new manifold is taken from the Golf's brother under the skin, the Scirocco. Increase in performance should be around 10 per cent although, if used in conjunction with an uprated camshaft, this can easily be as much as 20 bhp.

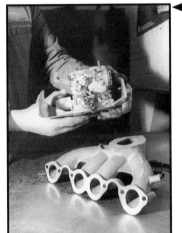

◀ MU8.4
Weber can supply a sports air filter for the 34DMTR as seen here. However, Volkswagen carbs have a habit of icing up in winter and as it does not have the heated air intake of the standard carb, it is a point to bear in mind.

Weber carburettor replacement

Weber 40DCOEs will bolt straight onto any larger (1600cc/1800cc) Golf and give GTi performance from a non-GTi engine, especially if an uprated camshaft is included. The impressive mpg of the GTi cannot be repeated with this set-up but, of course, it is considerably cheaper than buying the fuel injected car. It is important that twin carbs are correctly tuned, a task for the professionals if ever there was one.

MU8.5
Now these beauties **will** make your car go! From his Alladin's cave of a store room, Brian produced this pair of huge Weber 40 DCOE carbs on a manifold.
▼

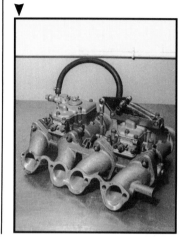

APPLICATION LIST

Weber Carb reference	Model	Part no
For 1093cc engine		
34ICH (2 stud flange)	Golf/Jetta '74 on	15290.994
34ICH (4 stud flange)	Golf/Jetta '79 on	15290.991
For 1272cc engine		
34ICH	Golf/Jetta '80 on	15290.992
For 1457cc engine		
34ICH	Golf/Jetta '77/'80	15290.993
For 1588cc engine		
2 x 40 DCNF	Golf '75/'78	17900.124
2 x 40 DCOE	Golf '75/'78	17900.121
Throttle body (F.I.)	Golf '76 on	15550.901

The last three are intended as mid-range performance kits and will be an improvement on original carburation and enchance further tuning. Where available, kits include manifolds and air filters and in some cases, slight modifications may be required in order to fit.

Heavy duty clutches

Having a highly tuned engine in your Golf, as described over the following pages, is only part of the overall tuning process. As mentioned elsewhere, suspension and tyres also play a major part but all this comes to nothing if the power cannot get to the road wheels in the first place. BR Motorsport supply and fit various Sachs clutches to the cars they work on.

Sachs manufacture a wide range of clutch parts and, as with their suspension products, much of the expertise has been learned on the race and rally scene. For the Mk I Golf, Sachs produce a heavy duty clutch which is capable of handling power outputs of up to 135 bhp. For those with really high powered engines, the next step up is the sporting Group 'N' clutch, which will handle almost anything from 135 bhp upwards. On this type of clutch the clamp load is increased by 20 per cent over the standard version. The first Mk Is had 190mm diameter clutches although this was changed to 200mm in some of the early 1980s models.
Diagram MU9a.2 shows the basic operation of the clutch mechanism.

◄ **MU9a.1**
Seen here is a Group 'N' clutch cover, photographed at BR Motorsport, which would be suitable for an 1800cc Golf GTi. The disc is also a Group 'N' item, on which the fibre is metal backed, bonded and rivetted.

MU9a.2 ▶

Top The clutch cover is bolted to the flywheel. The clutch disc is pressed up against the flywheel by the cover assembly which is fitted with several springs (either diaphragm or helical). Thus, the power from the engine is transferred to the road wheels by means of the frictional connection of the clutch disc. It is when this disc begins to wear that clutch slip occurs. Not surprisingly, uprated engines require uprated clutches.

Bottom To interrupt the transmission of power, the pressure plate must be lifted away from the clutch disc against the springs contained in the clutch cover. This is accomplished by simply pressing the clutch pedal inside the car. This forces a release bearing against the release levers (or diaphragm spring fingers) and the clutch disc is released. As such the power is then disconnected from the transmission. (Drawings by courtesy of Fichtel & Sachs AG.)

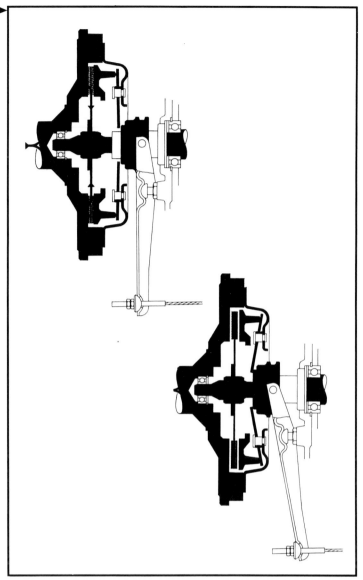

All Mk II clutches are 210mm, and Sachs can supply a heavy duty version for the Mk I. At the top of the tree is the Group 'A' clutch, although this is purely for competition use. It would normally only be fitted where a particularly torquey engine is being used, according to Brian Ricketts, supremo at BR Motorsport.

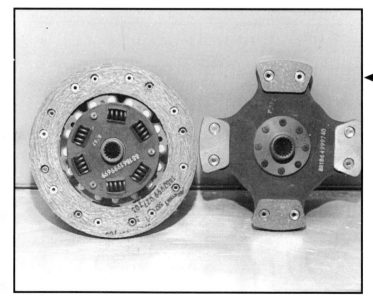

◀ **MU9a.3**

The ultimate. Alongside the Group 'N' disc is seen the Group 'A' paddle clutch. A paddle configuration is used rather than a solid disc because of the massive heat build up in competition cars. The friction area is sintered metal rather than fibre, again for reasons of heat dissipation. The metal used disintegrates at 1000 degrees C whilst fibre burns at 600 degrees C. These clutches are also available with a torsion spring centre.

Engine conversion

This Section deals with the process of producing a tuned engine for the Golf or Jetta, either by using relatively mild tuning procedures or by converting the engine to a larger capacity. To establish exactly what is involved we paid several visits to BR Motorsport of Leamington Spa. We don't even pretend to show you how to DIY this Section; it's strictly work for the specialists.

Obtaining extra power from the GTi engine is not easy, especially if the qualities that Volkswagen build in as standard are to be preserved. Many mass produced motor cars have engines that are effectively 'slung together' on the production line and therefore it is possible to obtain quite large amounts of extra horsepower simply by 'blueprinting' the engine, which means taking it apart and rebuilding to more exact tolerances. However, in true Teutonic style, the Golf is put together with considerably more care, which complicates the life of the Volkswagen engine tuner. Similarly, the fuel-injected Golf engines, particularly those of 1800cc, have a well-deserved reputation for being torquey, reliable and economical as well as powerful. Improving, therefore, on this excellent basic design, is no mean feat and to do so takes a mixture of skill, expertise and experience.

Brian Ricketts is renowned throughout tuning circles, as well as at Volkswagen UK themselves, as being the creator of many engine conversions for the Golf GTi. In 1987 he formed his own company, BR Motorsport, and continued his mission of perfecting the tuned engine for the Golf and Jetta and expanded his conversion programme to include several carburettored models. Brian was quick to point out that before any tuning work can be done, the engine must be in good condition. Ideally, it should have covered less than 20,000 miles. Any motor which has 50,000 miles or more will probably need some work to the valves/guides, etc. At this sort of mileage, the bore would have to be checked for wear as would the big ends and crankshaft. During our visits to the BR Motorsport HQ at Leamington Spa, we were able to see many engines at various stages of their development and to view the attention to detail that is so essential in this sort of work.

As can be seen from the BRM conversion chart, there is a wide range of conversions available. At one end of the scale is the relatively mild BRM100C, which takes the 1800cc carburettor engine up to 100 bhp. At the other is the 170 bhp, 2070cc conversion for the 16V motor.

BR Motorsport Conversion Chart

Standard engine size/type	BRM reference
1457/1588cc Carburettor	BRM135C 1760cc, BRM125C 1847cc
1588cc Injection	BRM125 1847cc, BRM140 1847cc
1781cc Carburettor	BRM100C 1781cc STD
1781cc Injection	BRM135 1781cc STD, BRM142 1892cc, BRM155 2070cc
1781cc Injection 16V	BRM160 1781cc STD, BRM165 1900cc, BRM170 2070cc

NOTE: Conversions for carburettor cars are denoted by a 'C' suffix. The number after the 'BRM' prefix indicates the BHP available from the tuned engine.

BRM125 (1588cc)

This is the lowest powered of the 8-valve fuel-injected engines and is designed for owners who have a worn standard engine and who may be thinking of replacing it with a service exchange unit. Installation of the BRM125, costs only slightly more than a basic 'recon' engine, but gives much more power and torque than the standard 1781cc engine. Note that the capacity is enlarged quite considerably.

Technical Specification

Cubic capacity	1847cc
Bore	82.5 mm
Stroke	86.4 mm
Output @ 5,500 rpm	125 bhp

The main work carried out to achieve this is that the cylinder head is rebuilt and the block rebored to 82.5 mm. In addition, an 86.4 mm VAG crankshaft is used, together with Mahle sports pistons. Finally, the ignition and fuel injection systems are modified to suit.

BRM140 (1588cc)

The specification for this motor is as above except where detailed below. This is a sporting engine which gives real sporting performance.

Technical Specification
As above except;

Output @ 5,500 rpm	140 bhp

In addition to the specification for the BRM125, the BRM140 features a fully gas-flowed cylinder head, inlet and exhaust manifolds and reprofiled inlet and exhaust valve seats and valves. A 276 degree sports camshaft is fitted with 11.3 mm valve lift.

BRM135 (1781cc)

This conversion is designed for the driver who wants noticeably more performance from his car but at reasonable cost. At 135 bhp, the BRM135 is more than 20 bhp up on standard figures.

Technical Specification

Cubic capacity	1781cc
Bore	81 mm
Stroke	86.4 mm
Output @ 5,500 rpm	135 bhp

The cylinder head is fully gas-flowed with the inlet and exhaust manifolds. A 276 degree camshaft is fitted together with reprofiled inlet and exhaust valves. A free-flow exhaust sytem is fitted along with modifications to the ignition and fuel systems.

BRM142 (1781cc)

Uprating the engine capacity to almost 1900cc, turns a pleasantly quick car into a real flyer. This is a high performance engine with more than enough power for most of us.

Technical Specification

Cubic capacity	1892 cc
Bore	83.5 mm
Stroke	86.4 mm (std)
Output @ 5,500 rpm	142 bhp
Torque @ 4,500 rpm	150 lb/ft
Compression ratio	9.5 : 1

The impressive figures shown on this page are achieved by fully gas-flowing the cylinder head plus the inlet and exhaust manifolds and reprofiling the inlet and exhaust valve seats. The valves used are 40 mm inlet and 35 mm exhaust. The cylinder block is bored to 83.5 mm and uses Mahle pistons. A 276 degree sports camshaft is used and, once again, the ignition and fuel injection systems are modified.

Deciding which tuning package to choose involves many personal elements of taste (and cost). Not surprisingly, the majority of work carried out at BR Motorsport involves fuel injected cars and of these there are four conversions in particular which prove to be popular. We have listed them here, with the basic ingredients.

Engine conversion

For tuning which involves work to only the head and cam (for example, the BRM135), the bottom end is not touched at all unless the engine is a high mileage unit. Therefore, there is no need to remove the engine completely; only the cylinder head is removed and stripped. Before any work commences, the head is thoroughly cleaned.

◀ **MU9.1**
The valves are replaced, especially if they are like the lower one here. The one above has been reprofiled and polished. New, standard valve springs are used. BRM do not find it necessary to uprate them unless the engine is to be used for racing or rallying where over 7000 rpm will be used.

MU9.2 ▶
This 16V head awaits porting and polishing. There is a great demand for tuning on this high performance motor, despite its relatively recent introduction.

◀ **MU9.3**
The difference between eight and sixteen valves is quite obvious in this shot showing both heads.

MU9.4 ▶
Porting and polishing involves the use of this special grinding tool.

156

◄ MU9.5
This polishing tool uses several heads, two of which are shown here.

▲
MU9.6
Polishing work is painstakingly slow but absolutely vital if the correct gas flow is to be obtained.

Both the BRM135 and the BRM142 conversions produce similar power outputs to the standard GTi 16V (which produces 139 bhp @ 6,100 rpm). For those who deem this amount of power desirable, then such a conversion could well be cost efficient when compared with the cost of trading up from an 8V GTi model. It should also be noted that the BR Motorsport engines give their peak power at some 600 rpm lower than the standard 16V motor.

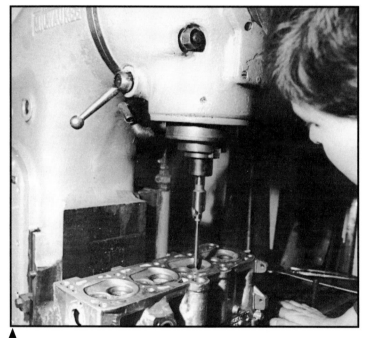

▲
MU9.7
The valve seats have to be machined using a milling machine which is also used to open the valve throats when required.

MU9.8 ►
The finished article, cleaned and polished. After the mechanical work has been completed, the head is checked thoroughly for any swarf or other foreign bodies which could cause problems. Oilways and all other passages are blown through using an air line.

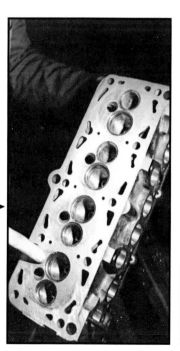

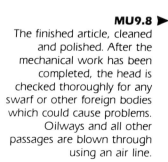

Engine conversion

At every stage of preparation, cleanliness is the keyword, not just with regard to the engine itself, but also the equipment used. Small particles of dirt included in a rebuilt engine will cause rapid wear and would result in a rapid decline in performance. Never entrust your car to a tuning specialist (or garage for that matter) with a dirty, unkempt workshop.

MU9.9 ▶
Another place where gas flowing is very important is at the inlet manifold. Here, the ports on the head have been machined exactly to match the inlet manifold so that the mixture will have a smooth, uninterrupted passage and thus be more efficiently carried into the combustion chambers.

MU9.10
Sometimes there are problems with simple things. Where a spark plug thread is completely stripped a helicoil thread insert is the only answer. However, if it is only partly damaged or just clogged with carbon the Sykes-Pickavant plug chaser can be used as seen here.

▼

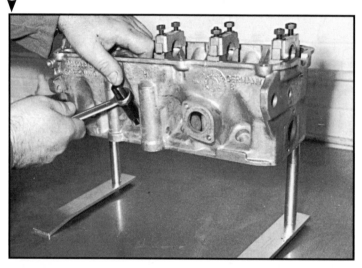

MU9.11
Camshafts play a very important part in the chase for more power. BRM uses only Dr. Schrick, a make they consider to be the best, although they certainly aren't cheap! These 16V cams are of 260 degree duration and suitable for road use. On the next page is a listing of Schrick camshafts and their applications as used by BRM on their conversions. Cams are also available for use in racing engines, but these are not normally used in road going Golfs and as such have not been shown. Schrick Rally cams can be used on the road, although the power delivery will be somewhat peaky and tractability will be severely compromised for outright power.

PART NO	CAM LIFT	VALVE LIFT	DURATION/POSITION/TIMING		
014.01.688	11.2	11.2	268/268/110		
014.01.720	11.0	11.0	272/272/110	ROAD	8-VALVE
014.01.762	11.3	11.3	276/276/110	USE	ENGINES
014.01.769	11.5	11.5	276/276/110		
014.01.886	11.2	11.2	288/288/105	RALLY	
014.01.960	11.2	11.2	296/296/105	USE	
220.01.600	10.3	10.3	260/260/112	ROAD	16-VALVE
220.01.660	10.6	10.6	266/266/110	USE	ENGINES
220.01.760	10.5	10.5	276/276/108	RALLY	
220.01.880	11.2	11.2	288/288/105	USE	

Schrick Camshaft applications for Golf/Jetta (1.6/1.8 litre only)

BR Motorsport recommend that the tuner uses only the best replacement parts. Schrick camshafts are expensive and they have to be ordered for each specific car but they are of superb quality and longevity is assured.

MU9.12 ▶
Before an engine is converted, it is removed and put onto a stand. The head is then removed and modified as shown previously. The rest of the engine is dismantled and checked over. Some parts, such as the pistons, are replaced as a matter of course whilst others are worked on. The crankshaft is checked for ovality and general condition. If it is within acceptable tolerances, the journals are polished in the lathe as shown here. If not, it is sent out to a specialist for regrinding. Whichever is the case, it is always dynamically balanced along with the flywheel, clutch and front damper assembly.

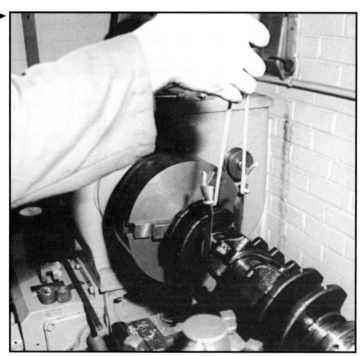

◀ **MU9.13**
The block is sent away to be bored out to the required size (a highly specialised task) and to be plateau honed, a treatment which results in fine scratching on the surface of the bore. This enables the bore and new rings to 'bed in' together as the engine is run-in. It is then thoroughly cleaned to remove all traces of dirt and swarf from oilways. This picture shows how the main bearing shells are inserted onto the end caps. The shells have already been put in place on the block.

Engine conversion

You must always remember to tell your insurers that you intend to modify your car. Many companies refuse point blank to have anything to do with uprated engines and it is best to know this beforehand so that you can go and find yourself someone more reasonable. Some may agree to insure the vehicle but only after a satisfactory engineer's report. Uprated brakes may well be a necessity with some companies (as they should be with yourself!). Bear in mind that policies are issued on trust and that not declaring modifications, however small they may be, could well lead to the policy being void in the event of a claim!

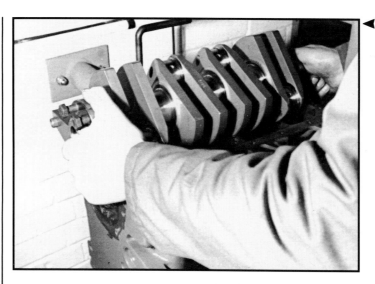

◀ **MU9.14**
The polished, balanced crankshaft is then oiled and lowered carefully into position.

MU9.15 ▶
Still at the lower end of the engine, the sump comes in for the BRM treatment. Early sumps had a capacity of three and a half litres and were very prone to oil surge. In later models the capacity went up to four litres which eased the problem. However, BRM baffle the sump, as shown here, to cut out oil surge altogether.

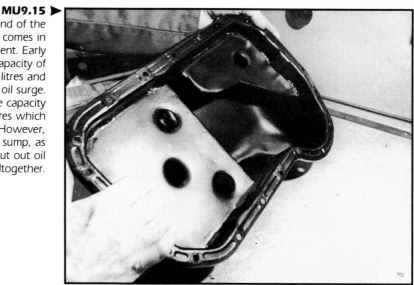

◀ **MU9.16**
The con-rods, little ends and pistons are balanced with the same precision as the rest of the conversion. BR Motorsport always use Mahle high quality pistons, one of which is shown here. Note the arrow on top of the piston, denoting which way round it should be fitted. The positions of the three piston rings is equally important; ring gaps should be spaced out evenly around the piston.

MU9.17 ▶
Fitting pistons is a job for the experts. Here, a Sykes-Pickavant piston ring compressor is used to close up the piston rings.

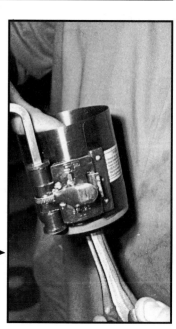

◀ MU9.18
With the rings thus held, the piston goes into position and is tapped carefully through the compressor. There are two compression rings and one oil ring.

MU9.19 ▶
When the piston has passed right through the piston ring compressor and the compressor has been removed, the piston can be tapped gently into position with a hammer handle. The con-rod can be fitted to its bearings and cap then torqued up to the correct poundage on the crankshaft.

BR Motorsport pride themselves on always using high quality tools and equipment. Many of the items used are of Sykes-Pickavant manufacture and most of the electronic tuning equipment are genuine VAG items as found in official dealerships. The latter area is one where the DIY enthusiast has to hand over gracefully to the specialist. Sometimes, getting the job done properly involves knowing what not to do yourself!

MU9.20 ▶
Here, a used standard piston is held alongside two of the new Mahles already fitted.

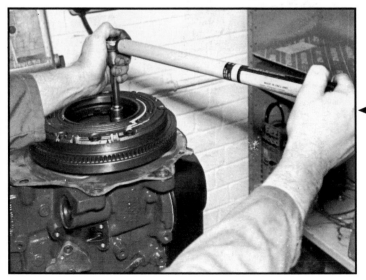

◀ MU9.21
In most cases, the clutch is replaced, either because it is worn or because it will not handle the extra power of the larger, more powerful engine (see later in this Section). Here, the Sykes-Pickavant torque wrench is being used to ensure that the correct poundage is obtained on the flywheel bolts.

Engine conversion

You won't find any reference here to tuning the smaller Golf engines. The substantial sum you would have to spend on tuning one of the smaller engines would be better spent trading up to one of the more powerful Golfs or Jettas further up the range.

◄ MU9.22
An 1850cc conversion sits proudly on the engine stand prior to being installed in an owners car. Note how clean it is! The cylinder block is now painted red.

MU9.23
Here the timing is being accurately set up using a dial gauge. One ingenious method of obtaining the correct setting is by using woodruff keys which have to be filed to the exact offset.
▼

◄ MU9.24
However, for those who can afford it, the much simpler way is to use the vernier pulley, shown here. It fixes in place of the top pulley and adjustment is made quickly via the six Allen screws around the inner circumference.

MU9.25 ▶
The last lap! A customer's engineless Mk I Golf GTi sits high on the ramps eagerly awaiting a new lease of life in the form of an 1850 cc, BRM140 unit.

Owners of smaller engined Golfs often ask whether they can swap their engine for a larger Golf/Jetta engine. Sadly, the answer is 'No'. Of course, just about any engine can be fitted to just about any car, but the cost and work involved in a Golf engine swap means that it is invariably less expensive and infinitely more satisfactory to trade up a model.

◀ **MU9.26**
The new engine is installed in the same manner as it would be on the production line; that is, lowering the car over the engine rather than putting the engine into the car. This process is carried out with great care and very slowly, for obvious reasons. Note that the first section of the exhaust is already connected.

MU9.27 ▶
With the engine almost in position, an engine lift is called into play to help manoeuvring over the last few vital inches.

Engine conversion

Getting to drive a car equipped with a BR Motorsport engine is an experience to be savoured. Brian uses his own car, a Mk I GTi, as a test bed for many of his products and it was that car, with a BRM140 engine installed, that is described on this page. It also runs with 6 inch alloy wheels, 185 x 60 profile Pirelli tyres, a full BBS body kit, a Sachs sports suspension kit and, to help cope with the extra power, an uprated Sachs clutch.

We feel that it is necessary to make several points to Golf owners who feel that they require extra power. The uprated engine places more demands on the car as a whole, particularly in the areas of suspension, brakes, tyres and clutch. It should be part of the prospective owners budget to allow for the replacement and/or uprating of these items. The tyres may well be illegal if they are not approved for the car's new speed potential. To check this, refer to Section 13. Improving the brakes is a must for all, even if it is a Mk II car that is being modified.

◄ **MU9.28**
When everything has been connected and the engine is running, Brian uses electronic technology to help him fine-tune the new motor.

MU9.29 ►
The final checks are made on BRM's sophisticated rolling road. None of the engines could be described as cheap, although the premium is not high where a tuned engine is being substituted for a worn out one.

On the road

From the instant the car is started it is obvious that something other than the standard 1600cc power unit lurks beneath the bonnet. The Jetex exhaust (see Section 2) produces a healthy burble which sounds suitably aggressive on tickover and which would warn an unsuspecting driver to handle with care!

What is truly impressive about this, and the other engine conversions in the BRM range, is their tractability. The car potters around town in commuter traffic quite happily and is totally fuss-free. The standard car's mid-range power is not only retained but improved upon, meaning that rapid, safe overtaking in third or fourth gear seldom requires a change down. With 140 bhp on tap, it doesn't take too long to appreciate the wisdom of fitting some of the 'extras' mentioned earlier. The uprated suspension is a must for this kind of power, as corners are invariably approached and taken at higher speeds than normal and similarly, the power and the higher cornering speeds place much greater loads on the tyres. Most important is the uprating of the brakes, especially on Mk I cars which were never renowned for their stopping ability! The test car is equipped with Brian's brake servo conversion which totally transforms it. It is easily as good as, if not better than, the four disc set-up on Mk II Golfs and that is high praise indeed.

The word 'turbo' is synonymous with power, speed and performance. It brings to mind vivid images of super powerful rally cars spitting flames as they blast down dark forest tracks and of Grand Prix cars performing similar pyrotechnics on the race circuits of the world. As is often the case, motorsport technology has found its way to the private motorist and there are now many companies offering turbocharger kits for the Golf. In principle, turbocharging an engine is a very efficient way of producing a lot of extra power. It uses the exhaust gases to spin a turbine which, in turn, 'force feeds' the engine and thus increases the power output. However, as the turbo cannot work until the exhaust gases reach it, there is a delay between operating the accelerator and receiving the power. This delay is called turbo lag. One other bugbear with turbocharged engines is that the power tends to arrive in a lump, rather than smoothly throughout the rev range. All turbo specialists, therefore, aim to produce smooth, non-peaky engines with minimal turbo lag.

Northampton based company Turbo Technics have a hard-earned reputation for producing high quality, well matched turbochargers and their work is recognised as being among the best. The VW Golf/Jetta range is, needless to say, among their specialities.

Whilst turbocharging is an accepted and very successful route to the goal of more power, it is interesting to note that Volkswagen themselves do not offer a turbo on any non-diesel version of the Golf.

MU10.1

In this numbered photograph, the component parts of the kit can be identified. The engine here is a Mk II 1800cc GTi unit fitted with a Turbo Technics turbocharger.

1. The Garret AiResearch T3 turbocharger with integral waste gate.

2. The multi-branch manifold has a high nickel content and is designed for pulse separation.

3. The downpipe, which is non-standard. Note the stainless steel 'bellows' section which allows flexibility. It couples into the standard exhaust system at the first junction although on later models, the rear exhaust section is enlarged to improve gas flow.

4. The air is drawn through the standard air filter into the compressor and then cooled by the intercooler. It then passes into the standard inlet manifold.

5. The fuel metering head is exchanged for a unit with a higher flow capacity and the air metering cone modified to suit.

6. The standard electronic ignition system is retained but with a modified advance curve. Wide heat range spark plugs are used and an overboost ignition cut-out is fitted to prevent engine damage in the event of a wastegate malfunction.

7. An oil supply is taken from the engine to the turbo, via a steel pipe, and then back to the sump.

8. The original engine mounting rubber is carried in a new mounting bracket, shaped to give clearance for the turbocharger.

9. A heavy duty clutch is fitted.

10. The pistons are machined to give a compression ratio of 9.3:1 and a special head gasket is used.

Apart from different spark plugs and ignition timing, servicing is unaltered. The use of a top-class semi-synthetic engine oil is strongly recommended, such as the celebrated Duckhams QXR.

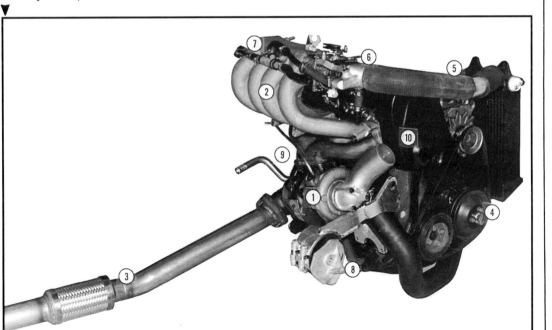

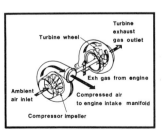

Turbocharging

Fitting a Turbocharger is anything but a DIY task. In common with other turbo specialists, Turbo Technics will only work on a supply-and-fit basis.

In common with most manufacturers, Turbo Technics only produce turbo kits for the fuel injected models, either Mk I or Mk II.

Turbo Technic's 150 bhp Mk II Golf GTi Turbo accelerates from 0-60 in 6.9 secs (9.4 standard), 0-100 in 18.5 secs (28.4), achieves 126 mph top speed (119 mph) - and there's a faster 168 bhp Turbo option as well!

This graph shows the effect of a turbo kit on a Mk I GTi. (Graph courtesy of Turbo Technics Ltd)

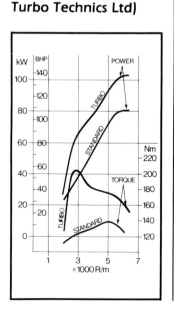

◄ MU10.2
The main component parts required to turbocharge an 1800cc Mk II GTi, seen here at Turbo Technic's Northampton base. One of an abundance of minor ancillary parts also used is a new vacuum pump which actuates the wastegate.

MU10.3 ►
The heart of the matter, the Garret T3 Turbocharger assembly, complete with compressor and wastegate.

◄ MU10.4
Possibly the most important part of the whole system; the integral mounted wastegate. The valve shown here is set to open at a pre-set pressure which is, in effect, a safety valve. If there is any problem with the system, or if it is in danger of being over-revved by an over enthusiastic driver, then the valve opens and prevents further boost from being obtained. Either way, it could save the engine.

MU10.5 ►
The cast alloy intercooler cools the air before it gets to the engine. The colder air increases efficiency and therefore power. The cooler the air, the denser the mixture, allowing more to be packed into each 'charge' of the cylinder. The intercooler offsets the heating effect of the turbocharger.

MU10.6
To cope with all the extra power, a Sachs heavy duty clutch is fitted along with the turbo.

MU10.7
Where necessary, T.T. will carry out additional work to a customer's engine. Attention to the cylinder head and valves is usually required on engines that have done 40,000 miles or more, before the turbo can be fitted. ▼

MU10.8
When we visited Turbo Technics, we were fortunate to see part of the development work for a kit suitable for the 16V engine. A different manifold has been made. It is on the right of this picture and as can be seen, is larger than the 8V version next to it.

MU10.9 ▶
Work had just started on fitting the turbo to the car. The intercooler is seen here mounted next to the radiator as on the 8V kit. None of the pipework had been connected at this stage.

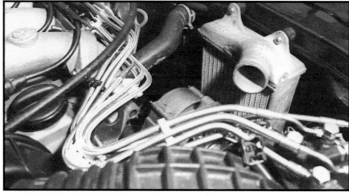

MU10.10
There's no mistaking what engine this is! The 'banana' manifold proudly announces to all that the motor has double its fair share of valves. As yet the turbo has not been installed, but note the huge heat shield in position on the bulkhead.

In keeping with the low key image that Volkswagen give all GTis, Turbo Technics restrict the badging to just one, fitted under the offside rear lamp cluster. Despite the 16V car starting with a higher base figure of 139bhp, the peak power will still only be about 170bhp. T.T. are of the opinion that, for all practical purposes, this is enough power to put through the front wheels. Their 16V fitting has concentrated on exploiting the better breathing characteristics of the engine to provide lots of low-down torque, making the engine feel as though it has more cylinders as well as more valves!

Using the Slick 50 treatment

Slick 50 is a highly specified product which, despite its appearance, is not an additive. It uses the oil in the engine as a means of reaching the metal surfaces. Effectively, the PTFE in the product sticks to the metal surfaces it touches and forms a protective coating approx two microns thick! The makers claim that once the initial thin coating has been applied, it will get no thicker and that the only way to get it off is to grind it off. Because of the reduction in drag and friction the engine should run cooler and quieter, need less maintenance and there should be an improvement in mpg. Thanks are due to BR Motorsport for demonstrating the use of Slick 50 in a 16V Jetta.

◄ MU11.1
Adding Slick 50 to the engine oil is straightforward. Drain the engine oil when warm and fit a new oil filter. The bottle of Slick 50 should be shaken vigorously and, if the weather is cool, should be immersed in warm water beforehand. The engine should be re-filled, using your usual oil (preferably a high quality branded product such as Duckhams) leaving enough room to add the pack of Slick 50. **Do not overfill.** The manufacturers recommend an immediate journey of around 30 miles or leaving the engine on tickover for 30 minutes. After this, the engine will have received its permanent coating of PTFE. Slick 50 only has to be added once and does not ever have to be topped up when the oil is changed.

MU11.2 ►
Here Slick 50 is being poured into the gearbox with the special filler nozzle supplied, where it has much the same effect as in the engine. Before filling or topping up, the level plug on the side of the gearbox should be removed and checked regularly to prevent overfilling. Note that the gearbox requires a different pack to the engine.

◄ MU11.3
Slick 50 also produce an aerosol spray can of their PTFE lubricant, ideal for things like window and sliding sunroof runners, and throttle linkages, like the 16V linkage shown here. Door locks and hinges could also benefit. In addition, there's a Slick 50 PTFE-enhanced grease for bearings and other longer-term lubrication requirements.

Uprating the suspension system
Fitting modified suspension units

As with braking efficiency, uprating the suspension should really be considered before carrying out any increase in performance. We took a GTi to BR Motorsport to watch a full Sachs Sporting kit being fitted.

Improving your Golf or Jetta's suspension can make it more positive to drive and more fun to own provided that you are prepared to lose some of Volkswagen's original compromise in respect of comfort. The choice is yours ...

◄ **MU12.1**
The attractive looking Sachs kit comes complete with springs, struts and comprehensive instructions.

MU12.2
For ease of fitting, the car was put onto one of BR Motorsport's two-post lifts and all the wheels removed. Starting at the front seemed logical and the picture shows the lower part of the original strut. ▼

◄ **MU12.3**
With the rubber dust cover removed, a socket is used to undo the top nut.

Fitting modified suspension units

Compressing a spring can be a highly dangerous operation. Ensure that the locating hooks are securely in place. Tighten one side of the pair of S-P compressors a little way, and then the other, never taking one side so far that the other side runs the remotest risk of slipping off. Release them with equal care and evenness. Unless you are absolutely sure of your competence and qualification to carry out this job, have it done by a garage or trained mechanic.

◄ **MU12.4**
This now allows the top plate to be removed. The rubber cover, top nut and the top cap are to be used again, so they need to be stored safely for a while.

MU12.5 ►
The strut is held to the wheel bearing housing by two nuts/bolts. Drawing these out, whilst supporting the strut, allows it to be removed altogether.

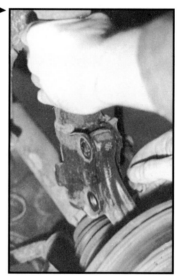

MU12.6
Once removed from the car, it is necessary to re-use the old upper spring plate on the new units. Remember to remove it from the old units. A spring compressor is used to facilitate this. The Sykes-Pickavant professional model shown here at BR Motorsport has a working load of 750 kgs. However, there is a simpler (and cheaper!) version, designed for use by the DIY owner shown towards the end of this section. It must be emphasised that the pressure required to move the spring is enormous and great care should be taken.
▼

MU12.7 ▶
With the spring compressor in place, a socket is all that is required to remove the upper spring plate.

This Sachs Sporting kit includes completely new springs and dampers for front and rear. The front are hydraulic struts with linear progression springs and the rear are gas pressurised with progressive springs, which means that the more they are compressed, the stiffer they become.

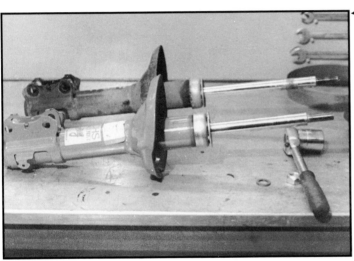

◀ **MU12.8**
There is very little external difference between the new Sachs strut (seen nearest the camera) and the old.

MU12.9 ▶
Using the spring compressor again, the BR Motorsport mechanic compressed the new spring to allow the strut to be inserted and the upper top plate to be attached.

Fitting modified suspension units

For both 16V and non-16V Golfs, both Mk I and Mk II, Sachs produce a choice of two Sachs Sporting suspension kits. One comprises a complete gas pressurised front strut and gas pressurised rear damper; the other comprises hydraulic front strut insert cartridges and rear hydraulic shock absorbers to give an economy option. Both come complete with four uprated springs. BR Motorsport can supply whichever you require.

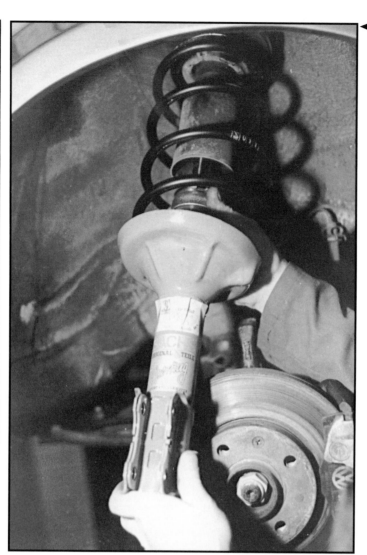

◄ **MU12.10**
With this done, the complete unit can then be refitted.

MU12.11
Note the difference between the new bolt, seen here at the top, and the original.
▼

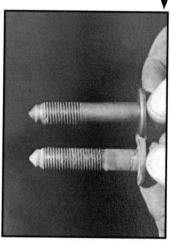

MU12.12 ►
After having positioned the strut correctly the bolts can be inserted. An important point to note is that the Sachs Sporting kit is TUV approved for use with all official Volkswagen UK wheel/tyre combinations. It is available only as a set, as the damper rates and spring rates are engineered for each other.

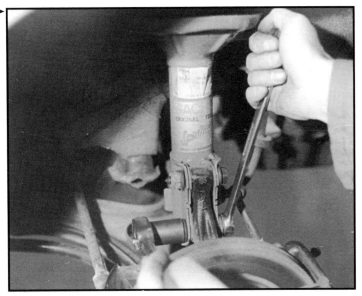

MU12.13 ▶
BR Motorsport's mechanic tightening the bolts from the strut onto the wheel bearing housing. As can be seen, a spanner will be required to prevent the bolt from spinning as the socket is turned.

There are, incidentally, two separate Sachs Sporting kits available: one comprises a complete front strut and gas shock absorber to give an economy option, both come complete with four uprated springs. Although the lower mounting bolts will probably have to be loosened later on, in order to adjust the camber, it is wise from a safety point of view to fully tighten them at this stage.

◀ MU12.14
Finally, the top plate can be refitted followed by the rubber dust cover.

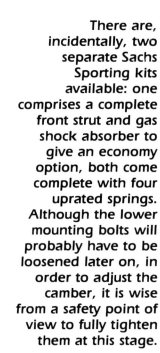

MU12.15 ▶
At the rear, access to the lower strut mounting bolt is from the inside, underneath the car.

Fitting modified suspension units

Whereas at the front, the dissassembly starts at the top, at the rear it starts at the bottom.

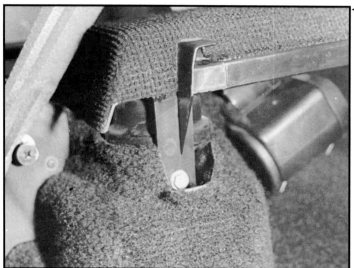

◀ **MU12.16**
At the top, inside the hatchback, the strut is hidden by the parcel shelf. This is held in place by five 10mm nuts (17mm spanner size), all of which have to be removed and the shelf taken out. Here, the front mounting is shown, which affixes to the suspension turret.

MU12.17 ▶
Here is the fixing above the rear lamp cluster (arrowed) with the nut removed. Where a speaker is fitted, care should be taken not to damage it when taking out the shelf or to snag the speaker leads. Specialists like BR Motorsport have developed their own time-saving methods of leaving the shelf in place, but there's no alternative if you're going to do-it-yourself.

◀ **MU12.18**
As with the front strut, the rubber dust cover should be taken off.

174

◄ MU12.19
This gives access to the nut and top plate, which should be undone with a socket as shown.

Whilst mounting both front and rear dampers, BR Motorsport's mechanic found a second pair of hands useful in order to hold them steady.

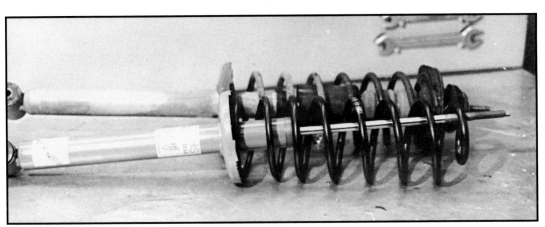

▲
MU12.20
The strut, complete with spring, will then just pull out of its fitted position. As can be seen here, there is, once again, little external difference between the old unit and the new Sachs item. Spring removal and replacement follows the same pattern as for the front and the fitting of the new strut is a simple reversal of the previous instructions.

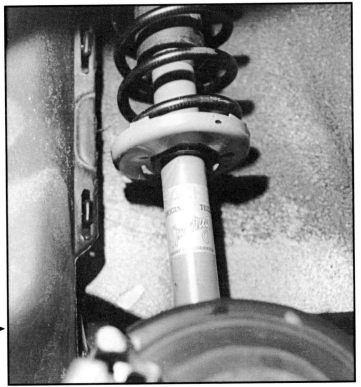

MU12.21 ►
The new Sachs strut can be inserted and bolted into position by a reversal of the previous instructions.

Fitting modified suspension units

It is important to realise that the fitting of a new suspension set-up may affect the camber and tracking. This should be checked and/or adjusted straight away as a maladjusted front end can be both expensive in terms of tyre wear and dangerous.

◄ MU12.22
With both front and rear Sachs suspension units fitted, the car can be lowered to the ground. The camber should be measured, as shown here using a special tool, by a specialist such as BR Motorsport.

MU12.23
Adjustment, which will certainly be necessary, is carried out as shown. With the lowered suspension, bodykit and very wide wheels, access is something of a squash!
▼

◄ MU12.24
When the camber has been checked and corrected, the tracking should receive the same treatment. Again, a special tool, shown here BR Motorsport, is required for accurate setting up. Having altered the camber and tracking, the steering wheel should be checked to make sure that it still points dead ahead. It may need to be moved round on the splines. (See Chapter 2, section 1).

MU12.25 ▶
The effect of the 30mm drop in ride height with the Sachs Sporting kit fitted is dramatic and can be seen quite clearly here, although the fitting of BBS 15 inch wheels, with appropriate tyres, and a body kit, has tended to accentuate this.

You should only work on your Golf or Jetta suspension if you are certain of your own competence. If you decide to DIY, have the work checked by a qualified mechanic before putting the car on the road. Otherwise, leave it to the specialists, such as BR Motorsport.

MU12.26
Earlier, heavy-duty Sykes-Pickavant spring compressors were seen in use at BR Motorsport. Sykes-Pickavant also produce these smaller coil spring compressors suitable for the smaller garage or the home enthusiast.

▼

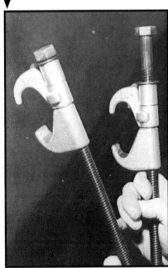

MU12.27 ▶
Make absolutely certain that the compressors are firmly located on opposite sides of the spring, top and bottom, and that they are tightened and loosened evenly. The released power of a compressed coil spring could kill!

Fitting modified suspension units

Sachs produce an incredibly wide range of suspension products with applications varying from rallying to caravanning! On this page we take a brief look at a few of those fitted at BR Motorsport.

▲
MU12.28
An unusual looking item, but this Sachs group 'A' Forest strut actually completed one third of the 1986 British National Rally series on a VW Junior Rally Team Golf. It is a hydraulic damper with adjustable spring platform. Not surprisingly, it is set much higher than for road use and the piston rod is thicker.

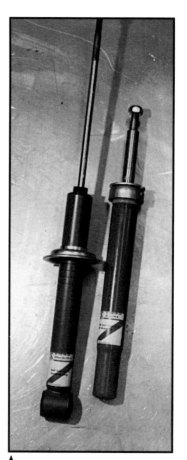

▲
MU12.29
A Sachs strut insert and rear damper for Mk I Golf. These provide damping at a rate more than 15 per cent up on the standard suspension units and are designed for use with the original springs.

MU12.30
For those who tow a lot or carry heavy loads, the Sachs Niveaulift suspension system could be the answer. Equally, it would be useful for those who have an extra fuel tank fitted. It is an adjustable system for the rear and maintains the standard ride height regardless of weight carried. It uses hydraulic shock absorbers although it is not actually uprated. The Niveaulift system is adjusted by means of either a garage airline or a small compressor, which can be fitted to the car. Obviously, the latter is a much more convenient solution for those whose loads are constantly changing. It is advisable, albeit not absolutely necessary, to uprate the front suspension.
▼

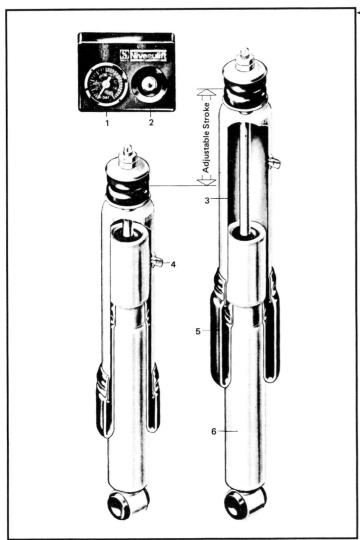

◀ MU12 Fig 1.
Nivaulift dampers, illustrating the amount of the adjustable stroke. The pressure gauge (1) and filling valve (2) are placed within the driver's sight. (Courtesy of Fichtel & Sachs AG)

The Sachs lowered suspension kit for the Golf and Jetta lowers and improves the suspension, so that cornering is much flatter with reduced body roll. On the other hand, although the suspension is a little firmer, the transformation is pleasant rather than spine-jarring. The same cannot, unfortunately, be said of some other after-market suspension kits ...

MU12 Fig 2.
Illustration of the pipework necessary for installing the Sachs Nivaulift into the car. (Courtesy of Fichtel & Sachs AG).
▼

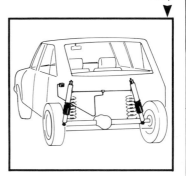

ROAD IMPRESSIONS

It has to be said that the Mk II GTi has a reasonable suspension set-up as standard. Having said this, the suspension on most cars is something of a compromise and although the sporty Golf is biased more towards driveability and less towards comfort, the sports suspension kit totally transforms the handling. The suspension will undoubtably be a little harder than before but the absence of crashing and banging may surprise you! This is regarded as one of the more subtle kits on the market. However, for those who enjoy **driving,** in the real sense of the word, the effect is a pure revelation. The almost total lack of body roll can be a little unnerving at first, but one soon adapts to it and cornering speeds increase proportionately. Safety also increases as there is never any doubt as to what the car will do in any given situation. It does of course place an extra workload on the tyres and the overall performance of the sports kit should be assessed with this in mind. In fact, handling performance as a whole will be further affected by choice of tyres. See 'Tyres' section on Page 182 to 184. For those who keep their cars for years rather than months, Sachs give the life expectancy of the units as being around 60,000 miles. One imagines that this is somewhat conservative.

If cost is a limiting factor, it is possible to fit both hydraulic front inserts or struts and rear dampers, both with the original springs. The handling improvement will not be nearly so dramatic as with the sports suspension and there will be no alteration in the ride height, of course.

How the suspension works

In this section we cover what is involved in replacing a standard suspension set-up with a Sachs Sporting kit. However, it helps to be able to relate the modified suspension components to those of the standard suspension. The units shown here are for Mk II Golfs, but units for Mk I cars are the same in principle, and the Sachs Sporting kit featured differs only in design details such as spring rates, tolerances, etc.

No small amount of thought should go into exactly which sort of suspension to fit into your car. It is possible to 'mix-n-match' springs and dampers in order to obtain the ideal set-up for your own needs (eg, sports dampers but with more forgiving springs), although, unless you are particularly skilled in this area, we would recommend that you consult a specialist dealer, such as BR Motorsport. We would also suggest that any potential buyer of uprated suspension drives a car so fitted before purchasing. This applies particularly with a sports kit which is **very** different to the original suspension!

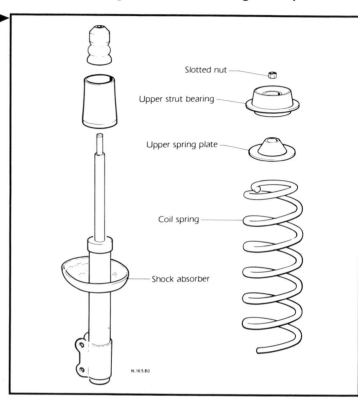

MUS12.1 ▶
At the front, MacPherson struts are fitted. These consist of a coil spring, in which is mounted a telescopic damper. The strut extends from the axle to the suspension turret, a specially strengthened area of the Golf wing. At the top mounting, the strut is flexible and able to swivel. The spring, when in position on the strut, is held under great pressure and under **no circumstances** should any attempt be made to remove it without the specialist equipment shown in this section.
(Diagram courtesy of Haynes Publishing)

Slotted nut

Upper strut bearing

Upper spring plate

Coil spring

Shock absorber

H.16580

Self-locking nut

Suspension strut

Clip

Anti-roll bar mounting

Anti-roll bar

Rubber bush

Eye bolt

Eye bolt bearing

Washer

Split sheet metal sleeve

Rear track control arm mounting

Subframe

Front track control arm mounting

Track control arm (wishbone)

◀ **MUS12.2**
This diagram shows the position of the front struts in relation to the suspension components. Note the anti-roll bar (fitted only to certain models, such as the GTi), which is, in effect, a torsion bar mounted at two points to the car's body and at each end to the bottom of the struts. When the car is cornering, the spring on the outer wheel is compressed. However, the other spring is not loaded so heavily and thus exerts a twisting force on the anti-roll bar. The spring already under compression is stiffened by this twisting and thus acts in a way which resists the car's roll.
(Diagram courtesy of Haynes Publishing)

When replacing faulty suspension items, it is important that they are always fitted in pairs, providing an opportunity to upgrade the system on an economical basis. Whenever front struts are replaced, especially if they have been uprated, the camber and tracking should be checked, and adjusted if necessary, before the car is used again on the road. Standard shock absorbers have an expected life of around 50,000 miles or four years, although this is very much dependent on the treatment they receive. Constant use on rough and unforgiving roads could lower this figure dramatically and the frequency of your safety checks should be increased.

Safety checks should be carried out at regular intervals. Both front and rear units should be checked to make sure that there are no loose nuts, while the rubber sealing shroud should always be in place on the piston tube. Should the unit be found to be leaking, replacement is required immediately.

◀ **MUS12.3**

The rear suspension units are similar to the front in basic design. They are, however, less complex as they do not have the steering or the driveshafts to cope with. Also, of course, on the front-engined Golf, they have considerably less weight to deal with. The spring is under much less pressure than those at the front although removal without a spring compressor could still be highly dangerous. (Diagram courtesy of Haynes Publishing)

Coil spring — Cover — Upper bearing ring — Cover — Lower bearing ring — Circlip — Packing — Spacer — Lower spring plate — Upper spring plate — Washer — Packing — Stop rubber — Shock absorber — Protective tube — Protective cap

H.16583

MUS12.4

As can be seen here, the units are held by one nut at the top and one bolt at the bottom, the latter passing through a rubber bush, which is an obvious source of wear after a large mileage has been covered. (Diagram courtesy of Haynes Publishing)

▼

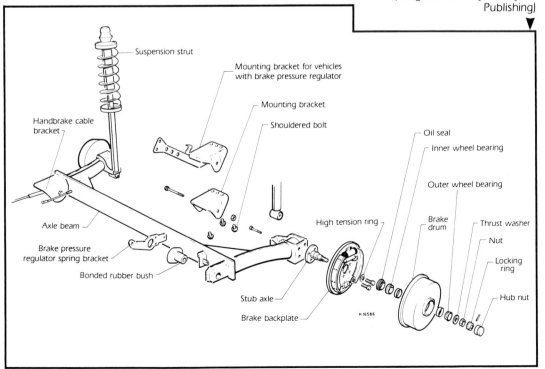

Suspension strut — Mounting bracket for vehicles with brake pressure regulator — Mounting bracket — Shouldered bolt — Oil seal — Inner wheel bearing — Outer wheel bearing — Handbrake cable bracket — High tension ring — Brake drum — Thrust washer — Nut — Axle beam — Locking ring — Brake pressure regulator spring bracket — Bonded rubber bush — Stub axle — Hub nut — Brake backplate

H.16586

Understanding

Tyres

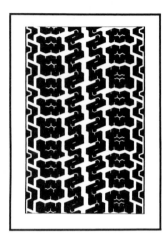

The original equipment Pirelli tyre contact patch shown in the diagram illustrates how the road would 'see' the tyre.

The Pirelli P700 is a high performance tyre with speed ratings of 'V' or 'Z' and is available with aspect ratios as low as 40 series. Many high performance cars, such as Porsche and Lamborghini, use these as standard fitments.

When you realise that your car's 'footprint' - the area in touch with the road - is in fact no bigger than a man's hand, you begin to see how crucial the selection and care of tyres can be. All your car's power and performance will come to nothing unless the tyres keep the car safely on the road.

Converting to ultra low profile tyres is one of the most effective and economical ways of enhancing many cars' looks and handling. However, don't choose on looks alone. At the extreme, you could end up with tyres that foul the bodywork or that cause a deterioration in wet weather grip, particularly at speed. You must also ensure that the tyre is not too wide for the width of wheel rim you are using and that the circumference is not so different from standard that the speedometer reading is greatly affected.

Specification

The tyre sidewall markings relate to both size designation and service description. Taking, for example, the groups of letters and numbers contained in the tyre description: 185/60R14 82H and reading from left to right:

'185' refers to the nominal section width of the tyre, whilst the '60' represents the aspect ratio. Aspect ratio is the ratio of nominal section width to section height. In this case it means, roughly speaking, that the distance from the bead of the tyre to the tread, is 60 per cent of the tyre's width. The lower the tyre's aspect ratio, the less sidewall flexing will occur, improving cornering grip and steering response. On the other hand, the tyre is less able to absorb bumps and could allow more road noise to be transmitted, while the ride could be a little firmer - although this is something that some owners prefer.

'R' indicates the tyre construction. Here, 'R' stands for Radial.

'14' refers to the wheel diameter in inches.

'82' is the load index, which is a numerical code associated with the maximum load the tyre can carry at the speed indicated by the speed symbol.

Finally, 'H' is the speed symbol. This is an alphabetical code indicating the speed at which the tyre can carry a load corresponding to the load index.

Tyre Choice

Car tyres purchased as replacements should have at least the same speed rating as those fitted as original equipment. The load index is also very important. While most ultra low profile tyres have at least the same load capacity as the base tyre, this should be checked before purchasing your replacement tyres.

When considering converting to ultra low profile tyres it is recommended that the overall diameter of the wheel/tyre package should not vary more than +3 per cent to –5 per cent from the original equipment tyre fitment. Remember, the percentage difference in the overall diameter will result in the same percentage difference in the overall gearing and speedometer reading. Larger tyres give lower speedometer readings; smaller tyres give higher speedometer readings. Most tyres fit a range of rim widths which will help you to choose the most suitable package for your needs, and for this, you need to speak to your supplier.

While increasing the 'tyre performance' on your car by fitting ultra low profile tyres, the wear rate may be affected due to your relying on the improved handling of the car. The more technologically advanced the tyre and car the more responsive the handling will become. The ultimate tyre Pirelli recommend for the Golf/Jetta is the 195/50VR15 P700. To gain the most from these tyres, alterations to the suspension may be required. Alternatively, the Pirelli P600 may be a more suitable and less costly compromise.

It is worth re-emphasizing that you should only deal with expert tyre dealers who will give you the best service and advice, such as Standard Motorists Centres or Central Tyre Company. Remember that quality of service is especially important when having expensive tyres fitted to 'exotic' wheels.

MU13.1 ▶
Pirelli's Vizzola test track, near Milan, showing a GTi; poised and under control at high speed in the wet.

◀ **MU13.2**
Wet or dry, P700 tyres are the ultimate performance tyres for Golf and Jetta, as Pirelli's tests would seem to indicate.

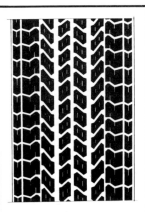

P6 and P600 are high performance tyres offering exceptional performance. The P600 is also part of the 'second generation' of ultra low profile tyres produced by Pirelli.

◀ **MU13.3**
The P4 is an everyday, 'family' tyre giving good grip, comfort and longevity.

MU13.4 ▶
P6 is a high performance tyre with outstanding levels of performance.

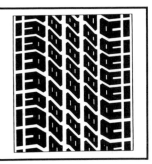

The Pirelli P700 tyre was a 'no compromise' development of the highly-acclaimed P7 tyre.

Pirelli are strongly associated with the AH4 (asymmetric hump) safety rim. Whereas a punctured tyre normally collapses into the rim (left), the AH4 holds the tyre treads in place (right), offering limited 'run flat' properties while still using normal tyres.

◀ **MU13.5**
P600 is part of Pirelli's 'second generation' of ultra low profile tyres, offering exceptional performance.

MU13.6 ▶
P Zero uses an asymmetric tread pattern, giving a normal block pattern across the inner 50 per cent of the tread width, an intermediate area for 28 per cent of width, and racing-type performance from the outer 22 per cent.

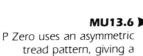

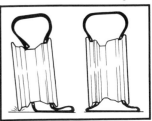

Tyres

Pirelli produce a Car Tyre Fitment and Conversions booklet for the tyre dealer to advise you in your tyre choice. Some confusion may arise from time to time regarding ultra low profile conversions and, in these instances, you should contact the Pirelli Performance Bureau where advice for your vehicle, and pocket, will be offered (see end of book for telephone contact).

Mk I Golf GTi/Jetta GLi (except Campaign) original tyre size, 175/70R13, 582 mm diameter. Alternative tyre sizes and diameters shown below.

OPTIONAL SIZES	(-5 %)	(-3 %)	(+2 %)	(+3 %)	RIM SIZE IN INCHES
185/60R13 P6	554				5
185/60R13 P600	552				5
205/60R13 P6		+581			5.5
205/60VR13 P7F		+581			5.5
165/65R14 P6		571			4.5
175/65R14 P6			584		5
185/65R14 P6				598*	5
185/60R14 P6		578			5
185/60R14 P600		578			5
185/60VR14 P6		578			5
185/60VR14 P600		578			5
195/60VR14 P6			592		5.5
195/60R14 P600			592		5.5
195/60VR14 P6			592		5.5
195/60VR14 P600			592		5.5
205/55VR14 P7F			589		5.5
185/55VR15 P600			585		5
195/55VR15 P600				595	5.5
195/50VR15 P7		581			5.5
195/50VR15 P700		579			5.5
205/50VR15 P7			+591		5.5
205/50VR15 P700			+586		5.5
205/50VR15 PZERO			+586		5.5

+ Untried fitment.   * Outside 3 %.

This chart, produced by the Pirelli Performance Bureau, shows size for size conversions of a base tyre size of 175/70R13. These are not recommendations but sizes based on overall diameter between the -5 per cent and +3 per cent variation on standard discussed previously.

Lubrication - oils, greases and fluids

Duckhams have been famous for producing the very best in engine oil, gear oil, grease and other associated products for a very long time.

Understanding lubrication

Back in the days of yore when knights were bold and rivers froze over in winter, the motorist didn't trouble his head about the type of lubricant in engine or gearbox. As long as there was plenty of the stuff around, the engine and gearbox chugged and ground along quite contentedly. Nowadays, the enthusiastic owner knows better! With increased performance, longer journeys and higher speeds, the demands on lubricants can be quite considerable and can be well beyond the capabilities of many of the 'economy' oils on the market. The wise owner gets to know what is required in a lubricant and makes darned sure that he or she uses only the best available. After all, to reduce the working life of an engine or gearbox because of penny-pinching or because of selecting the wrong lubricant for the job is not what any Golf or Jetta owner wants. Cheap 'n' nasty oils are best left to the cars to which they are best suited!

Engine oils

This section leans on the expertise of Duckhams, a company right at the forefront in oil technology. They have invested an enormous amount of resources in producing a range of engine oils that satisfies the requirements of all engines, including the most advanced, with some to spare. Before explaining how they have done so, it is necessary to take a look at some of the criteria that are applied to modern oils.

Many years ago, all engine oil was 'single grade'. It was given an 'SAE' rating which described how 'viscous' or 'thick' it was. An SAE 20 oil, being 'thin' was used in the winter months when the oil became heavier, making it more difficult to start the engine, while in the summer months a 'thicker' oil, perhaps SAE 40 or 50 was used so that the oil did not become too 'watery' to do its job. Then along came multigrade oils, introduced first by Duckhams themselves, way back at the beginning of the 1950s, and covering the spectrum from SAE 20 to 50 all the year round. These oils are still universally available, of course, along with variations such as 15w/50, 10w/40 and even 5w/50 in some cases.

It's relatively easy to make an oil which gives a viscosity of 20w/50 while it is new. The manufacturer just adds something called a 'polymer' which acts as a 'thickener' as the oil gets hotter. There is, however, a wide choice of polymers available and the old rule of 'you get what you pay for' applies. Cheap polymers lose their effectiveness quite rapidly as they are subjected to heat and 'shearing' effects inside the engine. The net result of using cheap polymers is that a 20w/50 oil loses the SAE 50 part of its viscosity which removes much of its effectiveness when the engine is working hard. The only way of avoiding the potential damage that this can cause is to only use a top-name

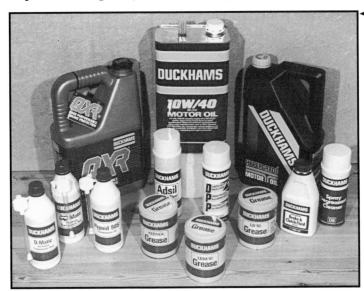

◄ UO1
Mention Duckhams, and most people immediately think of oil. However, there's also Spray Degreasant Cleaner, DPP penetrating and lubricating fluid, and Adsil Silicone Fluid which is wonderful for lubricating sliding rubbing parts. All come in aerosol packs. Check in your Volkswagen handbook to find which grade of Duckhams engine oil or transmission fluid will be required for your Golf or Jetta.

Where the lower 'drag' factor of a lower viscosity oil is required but without the additional features of QXR, Duckhams also produce '10w/40 Motor Oil'. Excellent for easier winter starting and marginally improved fuel economy when used with a newer engine, 10w/40 is not intended to replace Hypergrade 15w/50 in an older or high-mileage engine. Oil consumption could deteriorate noticeably if 10w/40 is used because it can find its way more easily past worn bores, piston rings and valve guides.

brand. Companies like Duckhams only use the best polymers in their multigrade oils because, they claim, they expect even more from their engine oils ...

Top brand 15w/50 oils, such as 'Hypergrade', are designed to satisfy the technical requirements of every engine used today. However, there is another oil, known as QXR, designed with the owners of modern high-performance cars in mind. These are probably fuel-injected engines in the majority of cases, quite possibly with multi-valve heads, while some are turbocharged, although of course, any engines powering the cars shown in this book can enjoy the benefits of QXR. The idea behind QXR was to develop an oil to meet the extra demands placed on a lubricant by these high-performance engines. Such an oil would cost more to buy than conventional oils, but would offer the very best protection from wear, the greatest possible freedom from deposits, excellent oil consumption control and the ability to perform really well over the widest extremes of temperatures and motoring conditions.

QXR is a 10w/40 oil, offering all the protection that could possibly be required along with a reduction in the 'drag' effect suffered inside an engine when 'thicker' oils are used. Ordinarily, a 10w/40 oil would have two huge disadvantages over conventional oils: it would tend to lose viscosity at higher temperatures, and it would tend to vapourise at high temperatures because 10w/40 oils are normally so much more volatile. The most expensive solution, and one which prices the oil beyond many enthusiasts pockets, is to use a synthetic lubricant in place of the usual mineral base oils. However, the route chosen by Duckhams is interesting! They have developed a special process through which the normal mineral oil is put at the refining stage to give it all the properties required but at far lower cost than that of synthetics.

Lubrication - oils, greases and fluids

Engines with turbochargers demand the use of the very best oil you can buy. Turbochargers themselves run at incredibly high speeds and are driven by the searingly hot gases passing through the exhaust system. They are also cooled, as well as lubricated, by the engine oil. Avoid loss of viscosity and gain turbocharger protection by using one of the top-line lubricants, such as QXR.

Oil companies are fond of saying that proprietary oil additives are at best useless and at worst harmful. After all, if there was a better additive, they would use it themselves! If you want the best possible level of additive in your oil, buy the more expensive oil: it's that simple! Take a look at the oil's designation number to determine additive level. For instance, the Duckhams swing ticket indicates that its 'API' classification is API SF and CD in the case of both QXR and 'Hypergrade'. The last letter indicates the degree of specification; the last-but-one indicates 'S' for petrol engines; 'C' for diesel engines.

Best of all, the tests which Duckhams carried out during development showed that in terms of performance, QXR proved to be comparable to highly expensive synthetic oils in some respects - and in other respects, even better! Pat Lelliott, Duckham's Technical Service Manager, is so proud of QXR that he says, 'Achieve all those standards and you have an oil of the high-performance class, such as QXR. Look around and see how many products attain such levels. There aren't many!'

◄ UO2
As this section indicates, Duckhams QXR is the very finest choice for high-performance engines. Here, it's being used in a Jetta GTi. On the Jetta's bulkhead there's a can of Hypergrade, a top-line lubricant in its own right.

UO3 ►
As well as being available in the large 'oil change' packs, QXR is also available in smaller top-up packs.

Gearboxes (manual)

The oil specification demanded by a gearbox varies according to its design and such factors as power transmitted, ease of gear selection and sealing, for instance. In the case of the Golf and Jetta range, Duckhams Hypoid 80 gear oil is recommended. Where low temperatures lead to a 'sticky' gearchange, a multigrade such as Hypoid 75w/90S might be preferred. Five-speed gearboxes sometimes benefit from the use of multigrade oil, especially under the adverse circumstances already mentioned, and in particular as an aid to low temperature gear selection. Don't expect the oil change to make an instant 'cure' however, as it takes a few hundred miles for the 'new' oil to displace all of the 'old' from every surface.

Rear axles

An oil such as Duckhams Hypoid 90S is, quite simply, all that is required to withstand the extraordinary 'shear' forces involved. Look at the specification of the oil. API GL4 is fine for every normal use, but if an oil with a higher level of additives is required, API GL5 may be considered, a higher last number indicating a higher level of additive treatment.

UO4 ►
There is a wide range of Duckhams grease types available and once again, you should check that you are purchasing the right type by checking in the vehicle handbook.

MU15.1
Three types of Bosch spark plug on display here are (left to right): the triple electrode plug specially developed to give highly extended service intervals for the VW range; platinum tipped plugs which are dearer to buy but are a good deal more efficient provided that they are accurately gapped before use and the standard Bosch Super plug, produced to original equipment specification.

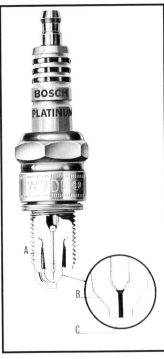

◄ MU15.2
Advantages of Platinum plugs are: ignition conditions remain practically constant all through recommended service life of plug; plugs warm up more quickly and so 'self-clean' earlier; heat transfer properties are improved; the centre electrode is virtually wear resistant, the property of platinum.
A Very long insulator nose ensures extension of the thermal operating range.
B 0.3mm dia. platinum centre electrode.
C Platinum centre electrode sintered gas tight in insulator nose.

Often under-rated and overlooked, the spark plug plays a decisive part in the efficient operation of any engine, and for a high-performance engine, the demands placed upon it are amazingly tough. Working at a pressure of up to 50 bar and in gas temperatures of up to 3000 degrees Celcius, the spark plug is expected to deliver 30,000 volts and above, no less than 100 times **every second** when the car is at speed. Not only that but the poor thing is expected to work happily, hot or cold, for months and thousands of miles on end. Indeed, Volkswagen's service intervals now demand a spark plug that will work well over a 20,000 mile period, and Bosch engineers have come up with a range of plugs that fulfil even that criterion.

Some spark plugs have a flat seating surface and make use of a sealing gasket; others have a conical surface and are self-sealing. Clearly, the correct type of plug seating designed for the engine has to be used; they are not interchangeable. Some types of spark plug are interchangeable, however. Where radio interference from spark plugs is a problem (which is unusual, to say the least, in the case of 'our' cars - although with radio interference, anything can happen!), it is possible to buy Bosch plugs with interference suppression (those plugs with an in-built resistor have an 'R' in the type number) and even fully shielded plugs.
Other special plugs include those with multiple electrodes to satisfy some manufacturers' extremely long service intervals, and those with precious metal electrodes. These plugs, with either silver ('S' identification) or platinum ('P' identification) electrodes are inherently more efficient than ordinary plugs, and the extra efficiency is especially useful in high performance engines, right up to racing spec.

Spark plugs

PLUGS IN PRACTICE

Spark plugs tend to break down, in the main, for one of two or three reasons. One is that the plugs internal insulation fails leading to internal shorting out, although this is usually because another problem has occurred. A plug working outside its optimum working temperature range will be prone to failing in this way, so it's important that the correct heat range is used in your particular car. If the engine is standard, just use the correct plug, the designation of which will have been determined by Bosch and the vehicle manufacturer. If the engine is tuned, however, the specialist concerned should be able to advise.

Leaving the plug in place for too long can also cause breakdown of the plug, of course. Again, the insulation can fail, or the centre electrode can become contaminated leading to reduced efficiency, or the electrode can become eroded.

TYPE NUMBERS AND FITTING

You can identify a Bosch plug by the type number on the box and on the body of the plug itself. Take a typical number, such as W 7 DP. (Plugs with resistors would have an additional 'R' after the 'W', by the way.) 'W' indicates the type of thread and seat, this being the most common flat seat, M 14 x 1.25 thread. '7' indicates the heat range - a critical measure, because to use a plug outside the correct heat range could damage the engine. 'D' shows that the plug thread length is, in this case, 19mm (or 17.5 mm if the plug is tapered), while the last letter indicates the electrode material, where 'C' would indicate the standard plug with copper electrode. You will find an application list detailing the correct plugs for your car wherever the plugs are sold.

MU15.3 ▶
Ensure that the plug threads in the head are clear. Use a Sykes-Pickavant thread chaser if necessary (see 'Engine conversion'). Screw plug in by hand until it is seated. New plugs with flat seats are turned a further 90 degrees with a spark plug wrench. Already used flat-seat plugs, and conical seat plugs, are turned by a further 15 degrees with the wrench. (Courtesty of Robert Bosch Ltd)

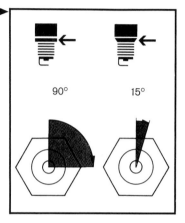

MU15.4
Using the Bosch spark plug gap-gauge:
A. Measuring the electrode gap. The measuring wire should pass through with only the slightest resistance.
B. Checking platinum plugs for wear: Bend the side electrode back; push measuring wire into hole in insulator nose; when wire goes in as far as plastic stop, wear limit has been reached.
C. Opening the electrode gap with the 'bottle opener' type bending devide on the Bosch measuring tool.
D. Close the gap by tapping lightly and carefully on a smooth, hard surface.

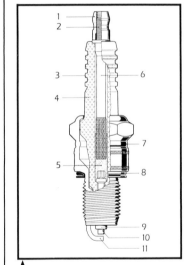

▲
MU15.5
CONSTRUCTION OF SPARK PLUG
1 Terminal nut
2 Thread
3 Current leak barrier
4 Insulator
5 Conductive seal
6 Terminal stud
7 Fitting: swaged & heat shrunk
8 Gasket (flat seat)
9 Insulator tip
10 Centre electrode
11 Ground electrode

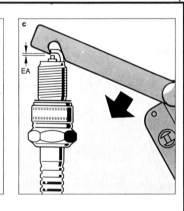
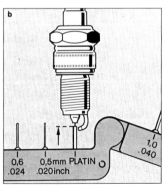
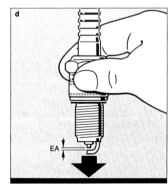

Improving engine bay appearance

MU16.1 ▶
Some of the range of Comma products for sprucing up your engine, both inside and out.

Cleaning and protecting the engine bay is an oft-neglected but very important task. Allowing it to become dirty and oily can put off the DIY owner from keeping up with those regular maintenance jobs. The importance of this is usually discovered at 2.30 am, on a wild and rainy winter's morning 10 miles from anywhere in a car with failed spark plugs, which, along with plug leads and the distributor cap, are far more likely to fail if coated in oily dirt. On an even more serious note, excessive dirt could easily conceal things which are potentially dangerous, such as loose nuts, worn cables etc.

◀ **MU16.2**
Easi-Flush is a quick and easy way to clean your engine internally. It should be used just prior to an engine oil change. With the engine warm, the whole bottle is poured into the engine which should then be run at fast idle for five minutes. The oil should then be drained and replaced as normal.

MU16.3
Rad Clean Plus works in a similar way to the above, except of course that it cleans the water cooling system! The radiator should be drained, flushed with clean water and then half filled. When the radiator is drained, Rad Clean Plus will be seen to have removed the build up of scaly deposits which accumulate over a period of time. ▼

MU16.4 ▶
Using Hyper Clean degreasant is one of the simplest ways to deal with an oily engine bay. Excessive grease and dirt should first be scraped off. It is reassuring to note that Hyper Clean contains a rust inhibitor. Before washing off, the electrical system could be protected by using Comma Ignition Sealer.

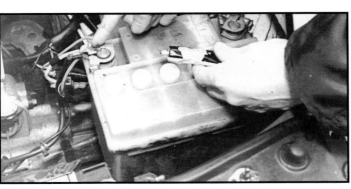

◀ **MU16.5**
Comma's Copper Ease improves sealing and facilitates easy dismantling of nuts and bolts. As shown in this picture, it can be used for protecting battery terminals from corrosion especially as it is an excellent electrical conductor.

Chapter Five
Techniques and tools

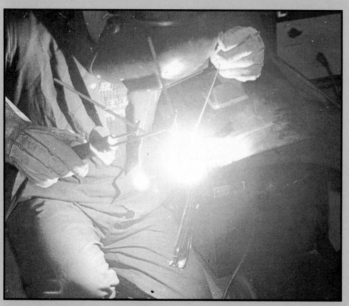

Hand tools

There seem to be two approaches when it comes to buying hand tools. One is to buy the cheapest Far East produced tools that can be found, preferably on special offer at the local filling station and, better still, given away free with 5 litres of engine oil; while the other approach is to buy tools with a sense of quality about them, tools that will last a lifetime. Some of the finest tools that can be had are made in the UK by Sykes-Pickavant, who are also the producers of the Speedline economy range. We examine some of them here.

It's possible to produce a higher standard of work with high quality tools than with poor ones. Not only do they fit better, causing no damage to the components that you are working on, such as nuts and bolts, but they're also designed to work efficiently. In addition there's the psychological benefit of working with high quality tools in your hands.

HT1 ▶

One of the exceptions to the 'Made in Britain' rule is the wide range of tool boxes and chests, which are made for Sykes-Pickavant in Canada. They're made of tough heavy gauge steel, are lockable, and contain separate 'filing cabinet' type drawers for tool storage. Some of the units are stackable.

HT2

Castors and fixing nuts and bolts come as part of the kit. Two of the castors swivel and are lockable, providing a stable base if you wish to use the cabinet top as a workbench. ▼

HT3

You have to pull out the top drawer and bolt the push-pull handle to the side of the cabinet.

▼

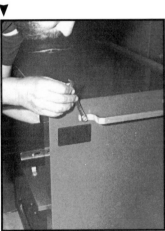

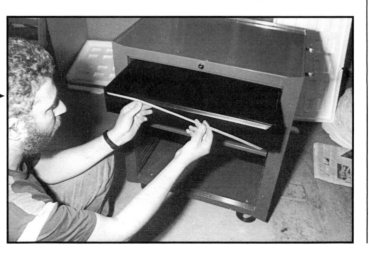

HT4 ▶

A nice touch this: SP also provide trim finishes for the drawer fronts which give an attractive appearance and do away with sharp edges. The Space Maker Chest seen in HT1 contains six smaller drawers and a lift out tote tray. It's designed to fit neatly on top of the cabinet bench.

Hand tools

With Sykes-Pickavant's surface drive sockets (see top figure), force is applied on the 'flats', not the corners, reducing socket and fastener wear and avoiding 'rounding-off'. The arrows in the lower figure show those parts of the nut or bolt where the socket applies its turning force.

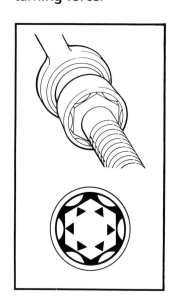

HT5 ▶

The tote tray from the Space Maker Chest with a selection of Speedline SP tools. Speedline are still of a very high quality, needless to say, but are designed to satisfy the enthusiastic DIYer's pocket.

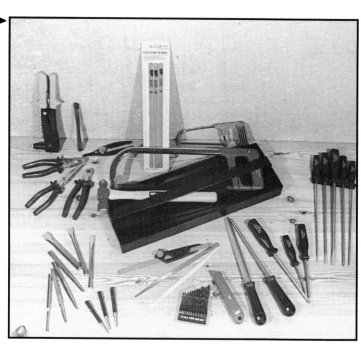

◀ **HT6**

There are no better looking or better handling ratchet sets than SP's Speedline tools. The 3/8 inch drive socket set is so well built that it's easily tough enough for most jobs yet it's lighter, easier to handle and less expensive than its 1/2 inch drive counterparts. Buy sockets in sets or individually bubble packed as shown.

HT7 ▶

In the old days everyone bought open-ended or ring spanners. Now we buy combination sets like the Speedline spanners pictured in the background. The extension set, pictured right, has a wonderful semi-universal joint end on each one; a boon in awkward spots.

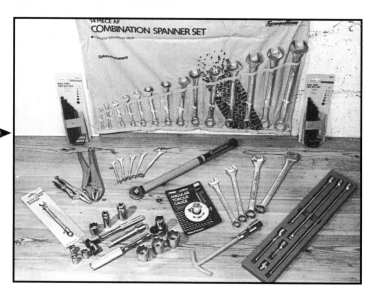

Engine diagnosis and tuning is relevant to engine modifications in two ways. First, it enables you to tell whether any reconditioning work will be required on the engine before uprating its performance, and second, it allows you to keep the engine in prime condition thereafter.

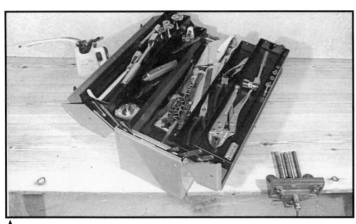

HT8
The SP Mechanic's Box has four cantilevered trays and an extra deep lower compartment. It's superbly built and there's no comparison between this and the average short-life accessory shop tool box.

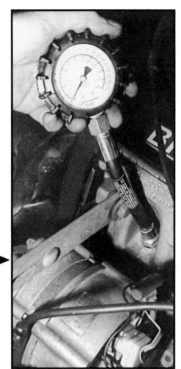

HT9 ▶
BR Motorsport use an SP Compression Tester to check the health of an engine before deciding whether it's a suitable case for modification or whether some reconditioning will be needed first.

◀ **HT10**
The engine will have to be cranked so it's important to remove the HT lead from the distributor cap to avoid the risk of an electric shock. However, on car's fitted with electronic ignition the HT lead must be earthed to prevent damage to the ignition system components.

HT11
The Speedline spark plug spanner has a UJ swivel which enables you to give extra leverage and aids access in awkward spots. See 'Understanding Spark Plugs' for correct tightening procedure.
▼

HT12 ▶
Faulty valves or piston rings will give variable compression readings and this indicates that some reconditioning may be necessary. A blown cylinder head gasket or - horror of horrors! - a holed piston will also give distinctive compression readings. Deep seated plugs require the accessory extension set shown here.

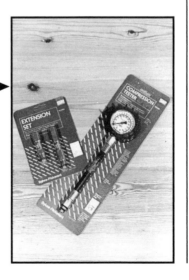

Hand tools

Here's a typical application of the 6-24V circuit tester, testing continuity in the ignition circuit. The ignition switch is in the 'start' position. You can also check for breaks in a suspect wire by clipping the crocodile clip to a good earth and pushing the sharp end of the probe through the insulation at various points.

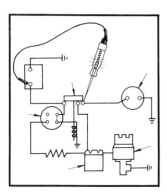

HT13 ▶

Apart from the compression tester and circuit tester already mentioned and the spark plug thread chaser (bottom right) shown under 'Engine Modifications', there's a huge range of other SP engine tools. Bottom left is the carburettor tool overhaul set while along the top (from right) are: oil filter remover, feeler gauges, piston ring compressor, and the odd-looking but extremely useful cylinder head stands.

HT14

It's absolutely crucial that clutch centre plates are aligned correctly. The Speedline clutch aligning tool set enables just about every clutch on the market to be lined up just as it should be.

▼

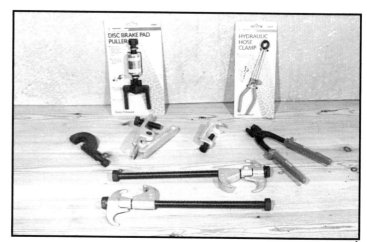

▲

HT15

For 'chassis' work, there's the Speedline disc brake pad puller, a nut splitter (a better alternative to a sheared bolt), and ball joint remover. There are also the tools seen in Chapter Four being used by BR Motorsport.

◀ **HT16**

Torx fasteners are found in a variety of applications on modern vehicles such as door hinges, locks and striker plates, window regulators, wiper motors, seat fixings, bumpers, etc. SP Speedline Torx drive bit sets solve the problem.

◄ HT17
Even professional electricians now often use wiring clips like the one shown for joining two pieces of wire together called 'Scotchloks'. These connectors will also join the end of one wire into the 'run' of another.

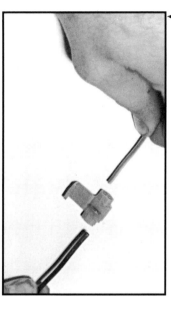

HT18 ►
Speedline insulated grip pliers are shown here squeezing the clip and making contact between the two lengths of wire. It's as simple as that!

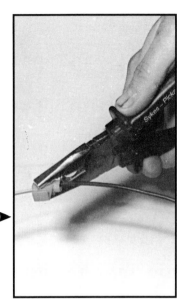

HT19 ►
The finished job is possibly only just about tolerable from the aesthetic point of view, but the electrical contact is perfectly acceptable.

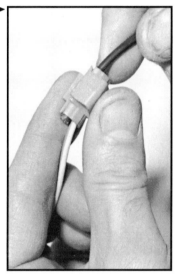

HT20
Sedan market an extremely useful box of wiring clips and fasteners shown in the background. The SP crimping tool is used to pinch a spade terminal to the end of a bared piece of wire. No soldering necessary.

HT21
Last in this sequence but perhaps first in priority, especially in respect of some of the items to come, is the Speedline safety kit. Goggles, gloves, efficient breathing mask and earplugs.

A Speedline long reach riveter will be invaluable when fitting body kits. When selecting rivets remember that the rivet should be 4mm (5/32 in) longer than the thickness of the material to be riveted.

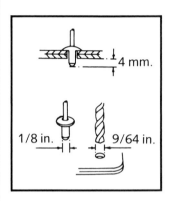

The correct selection of drill size is important: it should be 0.1mm (1/64 in) larger than the rivet. (Figures courtesy of Sykes-Pickavant)

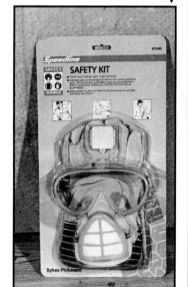

Arc, MIG and spot welding

Although, to be honest, the plasma cutter is only really relevant to the car restorer, it's worth looking at. Here is one of the latest developments in arc 'welding' technology. Costs of the smaller models such as the SIP Cutmaster 25 have fallen to the level where the keen restoration enthusiast who intends carrying out more than one job could afford to buy one.

It's only a few short years ago that the only way of cutting and welding steel was with messy and relatively dangerous oxy-acetylene welding. Now there's electric arc and MIG and spot welding and even electric cutting: quick, clean and efficient and best of all, affordable to the keen DIYer. For a combination of quality and economy, the smaller SIP unit shown here takes some beating!

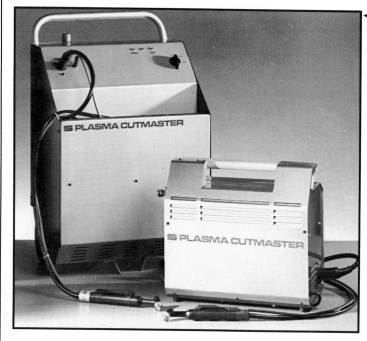

◀ **AMS1**
Plasma cutters demand coupling to a compressor to supply cooling air to the torch and cutting area. This cuts down significantly on distortion. Conveniently, the jet of plasma, which carries out the cutting operation, is also formed from air; no special gases here!

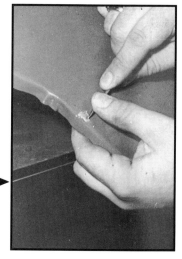

AMS3
Once you start (note gloves and goggles), cutting is amazingly quick and clean. Edges are clean and the torch moves almost as quickly as your hand will let it.

AMS2 ▶
Because electrical contact is needed, it is best to start cutting on a piece of paint-free metal with the smaller models.

AMS4 ▶
However, most of us are more interested in the practicalities of MIG welding. This Golf owner studies the 'MIG Welding Step by Step' handbook that accompanies his SIP MigMate.

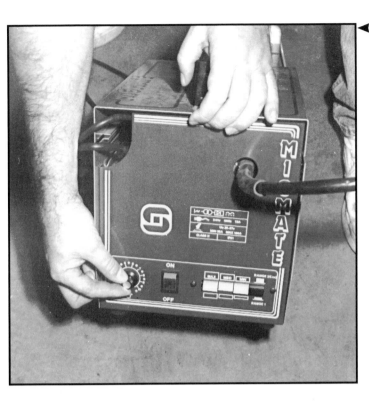

AMS5
Settings couldn't be simpler. There's a button, far right, relating to the type of gas you use (CO$_2$ or Argon-mix); three settings: 'Max', 'Med', 'Min'; and a wire feed setting being adjusted here. On later models, separate settings for Argon-mix and CO$_2$ have been deleted; SIP have found them to be unnecessary.

If you try MIG welding in windy conditions, the shielding gas, which is supposed to surround the weld, will be blown away leaving a weak and truly horrible looking weld. Weld indoors or put a wind shield around the weld area.

AMS6 ▶
Most DIYer's are happy to use the small disposable gas canisters shown here which are available from many DIY and auto accessory outlets. If you give the machine a lot of use, save money by obtaining a large cylinder from one of the major gas companies.

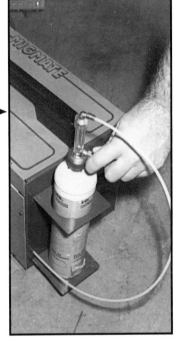

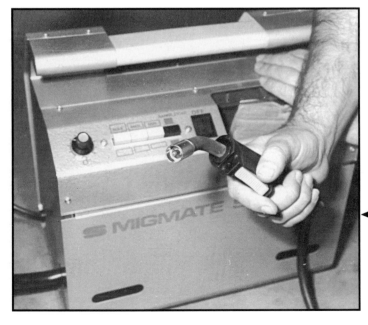

◀ **AMS7**
In the background, the British-made MigMate Super. Welding wire appears out of the end of the torch when the trigger is squeezed and that's where welding takes place.

Arc, MIG and spot welding

You'll probably find it easiest to hold the torch at the angle shown and move it steadily in the direction indicated. (Figure courtesy of SIP

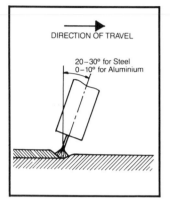

DIRECTION OF TRAVEL

20–30° for Steel
0–10° for Aluminium

◄ AMS8
After a little experimentation, the correct settings will be very quickly established. Tack-weld your two work pieces together at regularly spaced intervals then go back to the start and run a continuous seam weld, end to end. It has to be the simplest form of welding!

AMS9
You can even plug-spot weld two pieces of steel together. Drill a 3mm (1/8 in) hole through the top sheet, then weld down to the sheet beneath, 'plugging' the hole.
▼

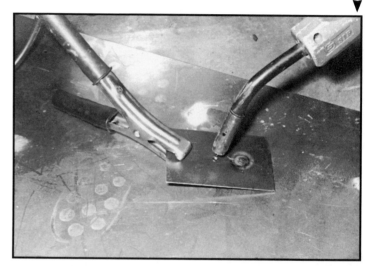

AMS10
The wire feed mechanism inside the machine. Wire is pushed along the feed pipe by the two rollers being pointed out here. Shielding gas (see pipes on left) travels along the same pipe.
▼

AMS11 ▶
Disposable cartridges of shielding gas; varying types, thicknesses and quantities of welding wire; gauges and fittings, all available from SIP.

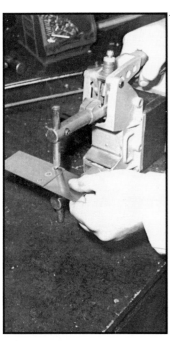

◄ AMS12
Spot welders, or 'resistance welders', fuse the metal only in the immediate area affected by the points of the spot welding arms. There is thus virtually no distortion whatsoever.

AMS13
The spot weld will only be weak if the current is not passed for long enough: test every now and again by trying to lever a spot weld apart. ▼

One of the smaller SIP spot welders also has a timer which consistently regulates the duration of the spot weld. It automatically compensates for slight rusting, paint residues and zinc coatings for best results.

◄ AMS14
The weld will also be weak if too much power has been passed, blowing a hole through the metal. The Automatic SIP model virtually refuses to do this, even when provoked!

AMS15 ►
Manufacturers put cars together almost entirely with spot welds. But access is easy on the production line; repairers can call on a variety of extension arms to help them get round obstacles.

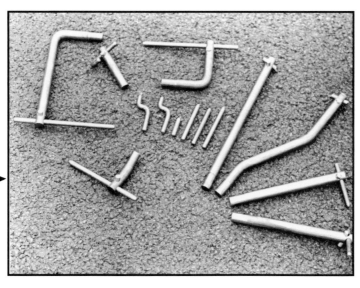

Arc, MIG and spot welding

'Strike an arc' by either stroking the end of the rod on the work piece or strike a hard blow with the end of the rod allowing it to bounce up to the correct distance away. It must be said that the procedure takes more practice than for MIG welding. Another problem is that you can't arc weld really thin sheet steel but the cost of the welders themselves start at less than half the price of a MIG.

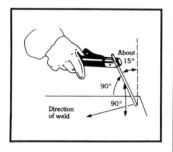

◄ AMS16
Current settings are easily controlled by using the sliding scale on Weldmate models.

AMS17
As with MIG, you have to tack weld first. The slag which forms on the top of an arc weld has to be carefully and meticulously chipped away using the chipping hammer which SIP thoughtfully provide. ▼

AMS18
A full seam weld can then be run from one end of the joint to the other. ▼

◄ AMS19
The layer of slag should chip away smoothly and cleanly. Erratic rod movements will introduce slag into the weld and weaken the joint.

◄ AMS20
All SIP welders come with full instructions to assist you in getting started. This one is also equipped with a carbon-arc brazing kit.

AMS21
The carbon-arc rods create a heat-only arc which heats the metal and melts the brazing rod held in the hand. This enables the arc welder to successfully braze-weld thin sheet steel. It's not suitable for repairing major structural components. ▼

Safety
Gloves should be worn when welding. The UV rays given off can be a health hazard and hot metal can burn! Sleeves should also be rolled down. It is **vital** that a full face mask is used at all times. Looking at a weld with the naked eye can cause an extremely painful eye condition short term; permanent eye damage long term. Keep children, onlookers and pets away. Looking through the safety glass provided rapidly becomes second nature.

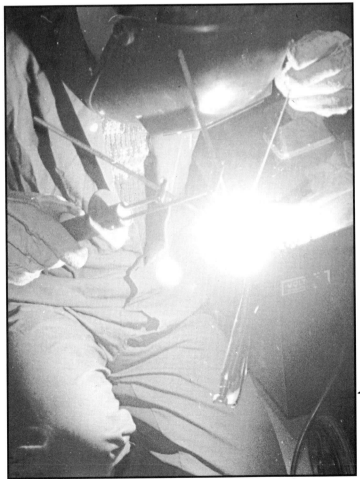

◄ AMS22
Repairing a stripped-down car door with carbon-arc brazing. Use of full head shield is essential because both hands are otherwise employed.

Power tools

We are only concerned here with tools that will help you 'improve and modify' your Golf/Jetta, but it's worth bearing in mind when selecting power tools that they can be put to other uses around the home. For instance, the Workmate 2 can be fitted with a circular saw and router table as an accessory, while the cordless tools shown, and the others in the huge Black & Decker range that we haven't considered here, are a boon for using all over the workshop, house or garden without having to worry about making the trailing lead reach far enough.

The range of power tools available to the DIY enthusiast has expanded greatly in recent years while old favourites, such as electric drills and jigsaws, have a far wider range of features not available in the old days. Black & Decker, probably the best known name in power tools the world over, are at the forefront in developments and we show several of their tools that relate to work carried out in this book.

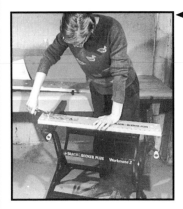

◀ **PT1**
Frankly, the Workmate is the sort of tool that, once you've got it, becomes the focal point for all your workshop activities. You can cover it in a cloth and respray small items, recondition engine components on it, varying the working height to suit yourself, or even use it as a vice when drilling or sawing. This new Workmate is shown being spannered together, following the simple instructions enclosed, although the winding screw assembly caused a little hard thought!

PT3
The Black & Decker 'Proline' drill (left) is designed to operate under the toughest of conditions and will last the DIYer for many years to come although its price reflects its 'professional' label. It's light and well balanced in use. The SR 910 RT, illustrated top-right, has a two-speed gearbox, electronic speed adjuster, ½ inch chuck, hammer attachment and reverse. The torque control allows you to drive in or remove screws and there's a depth stop incorporated. Its sheer size might be a problem in some tight locations, but its capabilities are awesome! Finally, there's the Cordless reversible screwdriver drill which has power for any drilling application up to 5/16 inch. In the background are some of the twist drill sets available from Black & Decker.

PT4
A cordless jigsaw (left), shown with charging pack, gives more versatility. The multi-speed power jigsaw has a pendulum action blade, which means that the blade swings forwards on the upwards cutting stroke for extra cutting power. The dust extractor has adaptors which connect to your domestic vacuum cleaner. Black & Decker also produce a full range of blades.

▲
PT2
The rearmost part of the table clips on to the base in one of three alternative positions, allowing you to clamp various widths or to support quite wide workpieces.

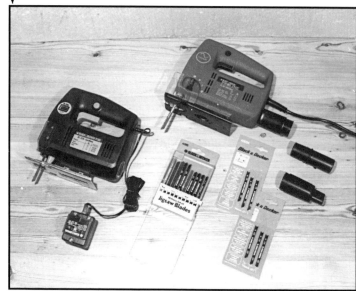

◄ PT5
Anyone tackling car bodywork repair or improvement should really consider investing in a mini-grinder. On the right is the Black & Decker PL80 4½ inch Sander/Grinder, 'Proline' tool, made to work hard for long periods of time at cutting, grinding or sanding steel or filler. On the left is the LUM sander and polisher. This enables you to sand, or polish paintwork to professional standards of finish with the lambswool polishing mop fitted.

Tools that were once purely the province of the professional are now within the price range of the keen DIYer. New technology has meant that, as features offered are on the increase, prices in real terms have fallen. The use of professional-quality tools makes it possible for the home enthusiast to achieve professional standards, saving on the cost of paying someone else to do the job and more than offsetting the cost in tools and equipment.

◄ PT6
The Black & Decker 180E Variable Speed Sander allows you to sand filler (or wood and plaster) at a rapid 11,000 orbits per minute, while slowing down to 6,500 orbits per minute for paintwork. '1/3 sheet' sanding papers are clipped to the front of the sander, after opening the paper clamp. Then, the clamp lever is returned to the 'closed' position . . .

PT7 ►
. . . and the paper folded round the sanding bed and clamped in similar fashion at the rear.

PT8 ►
The punched holes enable the bulk of the dust created by the sander to be sucked out through the outlet on the rear of the sander body. The dust-extracter is connected to your domestic vacuum cleaner via the adaptor provided.

Power tools

Sanding dust in the air can create a health hazard. It may not be necessary to wear a face mask if an extractor system is fitted, especially if your domestic vacuum cleaner is powerful enough to take away the bulk of the dust but, if your sander is not equipped for dust extraction, or if the substance you are sanding, such as glass fibre, presents a health hazard in itself, you should then **always** wear a mask.

PT9 ▶

The random orbit sander is wonderful for carrying out bodywork preparation! The sanding head spins in the normal way, but the spindle itself also rotates through a small circle. This enables the benefit of scratch-free sanding to be carried out. If you try sanding filler or paintwork with an ordinary sanding pad, circular scuff marks would be certain to show through the paint finish. Sanding is also carried out far more quickly than if the job was done by hand, to the extent that what would take days by elbow power, takes just a couple of hours using electric power.

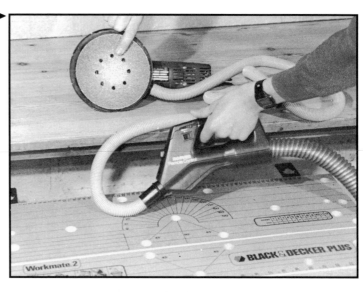

◀ **PT10**

In the background you can see the random orbit sander still connected to the dust extraction system. The sanding discs used are standard self-adhesive discs and, to allow the extraction system to operate, these have to be punched with holes. Black & Decker supply a pair of steel plates which locate against one another with the sanding disc popped between.

PT11

When you push through each hole in the plates with the cutter provided, using a slight twist of the wrist, a neat hole is punched in the sanding disc. It only takes a few moments, but it would probably encourage more people to use the excellent dust extraction system if Black & Decker were to make pre-punched discs available.

▼

PT12 ▶

Another Black & Decker sanding option is the Palm Grip Sander, a Proline tool designed for one-hand operation and very 'handy' (oh dear!) for smaller sanding jobs. The face mask is part of the Sykes-Pickavant 'Safety' kit shown earlier and 'seals' around the mouth much more efficiently than those with an aluminium backing plate.

On this page we start work on a project that cuts across several of the items in this Chapter. Fitting a power bulge to a bonnet involves the use of power tools, glass fibre and filler, some hand tools and the use of a wide range of aerosol spray paints.

PT13 ▶
The Black & Decker Powerfile makes short work of materials as hard as wood and steel. Fitted with bench stand and grinding stop and clamped to the Workmate, Powerfile doubles up as an excellent tool sharpener.

◀ **PT14**
The heat gun was shown in Chapter One helping to remove old styling stripes, but around the home its versatility extends to paint stripping, moulding plastics, soldering pipe joints or even lighting the barbecue!

PT16
After drilling a hole slightly wider than the blade, the Black & Decker jigsaw was used to good effect. This isn't the scrolling saw, so on tight corners it was necessary to do a couple of 'three point turns' to get round without the blade binding in the sheet steel.

PT15
Here's the power bulge that we fitted to our bonnet. After drawing around it, another line was drawn a **little** way in to allow for the width of the flange on the power bulge.
▼

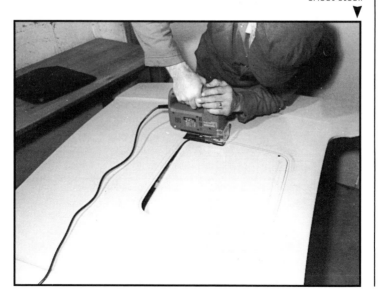

Fitting a power bulge to a bonnet may be necessary if you fit a taller carburettor - or even a taller engine! It can assist in heat extraction when a highly-tuned engine produces excessive heat, or you might find that the power bulge is an interesting visual modification in itself.

Power tools

Workmate 2 makes an ideal workbench for this sort of project. The jaws can be opened wide giving a stable support with enough room between them for the saw blade to pass with ease.

◀ PT17
Cutting out sheet steel with the jigsaw demands the use of the correct blade, but gives one of the cleanest types of cut in sheet steel.

PT18 ▶
The Black & Decker sanding disc attachment and medium grit sandpaper were fitted to the drill and used to clean paint from around the hole.

PT19
The bonnet was turned over and, after drilling pilot holes, the power bulge was screwed down using self-tapping screws. The Black & Decker cordless screwdriver SC450 provided an incredibly quick and easy way of driving the self-tapping screws fully home.
▼

PT20
We wanted to protect the edges of the power bulge so strips of masking tape were positioned all the way round it.
▼

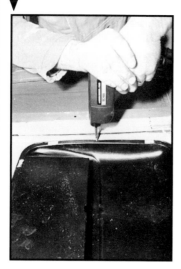

Working with filler and glass fibre

Blending in with resin, mat and filler

We chose Plastic Padding products for this part of the work, partly because they are readily available from just about any auto accessory shop and in quantities which are just sufficient for projects of this size, and also because Plastic Padding type Elastic filler is noted for its ability to flex and to withstand shock and vibration without cracking or coming adrift.

Weight for weight, glass fibre is stronger than steel and yet is far easier to work with. It can be persuaded to adopt any shape that you wish and yet bonds with great tenacity. Its close cousin, body filler, is the perfect medium for filling gaps and smoothing out imperfections to give a perfect finish.

FF1 ▶
This is part of the large Plastic Padding range and it's worth mentioning that they also sell aerosol cans of Stonechip Protect for spraying onto sills, valances and other vulnerable areas.

FF2
You won't get in too much of a mess if you carry out work in the right order. Cut strips of glass fibre mat to the width and length required before mixing the resin.

▼

FF3 ▶
Add the recommended amount of hardener with the resin in a suitable container (this is the lid from the tin of Plastic Padding filler) and stir thoroughly until the hardener is well mixed.

◀ FF4
Brush resin generously onto the areas to receive the glass fibre. Don't brush it out like paint; leave enough to soak into the mat.

Blending in with resin, mat and filler

Resin will come off hands after a generous application of hand cleaner, although it's best to use a barrier cream first as well. Alternatively, use disposable plastic gloves or even plastic bags tied around the wrists.

◄ FF5
Place the mat in position and add more resin. You're now at stage one, where you need to add a fairly generous amount of resin to break down the bonding agent in the mat allowing it to go floppy.

◄ FF6
After you've 'wetted-out' all of the mat, go back and stipple it vigorously with a brush. It will then follow the contours of the panel beneath, taking on its shape and the removal of any air bubbles will add strength.

FF7 ►
The SP craft knife comes in handy for removing any excess glass fibre but only if you catch the glass fibre **after** it has ceased to be 'wet', and before it sets hard.

FF8 ►
When the glass fibre has gone hard, the Black & Decker angle grinder comes into its own, but be careful not to go right through! You will see on page 210 that the Plastic Padding hardener is yellow in colour. If the resin and the glass fibre are yellow all through, this shows that you've mixed the resin thoroughly.

FF9 ▶
All glass fibre dust can be harmful if inhaled during sanding, and therefore you should always wear goggles and a face mask during grinding or sanding operations. This is the SP kit featured earlier.

If you find that you need more resin or more hardener separately (although you shouldn't if you use it in the proportions recommended by Plastic Padding), there are individual cans of resin available in various sizes from your auto accessory shop.

◀ **FF10**
Being determined to obtain a good finish underneath the bonnet as well as on top, we spread a layer of Plastic Padding type Elastic filler over the glass fibre and then sanded it smooth before painting it.

FF11 ▶
On the top side, the protruding self-tapping screws were trimmed by fitting a cutting wheel to the Black & Decker angle grinder. Plastic Padding recommend cutting off any resin that may have oozed through with a craft knife before it goes too hard. If left until later it would have to be ground away.

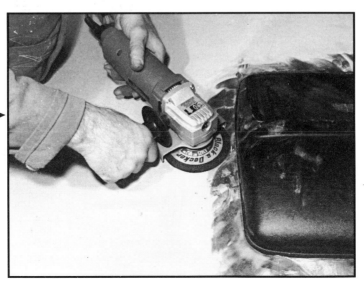

Filler 'goes off' (sets) by chemical reaction. The warmer the weather, the quicker the reaction and the less hardener you need; the colder the weather, the more hardener needed.

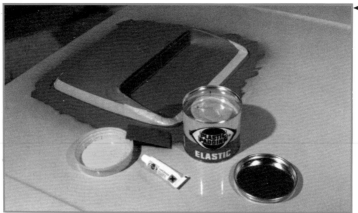

◀ FF12
Plastic Padding type Elastic comes in a tube or in a tin with its own spreader and sufficient hardener for the filler in that particular pack.

FF13 ▶
Take a piece of clean card, scoop out sufficient filler and squeeze on top as much hardener as you will need. Don't get hardener into the open tin nor, if you can help it, on your fingers since it can be toxic. Later, always wash hands thoroughly before eating or smoking.

Plastic Padding also produce aerosol Stonechip Protect for protecting sills, spoilers and the undersides of panels vulnerable to stone chipping.

◀ FF14
Again, the Plastic Padding trick of including a strongly coloured hardener pays off because you can see clearly when the pigmented hardener has been mixed thoroughly with the filler.

FF15 ▶
Carefully spread filler into the joint, leaving it very slightly proud but not so high that you have an enormous amount of sanding to do. Plastic Padding filler has the great advantage that it sands particularly easily giving a smooth finish. After sanding, you will invariably find a few dips and hollows which will have to be filled with a further application of filler.

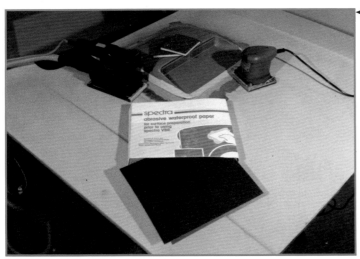

◄ PP1
As well as the aerosol paint itself, Spectra produce a whole range of ancillaries such as abrasive paper for rubbing down.

Aerosol paint is the ideal way of spraying anything up to a single panel at a time. After all, you don't need to buy any expensive equipment, only the can that the paint comes in.

◄ PP2
The Spectra 'wet-or-dry' paper was used with water to feather out the Plastic Padding filler, which left no trace of a hard edge.

PP3 ►
Before starting to spray, the Spectra primer was taken outside, shaken vigorously, and the nozzle cleared.

PP4 ►
The can was held about six inches away and red oxide primer sprayed onto the bare metal.

Spraying with aerosol

Illustration PP9 shows why it's essential to shake an aerosol paint can for several minutes before using it. The agitator ball has the job of mixing the paint pigment, which may be quite thick at the bottom, thoroughly with the solvent. In very cold weather you may also have to immerse the can in warm (not boiling) water for several minutes before use. Never puncture an aerosol can nor expose it to direct heat.

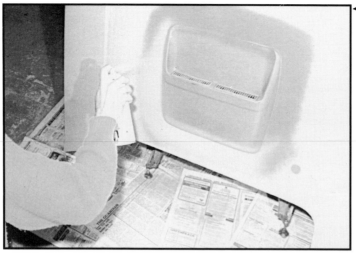

PP5
This was magic! (or at least, the results of sanding it later, were). Spectra High Build Spray Putty was sprayed onto the whole area . . .

PP6
. . . and then, extending a little wider than the area of the original red oxide primer, a second coat of spray putty was applied after the first had dried.

PP7
It's best to practice your spraying on a spare scrap of sheet steel. Hold the can too close and the paint will run; too far away and you'll have a 'dry' looking finish.

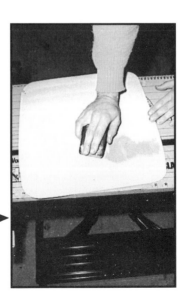

PP8 ▶
Very slight runs may be polished out but most will have to be sanded out when the paint is dry using fine wet-or-dry paper.

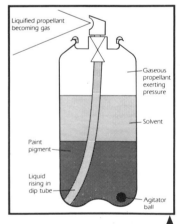

Liquified propellant becoming gas

Gaseous propellant exerting pressure

Solvent

Paint pigment

Liquid rising in dip tube

Agitator ball

PP9
How an aerosol works. If you tip the can upside down, the paint flow ceases. At the end of spraying, use this technique to clear the nozzle.

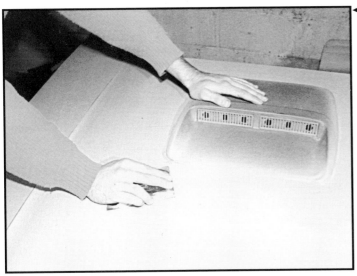

◄ PP10
Provided that the filler work was carried out properly, the use of High Build Spray Putty will allow you to remove every last blemish when you sand it out with fine wet-or-dry paper supported on a flat rubbing block.

When choosing your primer colour, go for red for dark shades, grey for lighter coats, and grey or preferably white for white top coats and metallics.

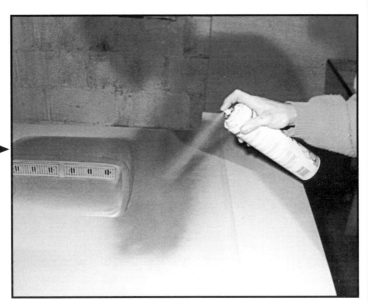

PP11 ►
By now, and for no apparent reason, we were working with the bonnet laid horizontal. We chose to spray on grey primer paint as a barrier colour between the yellow and the white top coat to follow. Red and yellow have a nasty habit of 'grinning through' white surface coats above them.

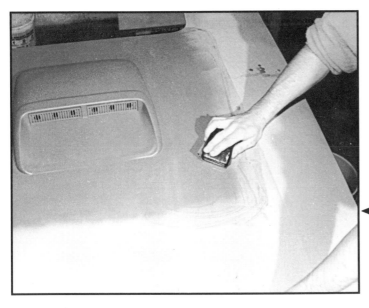

◄ PP12
Plenty of water, a few spots of washing up liquid, the finest grade of Spectra wet-or-dry and the final primer coat was prepared for finish painting.

One of the main reasons we chose Spectra for this part of the book was because their aerosol paint containers are specially designed not to clog and or spit blobs of paint onto the work. There's nothing more frustrating!

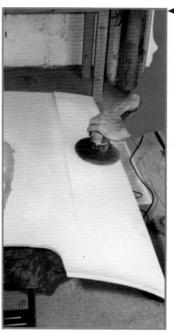

◄ PP13
To digress for a moment, the preparation of a large flat area can take quite a long time by hand. This is where the Black & Decker random orbit sander (see earlier item) was particularly useful.

PP14 ►
Now here's a tip from the experts. Holding a tin of black spray paint about a foot or more away from the job, a light coat was dusted onto the work.

PP15 ►
The idea is not to change the colour of the panel but just to put an even sprinkling of paint over the whole panel.

Obtain the correct finish colour with Volkwagen's own aerosol spray paint or touch-up.

◄ PP16
Sand the entire panel all over once more with the finest grade of paper and the guide coat, as it is called, will be sanded off in all but the lowest areas. After you wipe off with a dry rag, any low spots and blemishes will stand out like a sore thumb!

◄ PP17
It might look uncomfortable, but you should always hold the nozzle down with the very tip of your finger.

PP18 ►
If you do what comes naturally, the part of your finger sticking forwards catches the edge of the spray which builds up into a drip which is then shot forwards as a blob onto your lovely handiwork. Most annoying!

You can spray the first two finish coats on in fairly quick succession, just leaving a few minutes between them for the first coat to 'flash off'. The second coat should be at right angles to the first. (Diagram courtesy of Spectra)

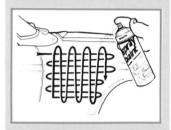

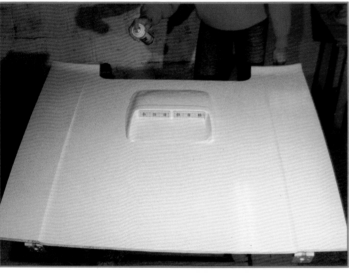

◄ PP19
The first coat was applied in regular strips up and down the bonnet, concentrating on obtaining an even coat without trying to blanket out the colour beneath. That's the way to achieve runs!

PP20 ►
The second coat, as already suggested, followed in a pattern which criss-crossed the first (see margin note), and this time the colour beneath really did disappear from view. Ideally, you may want to give another one or two coats. If any little bits of dust have landed in the surface, you may be able to polish them out with fine cutting compound, but be most careful not to go right through the paint and don't try it until the paint has had several days to dry really hard.

Using special paints

As well as the paint types already shown, Spectra also produce Extra High Gloss chrome or gold paint for customising, black heat dispersant paint for cylinder blocks, engines and exhaust systems to aid cooling and improve efficiency, and clear acrylic lacquer called 'Wheel Protector', for preventing corrosion on alloy wheels. Spectra recommend that you don't use heat dispersant paint on manifolds. The extra heat found there being just too much for it!

SP1
Some people rave over Spectras aerosol hammer finish paint. It gives an even hammer finish coat from an aerosol can without needing any primer beneath it. It also has good rust protection and easy-clean qualities.

SP2
Only the plastic components shown earlier would need plastic primer (see page 223). A second coat sprayed at right angles to the first, gives a full, even coat. Do it within a few minutes of spraying the first coat but after the first coat's solvent has 'flashed off'.

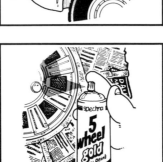

SP3
Spectra clear lacquer is a cellulose-based lacquered top seal for sealing styling stripes or for keeping the gloss on cellulose paint finishes.

SP4
Spectra wheel paints come in white, black, gold, silver and steel. You could mask off the tyre with masking tape and newspaper as shown in the drawing, or you could paint hand cleaner in a heavy layer onto the tyre before spraying on the wheel paint. As soon as the wheel paint is dry the hand cleaner can be washed off leaving the tyre good as new. For a final finish, paint with tyre wall black.

Do-it-yourself spraying

Cellulose paint is not as durable as the 2-pack paint which DIY enthusiasts must never use, but it has the virtue of being able to be sprayed on a DIY basis and it can also be polished to give the best shine of any paint.

DYP1 ▶
If many coats of paint have previously been applied, they will have to be stripped back to bare metal before being repainted. Sanding of any sort is far quicker with a random orbit sander, such as the Black & Decker electric unit shown here. This has the distinct advantage of not creating scratches which will show through the finished paintwork.

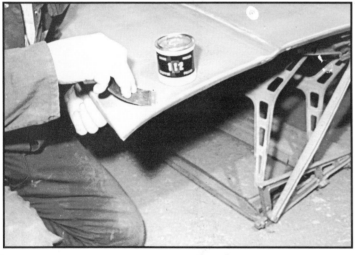

◀ DYP2
Very minor blemishes such as pin holes or scratches in the paint should be filled with a thin scrape of Valentine G112 stopper which can be sanded down after drying thoroughly.

DYP3 ▶
Hand sanding should always be carried out with the aid of a rubbing block, other than in the corners of fluted panels such as those shown here, where your fingers make an ideally shaped tool.

Safety
All filler contains skin irritants so you should wear gloves when handling them. When sanding paint or filler, particularly with a power sander, you must always wear an efficient particle mask, because otherwise the inhalation of sanding dust could damage your health. Nitro-cellulose paints, those made by Valentine for instance and shown here, are suitable for DIY work, unlike 2-pack paints which must only be used by a professional bodyshop. However, take full note of Valentine's own safety precautions and, in particular, never spray in other than a well-ventilated work area. Also, bear in mind that paint, thinners and spray vapour are all highly flammable. Do not use near flames, sparks (including those created by central heating boilers) or any naked flames.

PREPARATION

Tools required
Grinder, sander, P120 and P240 grit discs, P600 wet-or-dry paper, dust particle mask.

Materials required
197-1005 degreasing fluid (this is essential for removing silicones which will most certainly ruin the finished paint surface if allowed to remain on the work), G112 stopper.

Before using primer check the existing paint to find out whether it is compatable with cellulose. Rub a small area of paint with cellulose thinner. If the paint film dissolves go ahead; if the paint wrinkles it is affected by cellulose and will have to be sprayed all over with isolating primer 200-6 to seal it.

◄ DYP4
With no attachment on the end of the hose, you can use the SIP Airmate compressor to blow any remaining sanding dust off the panel.

DYP5
The Valentine Degreasing Fluid should have been used before you started and should now be used again to remove any traces of silicones or other grease contamination. Silicones, which are contained in all domestic polishes, cause dreadful and irremovable 'fish eye' marks in the final paint.

▼

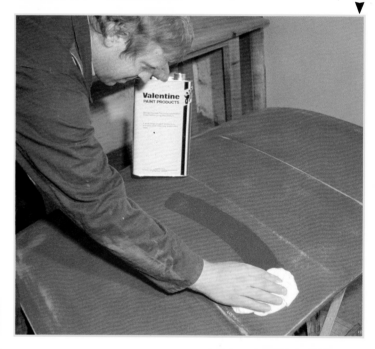

DYP6
The Cordless drill was used with a paint stirrer in the chuck to stir the Valentine Primer Filler to an even consistency. Note the steel rule placed in the pot to aid accurate measurement when thinning the paint. Go initially for 50/50 thinning, but be prepared to readjust to suit the requirements of the SIP spray gun.

▼

DYP7 ►
The SIP gun has two adjustment screws at the rear. The top one is for the width of the spray pattern, while the lower one adjusts the quantity which comes out of the gun.

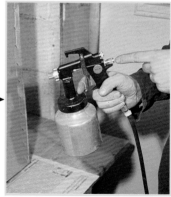

◄ DYP8
Adjust the two spray gun screws so that the spray pattern and spray density are as you require. Test it out thoroughly upon a piece of scrap board or a cardboard box.

DYP9 ►
The edge of this panel dipped away from the user so that part, the curved edge, was sprayed first. The SIP gun has a light triggering action and is easy to use.

◄ DYP10
The whole panel was painted in consistent, even bands, each one half overlapping the previous one.

DYP11 ►
The next day, after the two full coats of primer had thoroughly dried, a very light, heavily thinned coat of black paint was sprayed on with the SIP gun.

PRIMING
Tools required
Masking tape, masking paper (such as newspaper), paint strainer, SIP spray gun, SIP compressor, spray mask, tack rag.
Materials required
As well as those shown earlier and on these pages: cellulose thinner 199-207 for any additional thinning above 50/50 (don't use 199-6 thinner for more than 50/50), Valentine Red Oxide Primer.

219

Do-it-yourself spraying

TOP COAT
Tools required
The same SIP equipment and other 'hardware' as was used previously. Top coat paint must be strained. Add P1200 wet-or-dry paper and polishing compound for polishing out any dirt particles that may get into the final coat.

Materials required
Spragloss 178 solid colour paint; Spragloss thinner 199-18 (mix 50/50). For further thinning, add more 199-18 thinner.

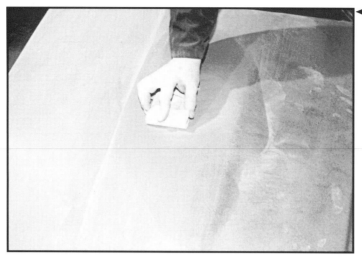

◄ **DYP12**
When the primer was 'blocked' down with medium grit paper, the thin 'guide' coat, which was sprayed on with the SIP gun (although you could have used aerosol for greater speed), was sanded off as the primer filler coat was made smooth. It remained visible in the low spots, however, picking them out.

DYP13 ►
Before spraying the top coat, wet the floor to lay the dust but take care to avoid electrical connections.

◄ **DYP14**
Use an air line to blow any dust from around the top of the tin. SIP produce a trigger operated 'air duster', if you prefer.

DYP15 ►
The Cordless drill is again used for several minutes to mix the entire contents of the Spragloss paint.

◄ DYP16
Use a steel rule ,if you haven't got the correct painter's measuring stick, to measure the correct amount of Spragloss paint and thinners.

DYP17
Pour in an equal amount of Spragloss thinner. Note: the supply of copious amounts of newspaper is essential! ▼

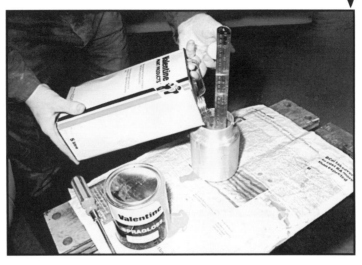

Always hold the spray gun at right angles to the surface you are painting, keeping it between six and eight inches from the car. (Diagram courtesy of Valentine)

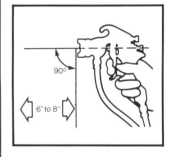

◄ DYP18
After using the Air Mate air line to blow off the panel once more, wipe it down yet again with Valentine spirit wipe ...

DYP19 ►
... followed by a wipe down with a tack rag to remove every trace of dust or dirt.

DYP20 ►
An accepted way of checking that the SIP gun is held the correct distance away (see margin note) is to use a hand span as a measure.

Keep your wrists stiff and avoid swinging the gun in an arc from your elbow, to ensure even spraying. Always spray at a steady, even pace. (Diagram courtesy of Valentine)

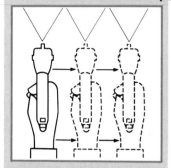

◄ DYP21
Robert started off by spraying a 'half coat' - a thin coat to aid adhesion without causing runs - sprayed in vertical, overlapping bands.

DYP22 ►
After this had 'flashed off' (ie, the thinners had evaporated), he sprayed a full coat in overlapping horizontal bands. The suspended panel reduces dirt contamination and an open door aids ventilation.

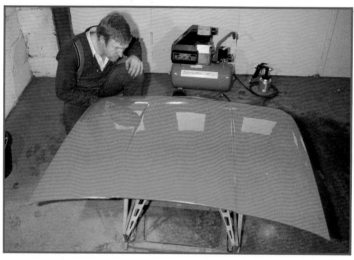

◄ DYP23
Robert surveys the wonderful depth of gloss which four coats of Valentine Spragloss solid colour had given, and proves that the DIY SIP equipment can give fully professional results.

DYP24
Valentine paints, shown here in their new livery, are professional paints perfectly suitable for the DIY enthusiast to use. Follow the safety regulations printed on every can.

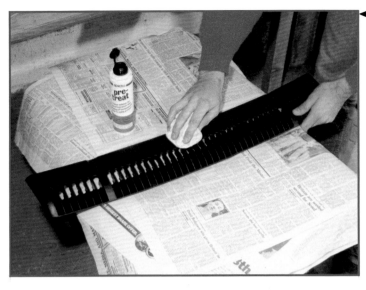

PL1
We used a Richard Grant air intake cover for the VW Golf for this section. Plastic primer treatment works just as well on any other plastic components, of course. Start by wiping over every nook and cranny with 'Pre-treat fluid' on a clean rag.

If you try spraying aerosol spray paint onto a plastic component without preparing it properly, the paint will simply peel off again very soon afterwards. Spectra produce a special plastic primer with a pre-treat solvent all in one pack. After using plastic primer, you can spray your finish coat straight on top. Aerosol tins of paint to match your car's body colour can be purchased from your VW dealer.

PL2
Shake, shake, shake, shake, shake ... Thorough mixing is absolutely essential.

PL3
The plastic primer can now be sprayed over the whole air intake cover.

PL4
Once the primer is dry, your car's body colour or any finish colour you choose can be sprayed on without fear of paint flaking off.

Bodywork preservation

Injecting rust proofing fluids

Although Volkswagen cars are far less prone to body corrosion than many other makes of car, any steel bodywork can and will eventually rust. Cars worth owning are cars worth keeping. Corroless Rust Stabilizing Cavity Wax is undoubtedly the best material available for preserving your older Golf or Jetta's bodywork. However, see page 228 regarding VW's six-year anti-rust warranty.

◄ BPR1
For enclosed bodywork sections and seams, Corroless produce their highly effective rust stabilizing cavity wax, while for exposed underbody areas and for paint chips there are other specially produced Corroless products such as Rust Stabilizing Body Primer, High Performance Finish and Stone Chip Primer.

BPR2 ▶
Each Corroless can comes with two spray nozzles. One is for injecting the fluid into enclosed sections while the other is for use as a conventional spray can.

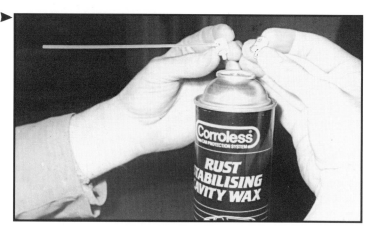

◄ BPR3
Much of the wax injection can be carried out through existing holes such as those found in the bottom of the Mk I Golf's sills.

BPR4 ▶
The only box section to be found is just rearwards of the engine bay and that too has a convenient hole at its rear end.

BPR5 ▶
Scrape heavy mud encrustations from under the front wings, then seek out strut support seams, and joints between the wing and the bodywork. You'll have to remove the plastic mud shield from underneath on later models.

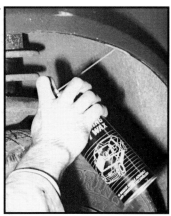

◀ BPR6
From the top side of the wing, look out for wing mounting flanges.

Corroless wax has two crucially important plus points in its favour. First, it 'creeps' particularly well, getting into spot welded seams where corrosion likes to take a hold. Second, it has unique rust **killing** qualities. Other rust proofers don't necessarily stop rusting that may have already taken a hold.

BPR7 ▶
Again, pay attention to wing-to-body mounting points and seams around the top of the strut.

◀ BPR8
Use the conventional nozzle to give a light coating inside the scuttle top.

Injecting rust proofing fluids

All rust preventatives evaporate over a period of time and 'topping them up' should be regarded as part of body maintenance. After all, bodywork is far more valuable than mechanical components, yet we think nothing of spending time and money maintaining **them.** Even Volkswagen-applied protectors harden in time, yet Corroless will creep into and seal any rust-inducing cracks or cavities. If re-treated every year your Golf or Jetta could go on and on, although it must be said that Corroless are adamant that annual retreatment is not necessary in enclosed areas.

◄ BPR9
You'll find more conveniently placed holes in bonnet strengthening rails and in the front of the bonnet in particular.

BPR10 ▶
Door bottoms have drain holes which at first should be cleared out if blocked before being injected with Corroless.

◄ BPR11
The long nozzle comes in handy for injecting more fluid into the door aperture after easing back the trim panel. Make sure that the nozzle has also found its way behind the stuck-down plastic sealing sheet behind the trim panel and that the window is wound up.

BPR12 ▶
The Golf tailgate has rubber bungs in it which can be used as convenient injection points.

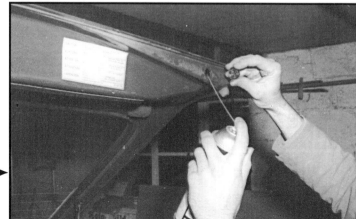

BPR13

Another pre-stamped hole is found behind a bung in the A-pillar. As you spray in the Corroless, you'll see it coming out of other holes and cracks as a light mist, showing how well it has travelled along the enclosed section.

BPR14 ▶

Another small bung which can be removed, this time in the four-door car's B-pillar.

Golfs and Jettas have more structural seams than box sections. Use your discretion: look for places in which body joints have been made and also spray the Corroless Rust Stabilizing Cavity Wax behind any chrome or body trim which could trap moisture. If you can get to the other side of the trim, spray the fluid into any fixing clip holes you come across. NEVER crawl beneath a car supported only by a jack. Use axle stands and chock wheels carefully.

BPR15 ▶

There are some places where you won't be able to inject Corroless without first drilling a hole. The Golf's inner sill is one of them. This hole would be hidden behind the carpet but if any extra holes you want to drill will show, you should buy some rubber bungs to seal them off.

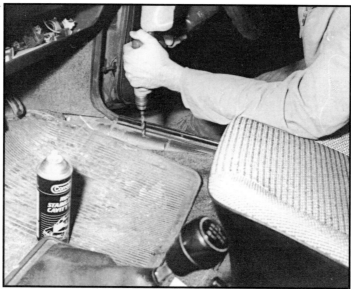

◀ **BPR16**

Why not stop the insides of wheels from going rusty by spraying them with Corroless using a conventional nozzle?

Using rust proofing primers and paints

Corroless Rust Stabilizing Body Primer contains the same amazingly effective rust killer as the Cavity Wax. By painting Corroless High Performance Finish on top, you'll give superb protection! This paint actually contains tiny glass flakes which gives it far more resilience than any conventional paint. Stones and hard objects simply bounce off! Remember that Volkswagen now has a six-year rust guarantee on new cars, so check that you are not contravening your warranty before embarking on additional protection. Check with your main dealer if your car is less than seven years old.

◀ BPR17
Rust Stabilizing Body Primer is just sprayed on in the conventional way after removing any loose paint or grease from the surface.

BPR18 ▶
Leave masking paper in place before brushing on the High Performance Finish but peel off before the paint has dried hard.

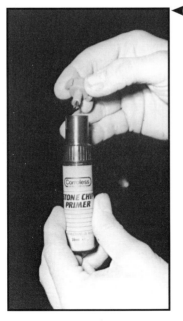

◀ BPR19
Stone Chip Primer comes complete with a tiny wire brush in the lid. Use it for cleaning loose rust out of a stone chip ...

BPR20 ▶
... before touching-in the Corroless Primer with the fine brush provided. Use Volkswagen's body colour on top for a perfect finish.

Chapter Six
Golf development

Golf development

1975

Six models - UK imports commenced: Golf N and L in three and five-door form; S and LS models with five doors only. Engines: N/L 1093cc/50bhp, S/LS 1471cc/70bhp. Brakes disc/drum all models. Wheels/tyres: N/L 4½Jx13 inch with crossply tyres; S/LS 5Jx13 inch with 155R13 radials. N/S rubber floormats, two-speed wipers, electric screenwash, heater fan, glovebox, folding rear seat back, luggage compartment cover. L/LS as N/S plus carpet replacing rubber mats, fully reclining seats, heated rear window, clock, temperature gauge, two-speed heater fan, cigarette lighter, lockable glove box lid, tunnel tray, armrests.

1976

Engine: S/LS new 1588cc/75bhp. Radial tyres, heated rear window and reclining front seats now standard on all models. LS now has rev counter.

1977

Base model designated 'Golf', N-designation deleted, the six models now Golf/L/GLS, each in three- and five-door form. Engines: Golf/L 1093cc/50bhp, GLS 1588cc/75bhp. Golf as N plus anti-dazzle rear view mirror, two-speed wipers, three-speed heater fan, gas strut on tailgate, added trim items. L: additional exterior trim and interior passenger equipment (grab handles, ashtrays, etc), intermittent wash/wipe operation. GLS as LS; plus tinted glass, halogen headlights, rear window wash/wipe, chrome hubcaps, higher quality carpet and upholstery, centre instrument console. Golf

By Peter Dickinson of VW Motoring magazine

The Golf family is as much a world car as its predecessor, the Beetle. The main difference between the two is that, while the Beetle evolved over a number of years, and was found to be suitable for so many diverse climates, the Golf was **planned and designed** that way.

Within three weeks of taking over the top job at Volkswagen Ag in October 1971, Rudolf Leiding scrapped five years of intensive development on what was to have been a Beetle replacement.

This left Volkswagen urgently in need of a replacement for the replacement. Another small/medium car scheme was already on the drawing board, along with two newly styled bodies from Ital Design - A square, 4/5 seat hatchback and a 2×2 coupe. These were rapidly and intensively developed into two completely new cars, the Golf and the Scirricco, both announced in 1974.

The Golf was available in three-door or five-door versions and there were, initially, four models; Golf N, Golf L, Golf S and Golf LS. The N and L models were powered by a new 1093 cc, 50 bhp engine, while S and LS models had the 1471 cc 70 bhp engine from the Audi/VW parts bin. The larger-engined cars were also available with automatic transmission.

Both Golf engines were essentially similar in design, four-cylinder, in-line units, with the crankshaft running in five main bearings. Cylinder heads were cast in aluminium, with overhead camshafts driven by a toothed belt from the crankshaft.

The differences lay in the valve gear; the camshaft in the 1471 cc engine operated via bucket tappets, with adjustment effected by shims machined to very fine tolerances, while the arrangement on the small engines was to have the valves opened by cam followers supported on fulcrum bolts with self-locking threads and a central recess, into which an Allen key could be inserted for adjustment purposes;

Ancillary drives differed, too. The oil pump, fuel pump and distributor were driven, on the 1471 engine, by an intermediate shaft at the top of the block, powered by the camshaft belt; while the water pump was conventionally driven from the crankshaft-driven vee-belt which also drove the alternator.

The arrangement for the 1093 cc unit was to drive the oil pump directly from the crankshaft. The fuel pump was operated by a cam and lever from the camshaft, with the distributor being directly driven off the end of it. The water pump was in the cylinder block, driven by the camshaft belt, and cleverly arranged so that it was also used as the belt tensioner.

The east-west transverse engine mounting was similar to that of the Minis, but VW chose to mount the gearbox, more conventionally, on the end of the engine, with the final drive located in the rear side of the transmission casing.

The clutch was the usual single dry plate type, but actuating mechanisms differed between the two engines. The smaller engine had the normal fork/thrust bearing method, while that of the 1471 cc was operated by a pushrod down the hollow gearbox mainshaft, not unlike the method found on some motorcycle clutches.

Power eventually reached the front wheels through unequal length driveshafts, fitted with constant-velocity joints at each end, the inner mounting onto a flange from the final drive, the outer terminating in a short splined stub axle. This fitted through the wheel-carrying hub, and was very firmly fixed by a self-locking nut which, for obvious reasons, was used only once.

◄ **D7.1**
Though UK registered, this Golf appears to be one of the first built and is in left-hand drive form.

Suspension for the front wheels was by MacPherson strut, fixed directly to the inner wings at the top, and located at the bottom by a wishbone. Light, precise steering was afforded by a rack-and-pinion steering box, and the suspension/steering geometry included a negative offset feature. This system ensured that the car would pull up in a straight line if, for example, a front tyre burst, or if an emergecy stop had to be made on road surfaces with different friction coefficients (eg, dry road/icy gutter). Nowadays, all VWs are made this way.

At the rear, similar coil-spring-over-damper struts were used, mounted on the 'free' ends of trailing arms. However, these were augmented by a T-section torsion beam fixed between the pivoted ends of the trailing arms, designed to give a stabilising effect, especially under cornering loads.

Braking on all of the 1500s was by front discs and rear drums, with servo assistanec. 1100 Golfs in Germany were all-drum, unless specified otherwise, although UK-bound models had the disc/drum set-up, apart from a few early examples, without the benefit of a servo. The braking was split diagonally into two hydraulic circuits, and the handbrake was cable operated, acting on the two rear wheels.

The Golf was, in effect, a small, strong box, based on the firewall, inner wings and engine mounting subframe, which carried all the front suspension, drive and steering stresses, and also a large proportion of the braking stresses. This box effectively towed the passenger-carrying box along behind it, along with the rear suspension, supporting the rear end.

This allowed the building of a light car (the original basic Golf tipped the scales well under 1,700 lbs), while safety was not compromised. Front and rear crumple zones were incorporated into the design, with a rigid passenger 'safety cell'. Additionally, the fuel tank was fitted in a safe area ahead of the rear axle, and the jointed steering column collapsed on impact, with additional driver safety coming from a deformable steering wheel. The dashboard and instrument panel were padded for crash protection, and the seats were themselves strong, and strongly mounted.

Overall, VW had come up with a formula that produced a roomy 4/5 seat passenger car, powered by engines of relatively small swept volume, but designed and engineered to give good handling and good performance, while remaining economy-conscious and inexpensive to service and repair. That this formula was right was borne out by the fact that the first million Golfs were sold in just 31 months.

With the success of the Golf assured, VW's fortunes took a turn for the better, and they enthusiastically went ahead, in 1978, with the development of a 'new' Golf, which made its debut in 1983. While it was a derivation of, and improvement on, the original Golf, it was, at the same time, a completely new car. VW had asked no less than ten design houses, to tender designs, but wound up using their own in-house offering.

Although the 'Born Again' Golf had been completely redesigned from the ground up, the initial response from the world's press, and the general public, was that the car was too close in appearance to the old car - which had, in fact, been the intention all along. That the new had been sired by the old was obvious; at a quick glance, the one could be mistaken for the other. Only by examining the new car closely could the differences be detected.

Golf 2 was bigger, in all directions. The wheelbase was increased by three inches, and overall length by six and a half inches, with just over two inches more width. The

1977 (continued)
Diesel announced, one model, LD. Engine: 1471cc/50bhp Diesel.

1978
Ten models: Golf/L/LS/GLS, three- or five-door; LD/GTi three-door only. Engine: LS/GLS new 1457cc/70bhp. All models: single-hand operable inertia-reel seat belts, brake warning light standard. L: plus adjustable head restraints. LS: plus rear wash/wipe, halogen headlights, rev counter.

1979
Nine models: Golf/L/GL, three- and five-door; LD/GLS five-door only; GTi three-door only. Engine: GL 1093cc/50bhp. All models: rear wash/wipe. GL/GLS: driver's door mirror adjustable from inside.

1980
Eleven models: Golf/L/LS/GLS, three- and five-door; LD/GLS Automatic five-door only; GTi three-door only. Engine: LS/GLS new 1272cc/60bhp, GLS Auto 1457cc/70bhp. All models: rear foglight.

1981
Eight models: Golf three-door only; L/LD/LS/LS Auto/GLS/GLS Auto five-door only; GTi three-door only. Engine: LS Auto/GLS/GLS Auto 1457cc/70bhp, LD new 1588cc/54bhp Diesel. All models: laminated windscreen, driver's shelf, anti-dazzle instruments, temperature gauge now standard. New facia layout. L/LS/LD: plus redesigned warning light layout, choke warning light (L/LS only), digital clock trip recorder, panel light rheostat, rev counter (not LD). GLS: with 4+E gearbox option.

1982
Six models: C three-door only; C Diesel/CL/GL/GL Auto five-door only; GTi three-door only. C as 1981 Golf; CL as 1981 LS; GL/GL

D7.2 ▶
The Caddy started life as the Rabbit Pick-up and is now also manufactured in Hungary.

1982 (continued)

Auto as 1981 GLS/GLS Auto; C/C Diesel as Golf plus halogen headlights; CL as LS plus locking glove box; GL as GLS plus headlamp washers, front door pockets, front armrests with integrated grab handles, twin-tone horn, colour-matched upholstery.

1983

Six models. All models: passenger door mirror now standard. GL: plus interior-adjustable door mirrors, upholstered door panels.

1985

Golf 2. Eight models: Golf/C/C Formel E/C Diesel/CL/GL/GL Auto/GTi; Golf/C/GTi three-door, all others five-door. Engine: Golf new 1043cc/45bhp; C/CL/C Formel E new 1272cc/55bhp; GL new 1595cc/75bhp; C Diesel 1588cc/54bhp. 4+E gearbox standard in all models except base and C models. Golf includes laminated windscreen, halogen headlights, heated rear window, hazard/reverse/parking/ rear fog lights, two-speed wipers, electric washers, plastic shields in front wheelarches, locking petrol cap, driver's door mirror, cloth upholstery and door panels, carpets, reclining front seats, folding rear seat, front/rear seat belts, three-speed heater fan, mono radio preparation with two speakers and aerial. C: plus rear window wash/wipe, intermittent wipe and automatic wash/wipe on front, passenger door mirror, front adjustable head restraints, luggage compartment cover, stereo radio preparation with four speakers and aerial, Blaupunkt radio fitted. CL as C plus exterior chrome trim and rubber bump strips, front door pockets,

D7.3
All Golf Convertibles are built at Karmann, not at the main VW factory and are based on the Mk I body shell.

similarity to Golf 1 was maintained with the wide C-pillars, stubby appearance and the square, boxy-looking shape, though now with the addition of some subtle curves, as well as a little rake in the front panel.

The space inside was significantly larger, for example by clever re-designing of the door trim panels, the interior elbow room was significantly increased by four and a half inches in the rear seats. There was also extra space fore-and-aft, with an additional inch and a half between the pedals and the rear seat giving much more legroom in the back. The boot benefitted by an additionally 30 per cent though there was no alteration made to the quite high lip, over which boot-bound items had to be lifted. In addition to the facility to fold the rear seat forward, there was a specification option on most models of a rear seat back with a one-third/two-thirds split, giving extra load space **and** passenger carrying capability.

The new car was not without its controversies, though. The increased boot space was partly due to a weirdly-shaped 12 gallon fuel tank, which had literally been designed around the rear suspension and underfloor and was made of plastic. That was all right, but the spare wheel well had been designed for one of the then-new 'spacesaver' wheels, which are still not wholly accepted by many in the UK. In the event of specifying a full-size spare, which made a hump in the floor, the production and fitting of a matching floor mat was necessary.

The instrument panel and fascia were very similar to the 1983 Golf 1, but the heater behind was very different. An air-blending type, meaning that the temperature was regulated by the mixing of heated and unheated air, made for a quicker response to the levers, all in the cause of passenger comfort. The disappointing bit, however, was the fact that there was no facility for cold air from the facia vents while hot air came from the footwells, which many people like to have. The occupants could have all hot air, or all cold; a situation which still remains at the time of writing.

Overall the interior trim was more luxurious, even the basic model having cloth door trim with moulded armrests, provision for radio or stereo systems, depending on model, with the front speakers in the top corners of the facia. Padded steering wheels, a storage shelf and passenger grab handles made it a far cry from the basic Golf of 1975.

The suspension layout was the same, with the track widened for the bigger car,. The significant improvement at the front was that the front lower wishbones were now mounted on a front subframe, rather than directly to the bodyshell.

At the rear, wheel travel was extended, the rear torsion bar was changed to V-section from the previous T-section, and toe-in compensating rubber bushes were used. This system made the Golf 2's cornering ability even more precise than its predecessor.

The disc/drum braking set-up was maintained, but they were much improved, having more 'feel' and requiring less pedal effort, something which Golf owners had been waiting for years.

Engines and transmissions were all new, starting with a 1043cc/45 bhp unit and going up through 1272/55 bhp, 1595cc/75 bhp to the 1781cc/112 bhp engine of the GTi, with the 1588cc/54 bhp diesel engine on the side. The new engines all had high compression ratios, although the smaller engines ran on two-star fuel, and the injected 1800 engine used four-star. All the engines' tuning was biased towards fuel economy and good mid-range toruque.

Standard transmission fittings were four-speed gearboxes for 1043 and 1272 models,

4E gearboxes for the diesel, 1600 and Formel E models. Gear and final-drive ratios were set to suit the performance characteristics of the cars and, again, optimised for fuel economy.

Golf 2 was a car of contradictions - bigger, heavier and faster, whilst at the same time more economical, quieter and far more comfortable. The luxuriously equipped - the basic model could almost have passed as a 'GL' five years before - upmarket versions had such creature comforts as electric windows and power steering! Truly 'Born Again'.

Since it first hit the road, the Golf GTi has been the charismatic face of Volkswagen. It was the hottest of the 'hot hatch' brigade when it first set the standard on its arrival, and has remained the leader that others must follow. VW engineers, however, have always had another ace up their sleeves when the opposition has threatened to take the lead. But its present role is far from what was originally intended!

The initial idea for a 'Sport Golf' came from a group of enthusiastic engineers working on a prototype in 1973. Time being of the essense with the development of the Golf in general, the engineers pet project was relegated to evenings and weekends in almost total secrecy. Not until after the launch of Golf 1 was the idea even shown to their chief. Only polite interest was evinced, especially as the sales people could not see a market for a 'sporting Golf'.

Sales and production had declined during the recent energy crisis, as with all car manufacturers, and no similar car existed on the racing circuit for it to compete with. However, eventually, on the understanding that only 5,000 would be built, for Group I homologation, sales agreed to unload the cars by spreading them thinly round European dealers. The 'Sport Golf' became an official project in May 1975.

The name 'GTi' was chosen, The GT tag being widely used for the sporting variants of many saloons, No one can remember how the 'i' was incorporated, but it **sounds** right - and it must be, for so many imitators to have borrowed it!

The first of the breed had a 1588cc engine, fitted with a Solex two-barrel carburettor, giving 100bhp. It was felt though, that a Golf with a hundred horses wasn't exactly going to set the world on fire, so they started work on uprating the California-specification engine. This had been adapted, using the Porsche K-Jetronic fuel-injection, to meet that 'states' stringent exhaust emission standards. This uprating boosted output to 110bhp, with which everyone was satisfied.

Originally the same four-speed gearbox as the other Golfs was used albeit with a slightly higher final-drive ratio, to take advantage of the increased torque. 1980 saw the GTi fitted with a five-speed close-ratio gearbox, which gave a set of gears suited to sporting use, while still maintaining overall economy. The GTi has remained with the five-speed box, with ratios altered from time to time to suit engine modifications.

As far as suspension and brakes were concerned, the VW engineers had got their sums right first time with the Golf, so the GTi's underpinnings were more or less left alone. Though the suspension was 20mm lower and a little firmer, anti-roll bars were added and wheels and tyres were only a little wider.

1985 (continued)

tunnel console, trip recorder, clock. GL as CL plus interior adjustable door mirrors, metallic paint, chrome hub caps, divided one third/two thirds rear seat back, digital clock, rev counter, heater duct for rear, courtesy light delay, boot light, twin-tone horn. Options included automatic transmission, power steering (GL only), tinted glass sunroof (all models). Formel E: fuel consumption indicator, gearchange light, automatic stop/start system, centre console.

1986
Seven models: C three-door; CL five-door; GL five-door; C Diesel five-door; new CL Turbo Diesel. All models (except Diesel): electronic ignition as standard. Formel E deleted. Engine: C 1043cc/45bhp; CL 1272cc/55bhp or 1595cc/75bhp petrol, or 1588cc/54bhp normally aspirated Diesel, or 1588cc/70bhp turbocharged Diesel; GL new 1781cc/90bhp. 4+E gearbox optional on all models auto option on 1595cc CL/GL. C plus side direction indicators, trip recorder, analogue quartz clock, luggage compartment cover, full stereo preparation, Blaupunkt radio. CL plus full width wheeltrims, Alpine Tweed upholstery. GL with tyre change to 175/70HR13 tyres.

D7.4
The Golf Driver limited edition, also based on the Mk I Golf.

Golf development

1987

Seven models: C three- or five-door; all others five-door. C/C Diesel plus side impact strip, height adjuster on driver's seat, height adjuster on front seat belts, stereo radio/auto-reverse cassette player. CL/CL turbo-Diesel plus interior-adjustable mirrors on both front doors, full-width wheeltrims replaced by flush-fit centre caps, padded steering wheel, heater duct for rear, Twill tweed upholstery, velour carpeting, cloth-covered head restraints. GL plus side impact strip with chrome trim, tinted glass, velour upholstery, sports steering wheel.

1988

New 'entry level' model, three- or five-door, 1272cc/55bhp engine, replaces Golf C. Specification as 1987 C, plus twin centre facia vents and tunnel console with ashtray. All models: windscreen wipers reset for RHD. False quarterlights deleted, door mirrors mounted further forward, new one-piece door windows, new aerodynamic five-slat grille, new steering wheel, side rubbing strips, minor detail changes.

GTi production modifications
1979

First official UK import. Specification as basic Golf. Engine: 1588cc/110bhp, Bosch K-jetronic fuel injection. Gearbox: four-speed. Brakes: internally ventilated front discs, rear drums, servo assisted. Plus halogen headlights, aerodynamic aid on driver's windscreen wiper, laminated windscreen, black surround to rear windscreen, intermittent wash/wipe, black internal headlining, sports steering wheel, golfball gearshift knob, centre console with clock and oil temperature gauge, water temperature

Similar size alloy wheels were optional extras. The front discs were abandoned for the GTi, in favour of internally ventilated discs of the same diameter in order to improve stopping power, and for the same reason, a larger brake servo was fitted. VW made one of their rare mistakes, however, when they elected to leave the standard drum brakes at the rear - a mistake not rectified until the Golf 2 GTi appeared.

When production started in June 1976 (with official RHD UK models arriving in 1979), the car was exactly as the engineers had designed it. There were no additional garish stripes, no extra gingerbread to enliven the image - on the contrary, other than the thin red line around the grille, and two discreet badges, the image was one of cool understatement. Neither decorated up to a market, nor trimmed to a price; the GTi was built for a purpose.

Far from being purely a homologation exercise, however, the car rapidly developed a cult following. Again, imitations followed from rival manufacturers and by the early 1980s the imitators were catching up with the innovator, and VW were looking at ways to keep their car one jump ahead.

The next step forward came with the 1781cc engine in late 1982. The GTi engine was extensively reworked, which resulted in a power increase of two brake horsepower! And this added to a higher final drive to take advantage of the greatly increased torque, made for better economy, quieter running and improved acceleration, while also giving a small increase in top speed.

The next reworking was of the whole car, in line with the 'Born Again' Golf 2. The larger car, although benefitting from better aerodynamics, was penalised by its weight. So the engine was breathed upon yet again, resulting in an even better torque curve, but with no horsepower gain. It was (and still is) economical, even when thrashed.

Everyone applauded the all-round discs now fitted, which endowed the car with stopping power to match its performance. Again, there were only minor differences from the mainstream Golf 2 package.

The latest development, still keeping one jump ahead of the opposition, is a 16-valve version. Basically, this is the 1781cc engine with a completely redesigned cylinder head resulting in galvanised power. The image is still one of understatement, outside show being limited to two discreet tags front and rear.

JETTA

The 'Golf with a boot' took VW into the largest sector of the car-buying market, the 'traditional' medium size and price three-box design.

Although the Jetta's popularity has never reached the proportions of that of the Golf, it has been sufficiently strong so to make production worthwhile. With the arrival of Jetta 2 ('Born Again' at the same time as the Golf), interest has increased, especially in the USA, where more Jettas sell than Golfs, and also where home production has recently been started.

In effect, the Jetta is a booted Golf (Jetta 1 even more so), but although the two cars share floorpans and mechanicals, many body components and most of the trim, enough changes have been made to the major body panels to regard the car as a model in its own right, as VW themselves do.

A glance at Jetta 1 will clearly show the Golf lines, but with an added box at the rear. Close examination reveals, however, the significantly different front wings, front panel, grille, indicators and headlights.

The front indicators are in the front panel/wing corners, instead of the bumper, and rectangular headlights have replaced the round units of the Golf, while the rear lights extend further round the rear wings. The roof does not have the slight upturn at the rear, seen on the Golf, therefore the rear quarter panels and bootlid must obviously be different. In fact, all that is left in common are the doors and windows and even so, the rear window is a Jetta part.

While, as already stated, the Jetta was based on the Golf floorpan, and therefore its wheelbase and track measurements, the car was, at 13ft 9 ins, 15 inches longer than its sister, and 66lbs heavier. All of the extra length was tacked on at the back, producing a boot of cavernous proportions. At 22 cubic feet, it was 70 per cent more capacious than the Golf's 13 cubic feet (rear seat up), which was the largest in its class (the Jetta 2 was claimed to have the largest boot to any production saloon car). Inside, dimensions and layout were virtually identical to the Golf, though the rear window was moved closer to the rear seat, which improved rearward visibility, especially when reversing.

Mechanically, also, the Jetta's specification has remained virtually the same as the Golf's, differing somewhat in the matter of wheels and tyres, where wider combinations may be fitted than on similarly powered Golfs. The spring rates, too, are altered, being a little stiffer to cope with the car's extra weight and additional carrying capacity. A rear anti-roll bar is standard on Jetta only.

As far as engine/equipment/trim combinations are concerned, the Jetta has always followed the Golf fairly closely. There have been, however, some Jetta engine/trim arrangements not seen on the Golf.

When the Jetta was launched in the UK in May 1980, there were five models available. The L and GL models were fitted with the 1272cc/60bhp engine, LS and GLS had the 1457cc/70bhp engine, and the short-lived GLi was fitted with the 1588cc/110bhp unit from the Golf GTi.

Jetta equipment was generally slightly more upmarket than the apparently equivalent Golf - FL Jettas, for instance, having the carpet inlays and bronze-tinted windows from the GLS Golf. The two larger-engined cars had steel wheels, and plastic wheelarch extensions effectively borrowed from the GTi, as were the side stripes fitted to all early Jettas.

The Jetta GLi was a bit of an oddity, but a very desirable oddity. Its life in the UK was brief, being deleted for 1981, and it is now a much sought-after model by the cognoscenti.

The advent of the Jetta Diesel followed the demise of the GLi. It was badged LD, and was mechanically identical to the Diesel Golf. Following on the economy theme, the Formel E Jetta arrived in mid-1981, with a high-compression 1093cc/50bhp engine.

1979 (contined)
gauge, fuel consumption indicator, twin-tone horn, fully reclining front sports seats, adjustable head restraints.

1980
Five-speed gearbox replaces previous four-speed. 5Jx13 inch alloy sports wheels now standard.

1981
Electronic ignition now standard.

1982
Door pockets, digital clock and locking glove box.

1983
Engine: new 1781cc/112bhp. Gearbox: internally revamped five-speed. Plus interior-adjustable door mirrors and MFA (onboard multi-function trip computor).

1984
New 'Born Again' bodystyle. Brakes: discs all round, solid rear, ventilated front, servo assisted. Wheels/tyres: 6Jx14 inch alloy sports wheels fitted with 185/60HR14 tyres. Equipment: as Golf GL plus wheelarch extensions, rear window spoiler, red trim strips on radiator grille, matt black body trimmings, steel sliding sunroof, front sports seats, sports steering wheel, MFA computor, fuel consumption gauge, gearchange indicator, water temperature gauge. Note: split folding rear seat optional extra (standard GL).

1985
No changes

◀ **D7.5**
What a clever move! Two very different car bodies that look so very similar.

D7.6 ▶
16V models were distinguished inside by a discreet small badge. A further two adorn the exterior, back and front.

Golf development

1986

Three models: GTi three- or five-door; new GTi 16V three-door only. Engine: GTi 16V new 1781cc/139bhp. GTi alloy wheels standard on 5-door only. Fuel consumption gauge and gearchange indicator deleted. GTi plus: twin-headlamp grille, twin exhaust tailpipes. GTi 16V as GTi plus green-tinted glass, electric windows, central locking.

1988

Body/equipment changes as for rest of Golf range. GTi eight-valve models now share standard spec. GTi 16V: new quality stereo digital radio/cassette player, new check cloth upholstery.

JETTA

Updates and improvements for the Jetta followed those of the Golf, with one or two exceptions. The car gained mini-headrests on the back seats in 1982 and the L/GL/GLS designations were changed to C/CL/GL. The Jetta GL of 1983, gained a 1588cc/85bhp engine and a high specification, including things like headlamp washers, a rev counter and luxurious upholstery and trim.

June 1984 saw the coming of the Jetta 2, in five models: 1300 C, 1300 CL, Formel E, CL Diesel, 1600 GL and 1800 GLX. All UK imported models were four-door. Current models include 1781cc/90bhp GL, 1588cc/75bhp TX, neither have a direct Golf companion. From 1987 the Jetta GT was available with Golf GTi performance; renamed later to the GTi.

The most desirable Jetta ever must be the GTi. This is, effectively, identical in all respects to the Golf GTi, sharing all the mechanical and interior appointments. The 16-valve engine has also been carried over to the Jetta range making, in typical VW understated fashion, a real street-sleeper of a car.

Jetta sales are increasing, showing that VW have found the right car for the format. The Golf scores for its versatility as everything from a shopping car to a 'sports' car, depending on model; the Jetta does exactly the same thing, but for the traditional motorist who prefers the three-box design but wants to experience the legendary Volkswagen.

Outside Europe, major centres of Golf production are the USA, Mexico and South Africa. The main difference between manufacturing centres, is the way in which the cars are packaged and presented to the public.

Detail changes here and there reflect local legislation and fashions - for example, the Mexican version was originally known as the Caribe, while the Rabbit, as the Golf is known in the USA, was characterised by its square headlights, big bumpers and side marker lights.

In addition, there have been over the years a number of other Golf-based vehicles. Various limited editions include the Golf Driver, based on Golf 1 and the all-white Match, its Golf 2, equivalent. More important variations are the Golf Convertible, the Golf Van and the Caddy.

The Convertible was based on the Golf 1 bodyshell and the model saw the light of day in 1979. It has never been built as a Mk 2 car but has remained, anachronistically, a 'Mk 1' up to the present day. Mechanically, it originally carried GTi equipment, but this was later supplemented by a GL-based additional model.

The Golf Van has appeared in both Golf 1 and 2 form. It is, in fact, the base model Golf as far as the B-pillars; there, the trim ends abruptly, giving way to painted metal and a flat load floor. The Pick-up version of the Golf has a slightly different history. It is, in fact, an American idea and started life as the Rabbit Pick-up built in the States. Now built in Hungary and sold as the Caddy, it is becoming increasingly popular in Europe and the UK. It can be fitted with a canvas tilt, or a glass fibre detachable body, converting it to a large van, and there are even caravan-style demountable bodies available, to make an occasional motorcaravan.

Volkswagen and the Golf are responsible for many 'firsts' - there is little doubt that the combination will come up with many more.

D7.7 The Jetta is particularly popular in the USA where it outsells the Golf.

Chapter Seven
Specialists

Specialists and Manufacturers

Acoustikit, Unit 2, Lowfield Road, Shaw Heath, Stockport SK3 8JS	061-480 3791
Ready-to-fit sound deadening kits	
Aeroquip, Think Automotive Ltd, 292 Worton Road, Isleworth, Middlesex TW7 6EL	01-568 1172
High performance brake hose components	
A&I (Peco) Acoustics Ltd, Sandford Street, Birkenhead, Merseyside L41 1AZ	051-647 6041
High performance exhaust systems, and air filters	
John Aley Racing Ltd, 7 Lime Tree Close, Hessett, Bury St. Edmunds IP30 9AY	0359 70954
'Aleybars', competition and road-use roll cages	
Automec Equipment and Parts Ltd., Stanbridge Road, Leighton Buzzard, Bedfordshire LU7 8QP	
Copper brake lines and Silicone Brake Fluid	0525 376608 & 375775
Autoplas, 90 Main Road, Hawkwell, Essex SS5 4JH	0702 202795
Suppliers of body kits and interior accessories	
Autotech, Nash Works, Belbroughton, Worcestershire	0562 730035
Volkswagen/Audi group approved paint shop and body repairers with design background	
Black and Decker, Westpoint, The Grove, Slough, Berkshire SL1 1QQ	0753 74277
Manufacturers of a huge range of professional and DIY tools	
Blaupunkt, Robert Bosch Ltd., PO Box 98, Broadwater Park, Denham, Uxbridge UB9 5HJ	0895 833633
Full range of VAG-supplied in-car entertainment components and systems	
Branyl Ltd., Unit 17, Kimberley Way, Redbrook Lane Trading Estate, Brereton, Rugeley WS15 1RE	088 94 76528/9
Self-adhesive car stripes, badges and decals	
Britax-Excelsior Ltd., Chertsey Road, Byfleet, Weybridge, Surrey KT14 7AW	09323 41121
Child safety seats and front and rear seat belts	
BR Motorsport, 8a Berrington Road, Sydenham Industrial Estate, Leamington Spa, Warwickshire CV31 1NB	
Audi-VW tuning and conversion specialist producing their own conversions and kits	0926 451545
Carflow Products (UK) Ltd., Leighton Road, Leighton Buzzard, Bedfordshire LU7 7LA	0525 383543
Wheel clean discs and locking wheel nuts	
Comma Oil & Chemicals Ltd., Comma Works, Denton Industrial Area, Lower Range Road, Gravesend, Kent DA12 2QX	
A full range of valeting products for the private and commercial market	0474 64311

Specialist manufacturers and magazines

Continental Coachworks, Spencer Bridge Works, Gladstone Road, Northampton VAG-approved paint and bodyshop	0604 54437
Duckhams Oils, Duckhams House, 157/159 Masons Hill, Bromley, Kent BR2 9HU Producers of high performance oils and lubricants for high performance engines	01-290 0600
Cruise U.K. Ltd, Sherborne Garage, Town Lane, Idle, Bradford UK distributor for 'after market' Cruise Control	0274 618756
Artur Fischer (UK) Ltd., Hithercroft Road, Wallingford, Oxon OX10 9AT C-Box range of quality cassette holders	0491 33000
Glasurit Valentine, Automotive Refinish, BASF Coatings + Inks Ltd., Colham Mill Road, West Drayton, Middlesex UB7 7AS Specialists in Automotive finish paints for the DIY (Valentine) and professional (Glasurit) markets	0895 442233
Hella Ltd., Daventry Road Industrial Estate, Banbury, Oxon OX16 7JU A wide range of general parts and accessories specifically for VW	0295 272233
Kenlowe Ltd., Burchetts Green, Maidenhead, Berkshire SL6 6QU Electrically-driven engine cooling fans. The 'Hotstart' engine pre-heater	062 882 3303
K.E.W. Industry Ltd., K.E.W. House, Gilwilly Industrial Estate, Penrith, Cumbria CA11 9BN K.E.W. Hobby Washer and accessories	0768 65777
Link-Sedan Ltd., Bone Lane, Newbury, Berkshire RG14 5TD Wide range of automotive accessories for the DIY enthusiast, customiser and family	0635 44796
Mitchell Marketing, 140 Leicester Road, Wigston, Leicester LE8 1DS Corroless products, full range of unique rust proofing fluids and paints. Also Slick 50, Protectalines and Backflashes	0533 881522
Mintex Don Ltd., P.O. Box 18, Cleckheaton, West Yorkshire BD19 3UJ High-performance brake and clutch lining manufacturers	0274 875711
Harry Moss International Ltd., 2a Lancaster Road, Wimbledon Village, London SW19 5DP Moss Professional Series accessories including central door locking	01-946 366301
Pacet Products and Co. Ltd., Wyebridge House, Cores End Road, Bourne End, Buckinghamshire SL8 5HH Oil coolers	06285 26754
Pirelli Limited, Derby Road, Burton on Trent, Staffordshire DE13 0BH Car, truck and motorcycle tyres and tubes	0283 66301
Plastic Padding Ltd., Wooburn Industrial Park, Wooburn Green, High Wycombe, Buckinghamshire HP10 0PE Full range of glass fibre and fillers for bodywork	06285 27912
Recaro Ltd. Available through all Volkswagen parts dealerships Wide range of VAG-approved car seats	
Richard Grant Motor Accessories Ltd., Moor End, Eaton Bray, Nr. Dunstable, Bedfordshire LU6 2JQ Wide range of body accessories	0525 220342
Robert Bosch Ltd., P.O. Box 98, Broadwater Park, Denham, Uxbridge UB9 5HJ Wide range of spark plugs and car electrical accessories	0895 833633
Rokee Limited, Unit 18, Central Trading Estate, Staines, Middlesex TW18 4XE Wooden dash and door trims, in various woods	0784 62588
Sachs Automotive Components Ltd., Avis Way, Newhaven, Sussex BN9 0DR High performance clutches, sports suspension kits	0273 515375
S.I.P. (Industrial Products) Limited, Gelders Hall Road, Shepshed, Loughborough, Leicestershire LE12 9NH Welding and spraying equipment	0509 503141
Spectra Automotive and Engineering Products plc, Treloggan Industrial Estate, Newqay, Cornwall TR7 2SX Aerosol spray paint	0637 871171

Sykes-Pickavant Ltd., Kilnhouse Lane, Lytham St. Annes, Lancashire FY8 3DU Manufacturers of DIY automotive and industrial service tools and Speedline hand tools	0253 721291
Turbo Technics Ltd., 17 Galowhill Road, Brackmills, Northampton NN4 0EE Suppliers of highly-developed turbocharging kits	0604 764005
V.A.G. (United Kingdom) Ltd., Yeomans Drive, Blakelands, Milton Keynes MK14 5AN UK distributors of Volkswagen cars and a vast range of improve and modify components	0908 679121
VW United States, 888W, Big Beaver, Troy, Michigan, 48007-3951, USA	313 362 6000
Weber Concessionaires Ltd., Dolphin Road, Sunbury, Middlesex TW16 7HE Weber and Solex carburettors	0932 788805

Clubs and Magazines

Club GTi, Membership Secretary, Cranhill Farmhouse, Cranhill Road, Street, Somerset BA16 0BZ	
National Volkswagen Association, PO Box 2291, Irwindale, CA 91706, USA	
Volkswagen Audi Car, Market Chambers, High Street, Toddington, Dunstable, Bedfordshire	05255 4019
Volkswagen Owners Club (GB), Dept E, 66 Pinewood Gardens, Iver Heath, Buckinghamshire SL0 0QH	
VW Club of America, PO Box 963, Plainfield, NJ 07061, USA	
VW Motoring Magazine, PO Box 4, Cirencester, Gloucestershire	0285 2185
VW & Porsche Magazine, PO Box 49659, Los Angeles, CA 90049, USA	

English/American terminology

Because this book has been written in England, British English component names, phrases and spellings have been used throughout. American English usage is quite often different and whereas normally no confusion should occur, a list of equivalent terminology is given below.

English	American	English	American
Air filter	Air cleaner	Mudguard	Fender
Alignment (headlamp)	Aim	Number plate	License plate
Allen screw/key	Socket screw/wrench	Output or layshaft	Countershaft
Anticlockwise	Counterclockwise	Panniers	Side cases
Bottom/top gear	Low/high gear	Paraffin	Kerosene
Bottom/top yoke	Bottom/top triple clamp	Petrol	Gasoline
Bush	Bushing	Petrol/fuel tank	Gas tank
Carburettor	Carburetor	Pinking	Pinging
Catch	Latch	Rear suspension unit	Rear shock absorber
Circlip	Snap ring	Rocker cover	Valve cover
Clutch drum	Clutch housing	Selector	Shifter
Dip switch	Dimmer switch	Self-locking pliers	Vise-grips
Disulphide	Disulfide	Side or parking lamp	Parking or auxiliary light
Dynamo	DC generator	Side or prop stand	Kick stand
Earth	Ground	Silencer	Muffler
End float	End play	Spanner	Wrench
Engineer's blue	Machinist's dye	Split pin	Cotter pin
Exhaust pipe	Header	Stanchion	Tube
Fault diagnosis	Trouble shooting	Sulphuric	Sulfuric
Float chamber	Float bowl	Sump	Oil pan
Footrest	Footpeg	Swinging arm	Swingarm
Fuel/petrol tap	Petcock	Tab washer	Lock washer
Gaiter	Boot	Top box	Trunk
Gearbox	Transmission	Two/four stroke	Two/four cycle
Gearchange	Shift	Tyre	Tire
Gudgeon pin	Wrist/piston pin	Valve collar	Valve retainer
Indicator	Turn signal	Valve collets	Valve cotters
Inlet	Intake	Vice	Vise
Input shaft or mainshaft	Mainshaft	Wheel spindle	Axle
Kickstart	Kickstarter	White spirit	Stoddard solvent
Lower leg	Slider	Windscreen	Windshield